Then the rain shifted direction, and I followed it, mouth open, trying to catch as much as I could. Something made me stop. In the back of my mind a warning sounded: *Hey, wake up, jerk. Something is about to happen. . . .*

I knew the surrounding jungle was filled with NVA patrols. We'd also learned from one of our CCN buddies back at FOB-1 that the NVA had been using counterrecon units, North Vietnamese soldiers trained as trackers and stationed at strategic locations along the Ho Chi Minh trail—which meant here, in the A Shau Valley. Once the gooks discovered the LRRPs' presence, within twenty-four hours the LRRPs would become the hunted. . . .

By Larry Chambers
Published by Ivy Books:

RECONDO: LRRPs in the 101st Airborne
DEATH IN THE A SHAU VALLEY: L Company LRRPs in
  Vietnam, 1969–70

Books published by The Ballantine Publishing Group
are available at quantity discounts on bulk purchases
for premium, educational, fund-raising, and special
sales use. For details, please call 1-800-733-3000.

DEATH IN THE A SHAU VALLEY

L Company LRRPs in Vietnam, 1969–70

Larry Chambers

IVY BOOKS • NEW YORK

An Ivy Book
Published by The Ballantine Publishing Group
Copyright © 1998 by Larry Chambers

http://www.randomhouse.com

Library of Congress Catalog Card Number: 98-92823

ISBN 0-8041-1575-3

Manufactured in the United States of America

First Edition: November 1998

10 9 8 7 6 5 4 3 2 1

To the memory of Joe Bielesch

Contents

Prologue	1
Commo Check	16
Short Arm Inspections	29
Discovered	32
Big Foot Lives in Vietnam	53
Ruong Ruong Valley	60
The Road to Bien Hoa	68
Fill the Pipeline	75
Shit-for-Brains	80
To Tell the Truth	84
Volunteer Number One	86
Pararescue	96
On-the-Job Training	103
Military Payment Certificates (MPCs)	107
Swimming Behind Nui Khe	113
Ammo Bunker Blowup	126
A New Year	131
Hiding in Plain Sight	135
Break Contact, Then Run Like Hell	142
"*Dung Lai*, Gook!"	149
Deep in Indian Country	155
Enemy Tunnel System	157
Buff "Brings Smoke" on the Gunkies	161
May 11, 1970—Tragedy	164

Contents

Epilogue   172
Appendixes   175
Glossary   231

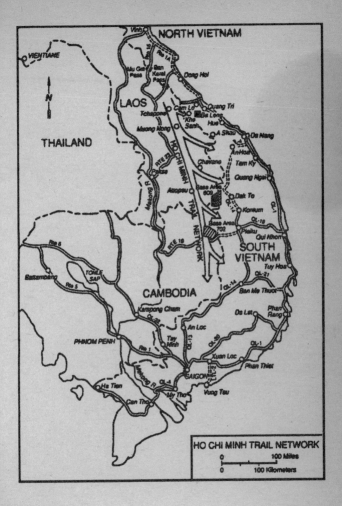

HO CHI MINH TRAIL NETWORK

0 — 100 Miles
0 — 100 Kilometers

DEATH
IN THE
A SHAU VALLEY

Prologue

My childhood prepared me for Vietnam. My dad had been a World War II hero and made a career in the army. My mom met and married him shortly after the war. A year later, I was born. My toddler clothes were made from my dad's cut-down officer's uniforms, and my childhood friends were twenty-year-old army privates. When I played army, I could hear the sounds of tank tracks. After Korea, my father was in charge of a radar site hidden in the hills overlooking the Golden Gate Bridge at one of the many missile installations that dotted the California coast.

I remember the three huge radar dishes slowly spinning and the concrete bunker under them. Inside, the room had no windows, and only an overhead light dimly illuminated its tightly packed equipment—radarscopes, controls, communication panels. The air was always warm and thick with cigarette smoke; ashtrays brimmed with butts. Men talked back and forth in controlled military voices.

Back then, Soviet planes routinely tested our air defenses. They'd fly down from the north, keeping low to avoid radar detection. Their bombers would try to find weaknesses in the radar and missile cover—openings to penetrate if the two superpowers were to go to war. The game was to get close but not get caught. We played the same game. Before reaching the coast, their bombers would turn back, but my dad was there in case they didn't.

He'd get phone calls in the middle of the night. Air-raid sirens would sound off. I often heard my mom and dad talking; my mom was scared. From our quarters, we could watch as the missiles went vertical. "There they go!" she'd say, then she'd put on a pot of coffee. I remember the sinister look of the Nike Hercules missiles as they slowly rose from their concrete underground bunkers. These images are burned in my mind. I knew then that what my dad did was important, and I wanted to be just like him someday.

As the cold war intensified in Europe, my dad's unit was sent to guard the West German border; I was sent to live with my grandparents on a ranch in northern California. It was very different from army life. I milked cows, hauled hay, and fished along the river. My uncle taught me to hunt. The first time I went bird hunting with him, I tried to shoot at all of them at the same time; not one duck dropped. So my uncle showed me how to zero in and shoot one bird at a time. I got so I could flick off the safety, bring the gun smoothly up under my chin, and fire the second it got there.

After high school, I enrolled in Shasta College. When I dropped two units during my sophomore year, football season, I lost my college deferment and was reclassified 1-A. That draft notice changed my life. It made me feel part of the bigger world. I don't mean to get heavy here, but I think it's important you know where I was coming from and how I got into the war. I wasn't completely crazy. Anyway, I cut a deal with my draft board—I'd volunteer if they'd let me finish football season.

After a grinding college football season, basic training and AIT seemed like summer camp. Nothing in the army bothered me. Besides, I was living out my childhood fantasy, fighting the Evil Empire. I was going to make the best of it. I used to piss off the other trainees; no one likes a guy who wakes up happy in boot camp or likes the food. I scored at the top in my physical fitness test, and tied for honors for best shot in the company.

While most of my friends stayed home, finished college, and got real jobs, I volunteered for Airborne training, earned my jump wings, and insured I'd be going to Vietnam sooner rather than later.

After training, I returned to northern California on a thirty-day leave, saw a few friends, but mostly spent my time fishing and pheasant hunting. My last week as a free man, I camped out at Lake Shasta, caught three huge trout, no less, and ate fish for breakfast, bird for dinner. I left the States with a good taste in my mouth.

Arriving in Vietnam, I realized this was a very different army from the one I'd known as a kid and experienced in basic training. Here, the Americans all seemed to be pissed off, from officers all the way down to privates. Orders were yelled at us as if they were jail sentences, and "old-timers" of a few months in country enjoyed the fact that the "new guys" had 365 days to go. I figured, since I'm here, I might as well go all the way.

I can still see the guy who recruited me into the LRRPs, Sergeant McDougal. He looked different from the other guys I met my first days in Nam. His shirt was starched. He wore a Combat Infantryman Badge above the left pocket and his jungle boots were polished though there was not much leather left on them. He wore a black baseball cap with a Recondo patch, his jump wings pinned above the patch. He reminded me of my dad. He gave us new guys a pitch about volunteering for one of the most dangerous jobs in the army—gathering intelligence behind enemy lines. My knees started shaking, and I imagined sneaking out the back of the tent. Instead, as if someone else had raised it, my arm was suddenly waving above my clean-shaven head. The next thing I knew, I was part of a special unit of recon scouts. An hour of excruciating buyer's remorse was drowned out by the mantra, *I'm tough, I'm tough.* I was actually excited. One other guy volunteered that night, Art Herringhausen, and he was sitting on the bench with me. At least I wasn't alone.

After a few more days of training, we were sent to Camp Eagle—which seemed to me like Dodge City. Muddy, unpaved streets, everyone carrying guns—like a real-life war movie. I couldn't wait to go out on my first combat mission. I imagined I was a military version of 007—James Bond in jungle fatigues.

On my very first mission, as I was sitting in front of my team, alone next to a trail, ten enemy soldiers walked within a few feet of me. I sat up straight to get a better view and realized I was trapped. I couldn't move a muscle or they'd hear me, they were so close. I held that sitting position for twenty minutes, telling myself over and over, *I feel no pain,* as my stomach muscles screamed. The enemy didn't see me and moved slowly down the trail. Back at the company, I was inducted as a full LRRP (long-range reconnaissance patrol) teammate: I had passed my first real test. I had kept my head and resisted a fearful move, which would have endangered the entire team.

When I was growing up, my dad did his share of drinking, so I was never sure what would happen next. When my dad first came back from war, he used to sleepwalk around the house carrying a machete. That used to scare the hell out of my mom. It taught me to be quiet and not to make fast moves at night. It also taught me to anticipate and prepare for the unexpected. Vietnam, in contrast, had clarity and simple rules. The enemy had a single purpose: kill me and my teammates. I got real good at spotting signs of the enemy before he spotted me. Some of the guys said I had a sixth sense, intuition, in the jungle, but the truth was my sensory awareness had already been fine tuned. I could see things immediately that were out of place. Walking through the jungle with me at night was a mystical experience, they said, because I could completely catalog anything that moved within a three hundred meter radius and instantly hatch plans to take it out.

I once walked around the backside of an enemy ambush. My team leader had sent me to scout the trail ahead. Things didn't look quite right, so I slipped off the main trail and found myself in thick jungle behind a group of enemy soldiers. I could hear them talking before my eyes adjusted to the darkness. Then, slowly, ten silhouettes—NVA soldiers sitting cross-legged on the ground—came into view. I pulled my rifle up to fire, but instead of shooting, slowly backed away from their camp undetected. Our team was able to escape unseen and unharmed. That was what a LRRP was supposed to do.

Most guys aren't cut out to be Rangers or LRRPs. Rational men, when faced with the concept of surviving in the jungle behind enemy lines, stop breathing. Surround them with enemy soldiers and most completely freak out. The problem is you never know if you're one of those until you're actually there. For others, the danger-induced adrenaline rush inspires even greater risk taking. The more missions you go on, the more you get off on it. It becomes an addiction. I personally reacted by covering my fear with a veneer of humor, but my humor was not always appreciated. Certain guys, like Marty Martinez, occasionally wanted to kill me for my positive attitude. One guy enjoyed it though—Gary Linderer. Gary was from Missouri, and aside from being part mule and a lot stubborn, he was one of the neatest and smartest guys I'd ever met. We would spend the nights in the rear area, mostly harassing each other. I'd try to convince him that his home state of Missouri should secede from the union; he would accuse my mother of impossible sexual feats.

Another guy who egged me on was Kenn Miller. Kenn first volunteered to come to Nam in 1967; he was with the 1st Brigade LRRPs and kept extending his stay. Kenn was an intellectual—a fish out of water in that environment. His father was the president of a major university, his mother a Ph.D., and Kenn had volunteered just to piss them off. Kenn and I became close friends after our chopper crash in the jungle. Rescued and safely back at the company, Kenn and I did battle after a few drinks with each other, landing us both in the hospital. As I recall, Miller broke my hand with his head. Yeah, we were buddies. Still are.

I really felt at home in the company, except for the food. Camp Eagle was near the end of the military food chain. By the time supplies in Vietnam made their way north, the food remnants resembled water buffalo dung mixed with sea shells. I can close my eyes and still taste powdered eggs and lime green Kool-Aid.

Camp Eagle was a huge military complex, 3½ miles long by nearly 1½ miles wide, just six miles south of Hue City. It was base camp to twelve thousand troops of the 101st Airborne Division and served as our rear area—slicks, gunships, trucks,

medical facilities, a PX, and miles of tents and bunkers surrounded by open fields pockmarked with bomb craters. Around
that was an Oriental landscape where farmers waded in rice
fields amid tiny hamlets and villages of thatch huts and ancient
pagodas were common sights. A gigantic cemetery bordered
the eastern end of the camp. At night, mortar illumination
rounds on the gravestones glowed a spooky green; they appeared to vibrate in our starlight scopes. It made some guys see
shadows running between the gravestones. I found that if you
looked off to one side, the shadows disappeared. There was also
a peculiar odor to the camp—and almost anywhere else GIs
lived in Vietnam—a mixture of diesel fuel and burning shit. I
never quite got used to that smell.

I did feel somewhat at home in the woods. The jungles of
Vietnam looked and smelled like river bottom. Living along a
river as a teenager gave me an edge. Summers back home had
been hot and humid, and the work never ended; Vietnam in a lot
of ways was no different.

In my second month with the company, we experienced a
major disaster: Two of our LRRP teams were attacked; four
men killed and eight wounded. Gary Linderer was one of the
wounded, and Art Herringhausen, the guy who volunteered with
me, was killed. The team I was on was stuck in heavy fog at the
time, down the side of a muddy hill and unable to help. We had
to just sit there, listening to the radio transmissions as our guys
were overrun. That was one of the worst days of my life.

We desperately needed replacements at that point. Aside
from losing the two teams, a lot of the original, experienced
guys had rotated home. I was one of only a few new recruits
who volunteered to refill the ranks. Gradually, more guys came
into the company, and we were back in business.

The 101st's Long Range Reconnaissance Patrol Company kicked off 1969 by becoming Rangers—in our case L
Company—in an army-wide paper shuffle to legitimize the
many LRRP-type units that had flourished in Vietnam. There
was no parade, no physical transfer, no change of command—
just a paper exchange of one scroll for another. Overnight we

became L Company, 75th Infantry (Ranger). We were, however, authorized by the reorganization to wear black berets. I tried one on but thought it made me look more like a French artist than a soldier, so I kept my tiger-stripe boonie hat for headgear. Anyway, we still had the same mission—to search out enemy troops in their sanctuaries and to bring down whatever tactical men and weapons we could upon them. We still functioned as the eyes and ears for the different unit commanders within the 101st Division.

Historically, the 75th Ranger Regiment had originated as "Merrill's Marauders," named after Maj. Gen. Frank D. Merrill. They were the first United States ground combat force to fight the Japanese on the continent of Asia during World War II. It seemed ironic to me that Merrill's Marauders worked alongside Chinese forces, fighting the Japanese. Now here we were, picking up where the Japanese left off.

In that year, 1969, the company conducted 310 long range patrols, almost twice the number of the previous year. Five Rangers were killed and fourteen wounded, and they were all my good friends. As the years went on, the statistics got much worse.

Also during that year, the South Vietnamese army was supposed to take on the majority of the offensive operations, and our troops were supposed to withdraw gradually from combat. All that really meant to us, however, was that our area of operations expanded. As the outlying firebases closed, L Company was working as far as seventy kilometers away from Camp Eagle, with fair to poor—sometimes zero—communications, and depending solely on 175mm guns firing at maximum range for support.

At that point, most of us were replacements, with only a few trained Rangers among us. Training for replacements became on-the-job. Every mission had one or two new guys along; this quickly weeded out the guys who couldn't handle the pressure. My team position was point man. I always wanted to be first, and I met little resistance from my teammates.

As the year dragged on, we pulled missions back-to-back

while our commanders worked on rebuilding the company's strength. Meanwhile, the North Vietnamese were infiltrating more units into South Vietnam, and our missions became evermore dangerous with ever-increasing enemy contact. By midyear, I had pulled twenty-seven recon missions, almost all resulting in enemy sighting or direct contact, and I was about to get a reward.

If an LRRP had spent at least six months in the country and had team leader potential, he would be sent to MACV Recondo School, the equivalent of a "finishing school" for recon men— and probably the finest of its kind anywhere in the world. The last week of school culminated in a three-day live mission in the jungles north of Nha Trang. You had to stay alive to complete the course and earn the school certificate, plus the right to wear the MACV Recondo patch.

As excited as if we were headed for an R & R, Harry Duty, Dan Roberts, Ron Reynolds, and I hitched a ride on a C-130 and hightailed it down south to Nha Trang, home away from home for the 5th Special Forces. After a weekend of drinking, we found our way to the gates of the school, where we were met by yelling, gravel-voiced Special Forces instructors. For three weeks, we worked eighteen-hour days in intense training. The first thing they did was give us each a thirty-pound sandbag to carry in our rucksacks. From the day we arrived, we were up at 4:00 A.M. for hard runs that progressively lengthened to eight miles. Heavy physical training, intensive map reading, medical instruction, prisoner handling, NVA attack strategies, and training with communist weapons followed. (The School was officially closed December 31, 1970, and had graduated 3,357 troops from a total 5,395 attendees.)

Our field training at Recondo school was conducted in the steep hills that rose behind the seaside base, one hundred miles northeast of Saigon. Viet Cong were still active in and out of the area. On my third day out, I was walking point ahead of my team when I suddenly came upon a group of fifteen NVA camped right in the center of a high-speed trail. I lifted my CAR-15, took aim, and shot the first enemy soldier just as he lifted his weapon. After a brief firefight, we pulled back. The following day, we went back with reinforcements to the same spot and came face-to-face with an NVA soldier who had gotten dislocated from his unit. We stood frozen for a split second, then I charged, threw a football tackle on the guy, and wrestled him into a headlock. He was struggling and screaming so loud that I stuck my rifle barrel down his throat and held him until our team leader, Sgt. Louis LaPage, got there. He yelled at me, "Don't pull that trigger." I looked down. The way I had hold of the guy, and the direction my rifle was pointed, I would have shot a hole through his head and my balls. I released my grip.

I was the first American that this young North Vietnamese soldier had ever seen, and he had thought I was Korean. That dispelled any illusions I had had about my Irish Heritage. The NVA's shiny silver belt buckle and the promise of an additional R & R were my rewards for capturing what turned out to be a fresh lieutenant who had just walked all the way from North Vietnam.

It seemed that whatever good news came my way was quickly overshadowed by the realities of combat. I returned to the company just in time to learn that S.Sgt. Julian Dedman's helicopter had been hit by ground fire, exploded in the air, and burned. The following month, on May 5, 1969, I was flying bellyman when our lead helicopter went down in the Ruong Ruong Valley, and my friend, Keith Hammond, was killed. Only three days later, a team led by Staff Sergeant Zoschak and Sergeant Reynolds engaged an enemy unit five times their number. Sergeant Reynolds was mortally wounded, and two other Rangers were also badly wounded. Next we lost Sgt. William Marcy, killed by small-arms fire. He was an admiral's son, so he was obviously there by his own choice, and he was highly respected by the other men because of that.

As the months went on, our missions brought us closer to the Laos border. North Vietnamese units had secured themselves in camps, which we were not permitted to touch, along the borders of Cambodia and Laos. Our commanding general, Gen. Creighton Abrams, believed the A Shau Valley was a staging area for the NVA and might be used for future attacks, so he ordered us to go in and see what was up so we did.

Everything about the A Shau was eerie, even the way it rained there. Rain clouds didn't have to form up and march their way into that place, they were just always there, waiting to loose a thick downpour—the kind unleashed if you pissed somebody off in the Old Testament. We're talking major flood! I remember thinking that no clouds could possibly hold that much water.

Because of the ever-present thick fog, fighter-bombers were often useless in the A Shau, and many of the mountaintops had been turned into small fortress bunkers by the North Vietnamese to protect their massive network of trails and roads through the valley. The peaks and ridges served as lookouts for communist antiaircraft gun emplacements. None of us were looking forward to going back in there.

In college, I'd taken a class in anthropology and knew something about the people who originally inhabited the A Shau—the montagnards. For thousands of years, dark-skinned montagnard tribes, similar to the aborigines and primitive tribes in the South Pacific, had inhabited the mountains surrounding the valley. The montagnards remained isolated from the French, but the communists had used them as guides, porters, and even soldier conscripts. During the Vietnam War, some of the lucky ones ended up working for our Special Forces units, but most of them were relocated to the lowlands or jailed by the South Vietnamese, who routinely mistreated montagnards because they regarded them as somewhat less than human. A lot ended up as slaves to the Viet Cong. The Vietnamese hated the montagnards, but the Special Forces loved them—which meant we did, too.

While the fighting continued throughout most of Vietnam, the A Shau Valley had remained untouched; it was a great hiding place for the NVA. They could slip in, roam around, then sneak back out undetected. The valley became an important NVA strategic way station for transporting supplies between base camps on myriad high-speed trails through the valley floor, leading from the north into any one of a number of South Vietnamese cities and villages, including Phu Bai and Hue.

During the Tet offensive in 1968, eighty-four thousand Viet Cong attacked sixty-four district capitals of South Vietnam, including the former imperial capital, Hue. Many of the North Vietnamese troops had bivouacked in the A Shau and struck out on that offensive in several different directions, avoiding American and South Vietnamese units. They took control of Hue, then embarked on an unbelievable orgy of death and destruction. The communists had prepared lists of enemy targets, which included just about anyone with even the slightest connection to the South Vietnamese government, including school teachers, artists, businessmen, students, and political leaders. Many people were killed on the spot; others were marched to isolated areas where they were clubbed to death and buried in mass graves. An estimated six thousand civilians were killed by "their own" VC.

Our mission was to insert near the old Special Forces A Shau camp and find them. I remember it being triangular, surrounded by minefields and rows of razor-sharp concertina wire. One of our higher-ups had the bright idea that we should insert *in* the minefield, reasoning the NVA wouldn't expect us there—a Vietnam version of military intelligence.

The old Special Forces camp had been overrun by NVA back in 1965. Only 180 men of the 434-man garrison survived; the rest were killed or taken prisoner by the NVA. Of course, I was not looking forward to patrolling where so many had been killed.

It was April 23, 1969, when Larry Closson, Gary Linderer, Marvin Hillman, John Sours, Mother Rucker, and I seriously *ate it* on a remote hill in the A Shau Valley. A bolt of lightning just about ended our young military careers. (Just three weeks later, that same hill became the notorious Hamburger Hill, when 70 men in the 101st Airborne Division died and 372 were wounded attempting to seize its fortified ridgeline.)

The mission began by making several false insertions in an attempt to deceive enemy observers, we landed near a spot labeled Dong Ap Bia on our map. The mountain was covered with a thick double- and triple-canopy jungle consisting of layers of vines, brushy trees, and stands of bamboo. The whole place was a network of trails and roads, and at night, we could hear gas engines running and what sounded like chain saws. During the day, we watched hundreds of enemy troops moving up the hill. We never moved to the bunkers at the top of the mountain, but stayed undetected on the jungle-covered ridges.

I remember lying with my face an inch above the ground, the smell of rotten vegetation filling my nostrils, peering through my binoculars at the men on the valley floor below. Looking uncannily like a column of red ants, one hundred or so NVA troops were climbing a jungle path.

Mother Rucker got on the radio to report the enemy movement. He had been careful to write out the coded message beforehand, and he checked the radio frequency as the rain started pounding down and I pulled a poncho cover over my head. When Rucker squeezed the radio handset, our world blew apart in a hundred different directions. A bolt of lightning tore through every piece of electrical equipment we carried, touched off the electric blasting caps in our claymore mines, and sent us all flying head over butt through the air. In my last moment of consciousness, I remember thinking, Oh shit, this is it! When I came to a few minutes later, I was unable to move and was completely disoriented. Finally, I reached down to feel if my legs were still there. They were paralyzed, but fear made me drag myself back up the ridge. When I got to the top of the ridge, no one else was there. That really shook me at first—but slowly everyone staggered back up that hill. We had no radio, and we were all hurt in varying degrees. Then a miracle happened: a chopper appeared above us out of nowhere, and thirty minutes later, a medevac pulled us out with a jungle penetrator. When the medevac landed back at camp, its tail boom was full of bullet holes.

After a couple of days in the hospital, I returned to the company—but I never fully recovered from the memory of being paralyzed, lying helpless on my back without a weapon, fully expecting that at any moment some teenage NVA recruit would simply walk up and cut my throat while I watched. I began having terrifying dreams of being chased, run to the ground, and killed by NVA, and then the gooks searching my lifeless body. Feeling alone on that muddy hillside was the first time during my tour that I'd felt real fear. Not the normal keep-yourself-alive kind of fear, but the kind that runs deep in your spine, is always with you, sometimes starts your legs shaking uncontrollably, and can even make a grown man piss all over himself.

While Mother Rucker and I were recuperating, we took a drive into Hue City. We parked the company jeep outside the old Imperial Palace, and I walked alone around the grounds. No one was around. Then an old papa-san opened a wooden door and smiled at me. He didn't speak any English, but waved me in. I entered a wide room filled with gold-leaf-covered tables and a huge ancient chair. I'd never seen anything like it—a Vietnamese museum. Rucker had to come get me and drag me back to the jeep. My major in college had been art.

That same month we got a new company commander, Capt. Robert Guy, whose primary job was to implement the concept of saturated patrolling. The company was to employ clusters of five and six teams to completely saturate an area. This was to help ensure that the regular troops were not attacked during the forthcoming withdrawal. Meanwhile, our guys would constantly be in the field. Morale was low, and bodies exhausted. Men with field experience were just shipped home when their tours were complete; they felt no incentive to return on extensions as other experienced soldiers had often done in the earlier years.

Back home, almost everyone—except my dad—seemed to be against the war. Between missions, we'd get news of the puzzling and infuriating events back home: Charles Manson's crazed killing, Bobby Kennedy assassinated, Martin Luther King shot and killed on a motel balcony, police teargassing and clubbing students in the streets or on campuses, students rioting in the streets and on campuses. It seemed safer and more sane there in the jungles of Vietnam than back in the States, so when my tour was up, I extended.

My new job was to recruit replacements for our Ranger Company. It was my responsibility to select men who could deal with the worst circumstances with the cards stacked against them. I felt the earlier guys had the advantage of some room for error, but that was no longer the case. In three months, I had recruited twenty-six replacements. After I left for the States, I didn't see or hear anything more about them. That bothered me.

Then in 1990, at our second annual LRRP/Ranger reunion, Gary Linderer convinced me to write a couple of chapters for his book about my experience in Recondo School. I did and sent them to his publisher, Owen Lock, at Random House. Owen responded that he would publish my story as well, which became *Recondo*.

Four years later at another reunion, Gary Linderer, Kenn Miller, and Rey Martinez decided to write a history of the 101st LRRPs. The finished book was so long, they divided it into three. Rey Martinez wrote about the early history and the original 1st Brigade LRRP Detachment, which became *Six Silent Men*, Book One; Kenn Miller wrote about the middle years, *Six Silent Men*, Book Two; and Gary Linderer wrote about the Rangers in the seventies, *Six Silent Men*, Book Three. (I strongly recommend all three.)

While Linderer was writing his book about the seventies, I told him I'd been wondering about what happened to the guys I recruited. It had been so long though, I didn't have the slightest idea about how to find them. I wasn't sure I could even remember all their names. A few months later, Gary called me. "You sittin' down?" Linderer barked over the phone. "You're not going to believe this, but I just got a diary in the mail from a guy who says that you recruited him." Linderer began to read aloud, "Sergeant Chambers recruited me into my Ranger company . . ."

The diary belonged to Frank Johnson. Johnson had kept meticulous notes—dates and places. The names were all there. I called Johnson and asked if I could use some of his notes, and he agreed to send me a copy. A few weeks later, Linderer called me with news of another guy I had recruited, Jim Bates. Of course, by this time, Linderer was saying he was making it too easy for me. The result is the book that you're reading. It took me a year to piece it together. I hope I haven't offended any of the guys.

There is another reason I wrote this book. I would have loved to read about my dad's combat during World War II. He never spoke about the war, and he died years before I became interested in what he had experienced. If he had written it down, it might have made a real difference in my life. Today's LRRPs are the Rangers who serve in the Long Range Surveillance Detachment (LRSD) of the 101st Airborne. This book is dedicated to them—and to my own children, when they're interested.

Commo Check

On a ridgetop just east of an abandoned 101st firebase, South Vietnam, May 10, 1970

The six men of the Ranger team had gone about their normal duties, made the required radio checks, secured their perimeter, formed a night defensive position (NDP), and laid out four claymore mines. They sat around before it was too dark to see, slapped at mosquitoes, and, in whispers, shot the bull about what they were going to do back in the World. They made their communications check at 0430 hours the following morning—*negative*. The team leader said he was going to move to a new location at first light.

Camp Eagle, May 20, 1969

My last recon mission was on Larry Closson's team. The team consisted of Closson, Mother Rucker, Marvin Hillman, Ricky "New Guy" Lawhon, and Doc Glasser. I had already been on four missions with Closson, including the one that nearly fried our butts.

The morning before that mission, we all sat in the 17th Cav mess hall telling stories and eating the usual breakfast of creamed chipped beef on toast, commonly known as shit on a shingle (or just SOS). Between lies, we updated each other with news from Stateside.

I remember standing in the chow line and flicking George Thomas's toast off his plate. It landed on the ground, and Dixie, our mascot dog, grabbed it, then ducked under the table. Thomas, who was as country as a turnip green, retaliated by pouring a pile of salt all over my beef—which didn't change the taste one bit.

Sgt. Larry Closson told us to get a leg on. Closson weighed over two hundred pounds, looked like he could lift a house, but wouldn't hurt a fly—at least not one on our side. He was a gentle, white-haired giant. Closson was what we called a "shake 'n' bake sergeant," meaning he had gone to an advanced version of AIT (advanced infantry training) and made sergeant before he shipped to Nam. Everyone resented the idea of making rank in ninety days, so the shake 'n' bake name tagged those guys.

Despite the fact that he was now a known lightning hazard, Mother Rucker was still the radioman on the team. Rucker couldn't carry an M-16 or a CAR-15 (a slightly shorter version of the M-16) like the rest of us. No, Mother always had to be different; so he carried a 9mm Swedish-K submachine gun that he had gotten in trade from some Special Forces guy over at FOB-1. Rucker also wore his hair longer than regulation, and from a side view, he had a slight resemblance to General Custer. He was "short," with less than two weeks left to serve in Vietnam.

I figured it would be fairly safe to go back out with Rucker and Closson since, according to the weather brief, neither of them would be making any unnecessary phone calls in a lightning storm.

Marvin Hillman was a shy, handsome, quiet black kid who made you feel welcome whenever he was around. He was about my height, five feet ten, and weighed 160 pounds—ten pounds less than I did at the time.

Ricky New Guy and Doc Glasser were two of my favorite guys to tease. Ricky New Guy had been on "umpteen" missions and had been in country for seven months, but we still called him *New Guy*. The name just stuck with him.

Doc Glasser was "a reject" from the Special Forces medical training and proud of it. He loved to remind us of that. It seems he got a little too drunk back at Fort Bragg, punched out a lifer, and ended up a PFC with orders for Vietnam, later finding his way into the Rangers. The nice thing about Special Forces was that they trained their recruits well. Even their rejects were a cut above. And with Doc, we had our own medic on the team.

I, on the other hand, had entered the service because I was fulfilling a lifelong dream—not mine, but my father's—to be in combat the way every male in my family had been before me.

Lt. Jim Jackson was in charge of the briefing that morning. Jackson wore a freshly pressed uniform and looked out of place as he walked in and moved to the front of the room with our CO, Captain Cardona, at his side. "Ten-Hut!" Closson shouted, protocol for a senior officer entering a room. But before anyone could stand, Captain Cardona answered back, "At ease."

Jackson talked in a slow, methodical drawl. He went over the weather report, which always seemed to be exactly the same. "The weather for the next six days will be hot and humid, with afternoon rain. Your AO (area of operation) will be foggy in the morning, cloudy during the day, with some rain in the afternoon and night. Winds will be out of the southwest."

I tried to remain attentive but was nearly asleep. Jackson walked to the side of a long table where a stack of SOI (signal operation instructions) booklets lay, containing all radio frequencies and call signs. The word CONFIDENTIAL was stamped on the outside of the booklets in red, large block letters. Inside, code words were neatly typed, and coordinates were drawn on a grid, so we could communicate by radio without giving away our positions. Jackson handed the booklets to the team leaders.

George Thompson asked, "When do I get a book?"

"You'll get yours when we attack Guam," I volunteered.

George looked at me, puzzled. "Guam?" The room cracked up. Then George grabbed me by the neck and almost strangled me. I loved to tease him, but I always had to pay a price for it.

Cardona gave the warning order. "Heavy enemy activity has been reported in the southeastern sector of your AO." He pointed at the map. "The A Shau Valley. You're familiar with the area. You are to conduct a BDA (bomb damage assessment)." With as little enthusiasm, he concluded, "We had an Arc Light (B-52 strike) in the valley three days ago. We have intelligence that an NVA regiment has a base camp in one of your AOs; we need to find out if we nailed it. Be at the chopper at 0530. Thank you, gentlemen."

This is great, I thought, a bomb damage assessment. We land in a freshly devastated AO to examine what's left after a B-52 bombardment. All I could think about was the possibility of enemy survivors; those guys might be a little pissed.

At 0530 the next day, puddles of water dotted the acid pad (helicopter landing pad). I mixed some camouflage with some insect repellent, to soften it, and covered the back of my neck and the shiny parts of my ears.

Then I watched Rucker add last-minute touches to his camouflage. He was extraordinary at this activity; in fact, he was the best. Rucker would really take his time contouring his face, and when he was done, his black and green tiger fatigues matched his skin. He looked exactly like a jungle leaf.

I was not as good at the special effects. The upper part of my face got a fast crisscross of dark green paint, which, now that I think about it, probably resembled a rifle target. My eyebrows looked like bat wings about to take off from the bridge of my nose. Even though Hillman was black, he still had to camouflage his face. When he was painted, he looked like an evil circus clown.

The whole idea was to break up the surface of the face, which really stood out in the jungle. But I knew, even as I amused myself with the exercise, that if any enemy soldiers got close enough to see us, we'd scare the shit out of them.

There was always something soothing about those last minutes of activity. I didn't think too much about the mission and what might be waiting for us. The rest of the team checked packs and smoked cigarettes. I was trying not to joke around this time and to just concentrate on the job at hand, but Ricky New Guy and Doc Glasser took one look at me and both started laughing.

I shook off the insult and pulled back the charging handle on my CAR-15, inserting a live round in the chamber, then rechecked my safety to make sure it was on. The CAR-15 fired a 5.56mm (.223 caliber, for those of you with a love of varmint guns) round. With most of the older weapons we had, the previous owners had filed down the trigger spring for the safety catch so we could slip from safe to auto without the metallic *click* that might otherwise tip off potential NVA casualties—perfect for walking point.

I always carried a sling on my rifle so it fit snugly around my shoulder. That way I could hold my CAR-15 in one hand, keeping it pointed straight ahead, and leaving my other hand free to clear the vegetation. My first three rounds were always tracers, so I could follow the tracers right into my target. My last three rounds were also tracers so I'd know when I was coming to the end of a magazine. Then I'd be ready to click in the next one. I loved that CAR-15. It just looked cool, and when it didn't jam, it was a great rifle. I wiped it down with my rag and set it down.

Closson handed me a starlight scope and a claymore mine. "Here. Stick these in your pack."

"Shit, I'll have to leave my Joan Baez pictures out," I said.

Closson answered, "Too bad."

I took the scope, opened my ruck, and set it where I could easily get to it. I closed and tightened down the flaps.

The starlight scope is a light-intensifying device, resembling a telescopic rifle sight. The scope magnifies the ambient light from the stars and allows the user to identify—and shoot—shapes in the dark. The starlight was well worth its added weight.

The claymores could be used for two purposes. If you get ambushed, it can blow an escape hole in the jungle. The other, more important, purpose was to blow a hole in the enemy. That it did by propelling several hundred ball bearings with deadly force in their direction.

I clipped on my K-bar knife and tied its scabbard around my right leg so it wouldn't bounce. Rucker stood next to me and turned back to the other team members. "Hey, you wimps, we may not be the baddest motherfuckers in Nam, but the baddest call me every morning just to make sure we're all still friends!"

"Yeah, Cheezedick. Get on board," Doc Glasser called to us.

Rucker held my rifle. I grabbed hold of the vertical brace that separated the door-gunner compartment from the cabin and pulled myself in. "I'm inside the chopper. We can go now," I shouted as I reached for my rifle. Rucker grabbed my arm and nearly pulled me out as he swung aboard and plopped down beside me. I looked between the seats at the new 17th Cav copilot; he looked eighteen or nineteen years old and his face was completely covered with pimples. *Oh, great!*

I turned back. Rucker was now crammed up against me, his white phosphorus grenade attached to his web gear was right up against my ear. "Get that thing away from me," I complained.

Every man on the team carried at least one white phosphorus grenade, as well as the SOP six baseball grenades. The old pineapple-shaped grenades of World War II had long been used up. The phosphorus grenades, or willy peters (for "White Phosphorus"), as we called them, were designed to allow us time to break contact with a larger enemy force. The grenade was a long cylinder with the letters WP on it. When you tossed that puppy, everyone came to a stop. When it explodes, it rains out splinters of phosphorus and no one was going to chase us through that rain because if any of it got on your skin, your only remedy was to try to pick it out with a knife. And if you didn't get it out, it would burn right through your flesh and out the other side. I had put some hundred-mile-an-hour tape (duct tape) around my grenade's handle so the pin wouldn't get caught on some wait-a-minute vine and explode the damn thing right on my chest.

I took a hard look at everyone, then turned back to yell in Rucker's ear as the helicopter began to lift, "Don't be coppin' no zees on me in the field, Mother; I'm too short."

"My ass is wired tight. Don't worry about it," Rucker fired back. "Smell that?" he said.

I took a whiff. It was the ever-present odor of aviation fuel.

"It smells like your sister," Rucker said.

"Rucker, you smell like my sister."

The chopper rocked back and lifted off the ground. The bird climbed, then dropped its nose to gain speed. Rucker did his infamous war holler above the ever-present high-pitch whine of the turbine engine. Then he scooted across the floor of the chopper to sit next to Closson.

"Rucker!" I yelled.

"What?"

"You looked like a dog dragging his butt down the driveway."

"I feel like it, too."

I turned back, released my grip on the metal frame and stared out the open door. I watched Camp Eagle disappear behind us.

The flight gave me a lot of time to think. I remembered the time we were in the middle of an ambush. We got away and hid from the gooks, then watched as the enemy team leader motioned to his men to flank us. One of the gook soldiers pulled out a piece of camouflage parachute, shook off the dust, then covered his back. At that instant, he became invisible. They had all kinds of crude tactics that no amount of firepower could defend against. I had heard back in Recondo School that the enemy had counterrecon units that roamed the A Shau Valley. They were NVA regulars, trained as trackers, to be called in whenever trail watchers discovered a Ranger team walking around. Their job was to hunt us down and kill us. Some of the teams had even reported hearing dogs with the NVA tracking them.

Twenty-five minutes later, the bellyman tapped me on the shoulder. "Get ready!" he shouted. The helicopter made a wide circle, descended, and made a false landing on a ridge near our intended target. I glanced over my shoulder at the door gunner, who was intently watching for any signs of enemy movement. I looked down at the row of bomb craters. The previous night's rain had filled them up, and they looked like mud-filled swimming pools.

The pilot circled back over the ridgetop, then headed toward an opening in the jungle. The LZ (landing zone) was a small field, fronted on one side by double-canopy jungle. I rechecked my rifle, pulling back on the charging handle to make sure that a live round was chambered, then carefully slid the handle forward.

We landed in saw grass and shrubs, underlaid by a spongy layer of peat and muck. I was the first one out, and dropped three feet to the ground. I tried to run, but each step felt like the mud was pulling my boots off. The monsoon season had found a receptive home there. But the team finally got off the LZ, and we set up a temporary perimeter. It took a few minutes for the sounds of the chopper to fade away. It wasn't our first time there, so we knew what to expect.

The usual procedure is to select an easily identified landmark. I chose where the jungle cut a pathway up the hill. Then I rechecked my compass. We were right where we should be. The biggest problem on any mission is knowing where you're located. In Vietnam, because of the need to pinpoint your own location to aid helicopter extraction and artillery plotting, being able to read a map and use a compass were absolute necessities. If you didn't know how, you would soon find yourself carrying a radio or walking slack or rear security. The team leader (TL), assistant team leader (ATL), and point man had to be experts at reading the terrain. If they weren't, you could find yourself lost, or worse—on the gun–target line of friendly fire.

The daylight was shrouded by the clouds, and only the North Vietnamese loved that because they could then travel day and night undetected, as if they owned the place—which they did. Shitty weather was their best friend because our helicopters had to sit on the ground. If you were unfortunate enough to be on the ground someplace else, as we were, you didn't dare move. You just sat on your ass and looked at nothing and hoped nothing was looking back. If you got into a firefight after the weather moved in, there was little hope of fast rescue. Your only hope was to break contact.

Trying to keep everything together was a constant fight. The slightest sound could travel hundreds of feet inside the jungle. Any metallic sound seemed to travel even farther. Talking was a no-no, and coughing was out of the question. If we were sick, we still went out. We just took extra Darvon and got over whatever it was—whether it was a hangover or a cold. That morning, I had the worst headache—it felt like someone had driven a stake between my eyes. Even so, I rechecked my ammo pouches, made sure everything was secure; then we moved out.

Most of the time, our communications were one way; the team's radios were turned off to conserve the batteries. At the designated sitrep (situation report) times, we'd stop and give the team a break while the team leader would call in, report the team's position and enemy observations.

This also gave your body a chance to get in tune with the jungle. We'd have to adjust to the sounds, smells, and sights, as well as changes in terrain. I'd stop every so often, just to look and listen. Moving through a new AO was like visiting an unfamiliar house. If you're there for a while, pretty soon everything starts to feel comfortable.

Then there were the sounds of the jungle at night. We'd get hit by droves of ravenous mosquitoes, which would fly inches from your ears and wait for your bug repellent to wash away so they could start their next feast. There was also the chirp of tree frogs; if they stopped, you got scared.

I was looking for shadows, silhouettes, or anything out of the ordinary. I'd try to move the vegetation in front of me without making noise. Our rear security, Hillman, was doing the same, covering our trail as we went. The idea was to put all the leaves and branches back where they were, as if no one had even been there. He had to do this at a slow pace, but fast enough to keep up with the team.

My biggest fear was tripping or falling and injuring myself because that would screw everybody up and could compromise our mission. So you try to balance speed with doing everything correctly. You also never wanted to silhouette yourself against the skyline. So my strategy was to walk below the ridgeline, just below the trail, even if that meant breaking brush. The good news was there was always an animal trail or two running parallel to a human trail.

Meanwhile, I was saying to myself, "What if?" What happens if you get attacked from the side or from the front? What if there's a booby trap overhead? Where is the best place to jump off the trail?

Like everyone else, I was carrying a hundred pounds of shit that kept getting snagged on wait-a-minute vines. Ricky New Guy was right behind me. Next came Closson, and behind him, on the radio, was Rucker. Doc Glasser was walking fifth, and the tail was Hillman. All morning, we kept hitting clearings, and I began seeing mirages of North Vietnamese jumping out from behind bushes. I was imagining the bastards popping up and down, like they were playing games with me. That day was the slowest I'd ever walked.

By midafternoon, it started raining; not the way it rained back home in northern California where you could see it coming for miles. I could remember watching Penner's cattle walk slowly toward the barn to take cover. My grandmother would yell at me to take the clothes off the line, and I'd still have plenty of time to roll the windows up in my Chevy.

Not in the A Shau; the rain never started slowly. The air was so wet, it simply burst into a downpour. Within seconds, every part of you was soaked, even those parts held tight by fear. Then every step became such a struggle that there was little pleasure in sucking in raindrops even though they tasted a hell of a lot better than the water in our plastic canteens. Purification tablets made the canteen water taste like liquid plastic.

Then the rain shifted direction, and I followed it, mouth open, trying to catch as much as I could. Something made me stop. In the back of my mind a warning sounded: *Hey, wake up, jerk. Something is about to happen.*

I closed my mouth, wiped the raindrops off my forehead, and brought my CAR-15 to the ready. I kept feeling there were gooks just around the next corner, or the next. I'd walk fifty meters and stop, seeing imaginary gooks running just ahead of me. Next, lightning lit up the mountains with giant luminescent explosions. I tried to clear my mind and didn't tell anyone on the team what I was experiencing. But it was difficult to not react. I knew the surrounding jungle was filled with NVA patrols. We'd also learned from one of our CCN buddies back at FOB-1 that the NVA had been using counterrecon units, NVA soldiers trained as trackers and stationed at strategic locations along the Ho Chi Minh trail—which meant here, in the A Shau Valley. Once the gooks discovered the LRRPs' presence, within twenty-four hours the LRRPs would become the hunted.

My mind raced, questioning both my map reading and my instincts. Our maps could be so far off that we could be in the wrong AO and not know it. The maps were compliments of the Imperial Japanese Army who had occupied Vietnam during World War II. I stopped again, rechecked the map, folded it up, stuck it back in my cargo pocket, and started moving again. Thumb-size leeches dropped from tree branches onto our necks and slithered up our pant legs. We kept moving. Finally, we found some good cover, with vines. We'd wait there for darkness. I looked back, Closson motioned me to go deeper in. It took a few minutes for my eyes to adjust to the darkness. I'd read that the cones in your eyes enable you to see colors and have depth perception in daylight, but they weren't worth a shit at night. But in the thick jungle, when it got dark, color and depth perception didn't matter much anyway.

I hoped Closson wanted us to stay put. I didn't want to stop unless it was to set up our night defensive position: during monsoon season, the temperature would drop into the forties and fifties and, after hiking with ninety-pound rucks, if we stopped, soaked with sweat, we'd start shivering. Closson told us we'd spend the night there. I was happy.

That night I whispered back and forth with Doc Glasser about what had really happened to Ron Reynolds. I told Doc that Ron and I were best friends and how he knew he was going to die. Reynolds told me that day, before we went out, "I won't be comin' back, man." He looked as if he'd seen a ghost. I tried to joke with him, but he had that far-off stare. When it happened, he must have walked right up on some well-hidden gook, because in the bush, Reynolds was one of the best. He was the last guy I thought would get it, but he did—in the chest, three rounds. My eyes fill with tears whenever I think about Reynolds going like that.

Glasser explained, "When an AK-47 round hits, man, it starts tumbling. And that damage is irreversible. Nerves get torn apart, and the body's nervous system goes into shock and begins to shut down consciousness. Blood pressure falls, then respiration, and all vital functions come to a complete stop."

Doc Glasser had witnessed Ron's last moment. "He just fell over backward like a rag doll the moment he was hit, then lay completely still in the middle of waist-deep elephant grass. Ron was tough and didn't die right away. I held him in my arms, waiting for a medevac. The last thing Ron said to me was 'I'm thirsty.' Then he closed his eyes and died."

Even near death, water had a high priority. I opened my canteen and took a drink.

Later that night, we moved again in case we'd been seen by a trail watcher. We crawled farther into the murky, triple-canopy vegetation of the fucking A Shau Valley. Unfortunately, I set us up right next to an anthill, a huge sucker that looked like a miniature, mud-covered volcano. So I got up and moved the team around until we found a flat spot. Then I set out my claymore, opened an LRP ration, and sat on a mossy log with my CAR-15 in my lap. Relaxing might mean death. It was clear that the fun and games had ended for me; I didn't want to do this anymore.

After five miserable days of humping and sitting in the rain, pulling leeches off at every stop, we were about to concede that the AO was clean. No traces of the enemy, just a waste of another B-52 bombing run.

The night before we were to extract seemed longer than any night I'd ever experienced before. When it was my turn to pull guard, I spent the whole time staring at the second hand on my luminescent watch dial. Then, when my watch was over, I couldn't sleep. I listened to the drone of approaching mosquitoes. They kept swarming around my ears. My hands were itching like crazy, so I just lay there under my poncho liner thinking about everything and nothing.

That night I decided I'd had enough.

Short Arm Inspections

Later, back at the hootch, I sat under the mosquito net draped over my cot, reading a letter from my cousin, Donna. Dixie dog was gnawing on a bone, while Jim Peterson and Steve Passmore argued about the Beatles. Stateside they had served in the Special Forces together, but they'd gotten drunk one too many times and ended up in Nam, reassigned to the Rangers. Passmore was trying to convince Pete that there was a coded message in one of the Beatles' songs. Peterson had to explain to him that Paul wasn't really dead.

Frankly, I wasn't interested. My concern was my forthcoming R & R trip to Australia. I was counting the days. Each night as I drifted off to sleep, I kept hoping I would wake up and find myself on a civilian plane. I was also doing some serious soul searching about the fear I was experiencing. I didn't want to be thought of as a coward for leaving my team. Since we were all volunteers, it wasn't hard to get off a team—pride was the motivator that kept guys going back out in the field. But if you stayed too long, you began to make stupid mistakes.

Foul weather kept our teams out of the jungle long enough for my R & R to finally arrive before I had to go out on another mission. I didn't want to miss my flight out of Bien Hoa, so I left the base two days early and hitched a connecting flight on an empty Marine Chinook. At least it was headed south.

I was sitting on the nylon seats, watching the crew chief scan the open window with his M-60. Suddenly we made a hard turn back to the north and started to drop. I asked the crew chief what was going on. He told me that unless I wanted a front row seat on a CA (combat assault), I had better get off at the next stop. The huge helicopter landed at a firebase near Da Nang, and I jumped out the back as thirty Marines in full combat gear ran aboard. The crew chief waved as the back door closed and the heavy bird flew off.

Now I was stuck on some remote Marine firebase without a weapon, and it was getting late. I wandered around until a Marine gunnery sergeant spotted my army uniform. "How did you get here?"

"I walked," I quipped. He didn't laugh, but he did tell me where I could find the base NCO club.

I walked inside and heard a bell ringing. The bartender pointed at my black Ranger baseball cap. "No covers in the bar, Sarge." In Marine jargon that meant that I couldn't wear my hat inside. Then he announced, "Hey, army, it's required for you to buy the bar a round!" That hat cost me ten bucks. After a few drinks and some serious bullshitting, I arranged for a place to crash and a ride out the next morning.

It took a series of zigzag connections before I finally made my flight to Australia, none the worse for wear. Before boarding the plane to Australia, we had been ordered to drop our pants. Then a medic examined us by eye to confirm that we didn't have the clap. This was one of the infamous "short arm" inspections, famous among GIs since World War II. It was a mandatory test required by the Australian government before they'd allow us to run free among their women. Probably not a bad idea given the VD (i.e., STD) rate among GIs in Vietnam.

After a day of walking around the wet streets of Sydney, I caught a flight to the capital of Australia, Canberra. I hopped a bus for a three-hour ride to the Snowy Mountains, then checked into a hotel at the ski resort village at Mount Kosciusko. It was winter there, and I tried to blend in; I bought ski clothes, rented all the equipment. But I couldn't disguise my eyes. They reflected eight months of Vietnam.

It was a totally different world. No one carried a submachine gun or said the word "gook." I spent my entire R & R skiing, sleeping, and pretending I was not an American. Fortunately for me, the pretending part didn't work. I discovered that Australian women really like American men, even GIs. I nearly missed my flight back home. I couldn't believe it; I was now calling Vietnam "home?"

Discovered

I returned from Australia to meet our new sergeant first class, Robert "Top" Gilbert. He was in his late thirties and had fought in Korea. He was on his fourth tour in Nam. He'd also been with Special Forces and seemed like a regular guy. Top was interested in everything, especially whatever he could do to make our lives better.

Unfortunately, we had also picked up a replacement platoon leader, a second lieutenant new out of OCS (Officers Candidate School). An officer's tour in the field was only six months long, so most of them barely had time to learn where the shitter was let alone what to do in the real war in the jungle.

The second lieutenant invited me on an overflight with him. At first I thought he was going to ask my advice on missions in the jungle; I couldn't have been more wrong. In fact, he never asked me diddly-squat. He kept studying his map and bothering the pilots with stupid questions.

I shook my head, put on my flight helmet, plugged in my mike, and sat back—hiding my face so the pilots wouldn't recognize me and connect me with that bozo. Finally he tapped me on the leg, pointed at his topo map, and asked me if that place looked like a good DZ (drop zone—where parachutists land). I politely corrected him, informing him that here we called it an LZ (a landing zone, a place suitable for landing a helicopter and

32

debarking troops). He fired back. "I know what an LZ is, Sergeant. I'm looking for a drop zone." Then he let me in on his grand plan. His goal was to trap the 5th NVA Regiment (about one thousand men). He planned to spring a huge ambush along route 547. Then he'd chase the gooks into Laos and have a *platoon* (maybe thirty men) do a parachute drop behind them.

Because I wanted to be sure not to be there, I asked him how soon he was planning on doing this. I thought, This is the final straw. We had back-to-back missions, and now we've got a John Wayne–type second lieutenant who wants to really kick some NVA ass. Anyone with any sense knew the cost was too high for that kind of maneuver.

When I was a cherry paratrooper, I may have had a fantasy of making a combat blast behind enemy lines—guns blazing, enemy dying. But in the A Shau Valley, that would have spelled suicide. The gooks would know about it before we boarded the planes and would be waiting with antiaircraft guns.

When we returned from the overflight, I made a beeline for the tactical operations center to keep my appointment with the new "first shirt," First Sergeant Gilbert. I was apprehensive as I walked down the short ramp and into the TOC. I couldn't figure out why the first shirt singled me out to talk. I thought it had to be about that bozo's air assault plan. I walked into the radio room.

After a handshake, Gilbert got right to the point. He needed a replacement radio-relay team leader, somebody who had already been in the field. He wanted me to take out the next team. Because of how deep into enemy territory we were inserting our teams, the radios that the Ranger teams carried wouldn't reach Camp Eagle. The solution was to place a radio-relay team with a bigger antenna somewhere on higher ground near the area of operation. We went over strategy, and Gilbert told me to pick the guys I wanted for the team. Boy was I happy. He also told me I was a new sergeant; I was even happier.

The first guy I picked for my team was Saenz. Larry Saenz was a stocky twenty-year-old from Michigan. He wore an old tiger-stripe beret, laughed a lot, and looked more like a fullback than an infantryman. I located him, and we walked together to get dinner and talk about the upcoming mission until we heard a scuffle on the berm.

We went to check out the noise but stopped dead in our tracks when we saw Steve Passmore running naked, except for his combat boots and a red Superman cape. He was chasing after Peterson, trying to stab him with a bayonet. When I recovered the ability to speak, I turned to Saenz. "I guess it is true that saltpeter can change a guy's personality."

The next day, Saenz and I took a drive down to China Beach for a short break. The weather was really hot, even in the shade. We sat on an embankment overlooking the beach and talked with some local Vietnamese kids. We were just killing time, waiting to go out on the radio-relay mission. Every few minutes, a helicopter whizzed overhead, and we'd both automatically stop talking and look up. Even the Vietnamese kids got that thousand-meter stare when a chopper flew over.

I could relate with those local kids, but I wasn't sure why. They were just a bunch of stinky, dirty, flat-faced kids with mud ground under their fingernails and so much dirt worked into the skin of their feet that their toes were permanently darker than the rest of their skin. They were sitting around with us, talking and smoking cigarettes. They'd been harassing and begging the GIs walking by, but they didn't ask us for anything. I guessed they'd already harassed their quota of GIs that morning and were taking a break.

One of the older kids offered me a cigarette. He told me his name was Danny. I'm sure his real name probably was Dong or Nguyen or something, but he answered to Danny. I'd guess he was eight or nine years old. On either side of him were two kids he claimed were his younger brothers. Danny sat with a carton of Camel cigarettes just under the back of his shirt, watching my every move. On my left was a tall skinny kid who looked as if he could have been a young VC in training. We sat for a while in silence, then Danny asked in broken English, "You have a car, GI?"

"A car? Sure," I said.

"What you got, Cadillac?"

"No, I've got a Chevy."

"You married?" Danny asked.

I started to laugh. "No wife." All three kids laughed, too.

"You rich number one GI." Then Danny translated to his "brothers" what he said.

"I wish! You think every American is rich?"

He looked very serious. "You have car, right?"

"So what, everyone back home has a car. That doesn't mean nothin'."

"See, rich! No one here got car. No one in family, no one in village got car. You probably very rich."

I'd never thought of it that way. Maybe I was rich. At least Danny and his brothers thought so. As if from another life, I heard my name called. I looked up and saw Larry Saenz motioning to me.

"I have to go, Danny. So long," I said as I jumped to my feet.

"You leave Vietnam?" Danny asked.

"Yes, but not for three more months."

"Today?"

"No, not today."

"Too bad. You number one. You number one GI. When you come back, bring me big car." They all laughed as Danny lit up another cigarette and passed it around. "Big *red* car." He put his hands on his flat stomach, laughing a huge belly laugh, almost falling over backward.

"Yeah, right—when I come back!"

I had only known that kid for a few minutes, but I felt as close to him as anybody I'd met in Nam. I liked being around those kids. I shook the dust off the bottom of my pants and started walking slowly back to our ride.

Danny called out, "Hey, what your name, GI?"

I turned slowly around. "Bond, James Bond."

They all laughed again. I wondered if they understood my joke.

Saenz and I hopped in the jeep and headed back to the company area. That night I packed for the mission—the radios, my gear, CAR-15, two bandoliers of M-16 ammo, extra tiger stripes (camouflage fatigues), and a willie peter bag full of odds and ends.

At first light, we flew out to a hastily constructed outpost guarded by a rifle company of the old Deuce (2d Battalion, 502d Infantry, 101st Airborne).

Before any Ranger team inserted, all objectives were known. Our guys didn't just go hop on a helicopter and fly around for an hour or two until we found a nice village to attack. We knew exactly where we were going and pretty much what to expect. The team leader studied every possible contingency and planned for problems associated with reaching the objective. The objective could be, say, to recon a suspected enemy base camp, or a trail used to bring troops into the country. Each objective was marked on the map and planned for, but sometimes things went wrong.

After the chopper dropped Saenz, Jimmy Walker, and me on the firebase, we hunted around for a position for our radio-relay site. The outpost we'd been sent to was a real shithole that had, at one time, contained a French villa that overlooked the whole valley. Abandoned, the ruin made a perfect combat lookout, high on a hill overlooking Elephant Valley. We'd been sent there for two consecutive six-day missions, which in army-math meant fourteen days.

Earlier that week, army engineers had been flown in along with a caterpillar to carve a ring around the side of the hill. Then the whole place was wrapped in concertina wire. But no matter what "improvements" they made, the place was just one big mud slide where two rifle companies were encamped.

I was impressed at how the villa had been built there. Most of the lookout sprawled across a hill rising above the fog-covered valley. Below was a vast sea of five-to-eight-foot-high elephant grass, bordered by bamboo. The hill sat between the coastal plains to the east and the open, rolling piedmont to the west. No roads, no path.

We were the only Rangers on the firebase, and we were wearing our black hats with jump wings—big ego-gratifying signs that shouted, "I'm a Ranger and you're not!" Unfortunately, I had to take orders from another cherry second lieutenant, of the rifle company, who allowed us the privilege of bivouacking right along the perimeter.

The compound's perimeter would hardly have presented a serious challenge to an NVA sapper team bent on penetrating the compound because elephant grass was the perfect concealment for a large NVA force moving up to attack. But in spite of the obvious weaknesses of our fortress, there were also some strong points. One of the infantry companies provided perimeter security for the compound, and it made me almost feel safe.

"Grunts." Saenz spit, looking out over the compound. The infantry grunts were strung out on both sides of the saddle. Most were busy playing radios, eating C rats, or boiling canteen cups of water for coffee or cocoa. They had posted security out over the edge of the ridge at a number of places.

When the receiving officer saw us standing off to one side, he stopped his conversation, introduced himself, and shook our hands. He filled us in on enemy troop movements and the weather report from division. He promised us a good week of heavy fog. The high humidity, cool weather, and total absence of surface winds were responsible for the thick overcast. Our own intel reports had enemy activity in the area, possibly a base camp somewhere, below and south of the ridgeline, less than two klicks out.

I found a spot next to their CO's command bunker and told some shit-for-brains leg second lieutenant that we would save him a canister of vanilla ice cream if he'd let us move. We got the flat spot to set up our tents. Of course, I was lying; I hadn't seen ice cream in a year.

I carried over two extra radio batteries, and Saenz hauled a couple of jerry-cans of water. A Huey flew over, and I flashed him a good-luck wave, then watched the aircraft fly over the overhanging clouds and disappear.

While we set up our tents, I told Saenz how we used to screw with the new recruits back in basic. "The cadre would have us up all night doing some E & E (escape and evasion) training, playing hide-'n'-seek. They'd make us take off running through the woods just after dark; the object being to get to the other side before daybreak. To make it interesting, the DIs (drill instructors) would pound the crap out of you if they were able to catch you, then toss you in a wet pit to spend the rest of the night. I never got caught. I figured that survival was what E & E was all about, so I got creative. I'd take off like everyone else, running like hell. But then I'd stop, double back, and low crawl back to where the next group of trainees would be waiting patiently.

There I could see what the DIs were up to. They had flashlights and M-16s with flash suppressors, and they'd scare the hell out of the guys. I'd get behind the group of guys whose job it was to harass the shit out of us, then head in the opposite direction. I'd find a safe spot under a huge tree, lie down, and go to sleep. I would stay there until first light, then head to the main road that circled around the forest.

It would have really pissed them off if they had found out, but I didn't care. I'd come out on a road a couple of hundred meters ahead of the bivouac. I could see silhouettes of soldiers sitting on the ground like a bunch of captured enemy. I'd sneak in close to their position, then low crawl up close to the group. Then I just laid back in the tall grass and waited for the last guys to pop out, so I could casually walk over to the group. I wouldn't even be tired, and everyone else would be shivering, cold, and wet. We would form a file and march back to the barracks.

"You didn't really do that?" asked Saenz, wearing his I'm-not-buying-it look.

"Of course I did, Saenz-man," I replied matter-of-factly. But as we spoke in Vietnam, it seemed more like a long-ago dream.

I spent some time setting up the artillery radio. Then I left Saenz in charge and headed over to the CO's bunker, which was set up inside the abandoned villa, to check in and tell the legs where we'd be sleeping.

The villa had thick concrete walls and twelve-foot-high ceilings. The roof had been blown off long ago. The old dining room floor was buried under thick mud and had been converted to a command post. I walked in and immediately caught a whiff of cigar smoke. At first, no one paid any attention to me as I stood there reading the major's name tag, "Beasley." He was approaching early middle age, maybe thirty-six or thirty-seven, with sunbaked dark skin. As he wrote intently in a spiral note-book with the stub of a pencil I saw that he was short, with a face like a bulldog, and he was chomping on a cigar.

I came to attention, saluted, then introduced myself. "Sir. Sergeant Chambers reporting in for L Company, 75th Rangers. We have three teams in your AO." Without even looking up, he said, "You and your men will be required to be at all meetings, and you will stay out of our way. Briefing every three hours." A really fucking friendly conversation. I returned to the tent and briefed Saenz that this was going to be a real pleasant stay, thanks to Major Asshole.

On the east side, the grunts had established a long oval perimeter along the crest of the ridge. They set out a few clay-mores and a similar number of trip flares, then curled up and went to sleep. It was the dark side of the moon, except for the occasional flare string of tracers that formed a red line into the valley below. The night was filled the sounds of 155mm how-itzers blasting away, as teams, squads, and companies of in-fantry called in artillery support.

It rained so hard that night, we couldn't sleep. We spent most of the time monitoring the radio and moving to avoid the river of water that found its way into our tent. The weather and ter-rain were making radio communication all but impossible. Even command was coming in very, very faint. At the first briefing, we got word that two battalions of NVA were present and moving in the valley below us. During the night, frequent aerial flares from the firebase illuminated the surrounding countryside. I tried to focus my eyes in the eerie light that made its way through the cloaking ground fog. Flitting shadows cast by the descending flares as they oscillated back and forth played tricks with my night vision and kept me on edge.

"Man, I can't sleep. My feet are itching so bad I'm going to tear off my boot laces and floss between my toes," Saenz com-plained. He kept getting up and sitting down in an attempt to find some comfort.

"At least we're under this piece-of-shit tent," I said, trying to find something positive in our situation.

"I'm going to see if one of the line doggies has a can of foot powder I can borrow. I'll be right back." Saenz got up to leave. Walker said, "I could use a stretch," and went with him.

It was 1900 hours. I had nearly dozed off when I heard the clang of another American 81mm mortar spitting illumination rounds into the air over the perimeter. An empty cannister hit the ground nearby. Then the rattle of small arms split the silence. Then the whole west side of the perimeter opened up. I thought it was what the grunts called a "mad-minute." That's when everyone on the line shoots for a minute or two. Kind of an infantry way of pounding on their chests to scare away the enemy. I'm sure it worked great for gorillas and monkeys, but I thought it just gave away your position.

"Saenz." I looked around. He and Walker were still gone. A loud explosion sounded—a mortar hitting the perimeter. I immediately lay flat on the ground. A piece of shrapnel flew over my head and thudded into the ground about three meters behind me. They must have been firing HE rounds into the valley. I looked back and adjusted my eyes. It was jagged and shaped like an upside-down teardrop, about the size of my fist, and glowing dark red. I could almost feel the heat from it.

I pushed off the ground and low crawled over to get a closer look. Another flare popped overhead and drifted under a small parachute over the concertina-wired perimeter. For the moment, the valley was flooded with a dim light, but I couldn't see any enemy attacking.

I reached for my CAR-15. "Saenz," I called in a low voice. No response. I couldn't take my eyes off the valley, but I had to turn back and see if the shrapnel was real. It was real, all right. I started thinking about what it would have done to me, had it been just a little lower. I could hear the sounds of our machine guns on the backside of the perimeter and the popping sound of more mortar firing.

Saenz and Walker were still nowhere to be found. The radio was silent. I knocked over one of the extra batteries and a box of

C rations as I crawled over to the radio. There I was, alone, hunched down on someone else's firebase in someone else's country. I thought about how stupid the infantry was; they almost blew me up.

A thought suddenly raced across my mind like a ticker on the New York Stock Exchange: I could get out of here, early. No one would know. I could crawl back to that red-hot piece of shrapnel and drive it into my calf, like a stake into the heart of Dracula. I contemplated which leg it ought to be, my right or left, and took a breath. Then a rush of adrenaline filled my body as I realized what I was about to do. No one would know. I would sever the tendon just above the ankle, at the back of my calf. The metal was still glowing, so the heat would cauterize the wound. Then I would roll on the ground and yell, "I'm hit! I'm hit!" I'd wrap the wound with an aid pack if I could, and no one would suspect I'd done it myself. The medevac would take me to the aid station, or maybe to a hospital ship, safe and off the coast, to spend the last of my tour in luxury. The whole scenario played out as the mortar shrapnel's glow ebbed from dark red to just dark. Then it just disappeared into the mud. Of course, by then, I had changed my mind.

A few minutes later, I heard voices from up the hill. Saenz and Walker were crawling down the trail. "Chambers," Saenz whispered.

"Here. What's the password?"

"Your mother's the password." He squatted down behind me. "We've been mortared," Saenz said, as if he had been on a paid vacation to the moon.

"No shit, Cheezedick. But it was our own guys." I told him a piece of shrapnel flew within inches of my head. "Look back there," I pointed. "It was red-hot, man. Can you dig it? The gooks can't kill me, so now my own side is trying."

Then Saenz stepped into the hole under the soggy tent. "You're so full of your own bullshit, man." He moved the batteries. "You think you're Audie frickin' Murphy."

"That's Mr. Murphy to you, assbite. Did you get your foot powder for your little tootsies?"

"No, but Walker scored a turkey loaf C ration and three warm cokes."

With the dawn, a thick gray fog filled the valley all the way up to the perimeter, and I was shivering from the dampness. Saenz relieved Walker at the radio and answered one of the team's sitreps, "I roger your transmission. Over. Negative sitrep. Two-six. Over."

I looked over at Saenz. "Everything's quiet?" He nodded his head. It was 0500, and nobody spoke again for an hour. That was the morning we lost radio contact with Frank Anderson's team.

I was sitting on a flat spot about to light a ball of C-4 (plastic explosive). I had just opened the can of turkey loaf. I thought it might make a good breakfast meal, but the smell made me sick. Even cooking that shit couldn't change its taste to turkey. I tossed the turkey loaf can down the hill and lit the C-4. "Hey, Saenz; ever wonder who lit the first ball of C-4? Pretty gutsy, huh? I want to find him and say, 'Thank you, you made life a little easier.'" Almost instantly, the water came to a boil.

Cooking with C-4 eliminated the problems of odor and smoke that you got when army Sterno cans boiled water. That was one of the first skills I learned as a cherry—how to cook without smoke. Snuffie Smith taught me the ritual. Take about a half-inch piece of C-4, roll it in a ball, and set it between a couple of rocks; light it, place a steel canteen filled with water on it, and within seconds, it will be boiling. No odor or smoke. Nothing.

Before each mission, I'd put a couple of balls of C-4 in my pocket. The hot water we boiled was the source of one of the few pleasures we had out on patrol. You won't find that tip in any army field manual, and it will never show up in a Ranger handbook; but every grunt, Sneaky Pete, or LRRP who spent a night in the jungle knew about it. Unfortunately, lifers—who generally went by the book—would go ballistic if they caught you. A Sterno can was the army way.

Of course there was a downside to this technique: You had to be careful to check your claymores before packing up. Nothing was worse than blowing an ambush with a half-empty claymore because someone had been cannibalizing the C-4 blasting charge. Still, the pleasure of having a cup of coffee was worth the risk.

Usually in the early morning when on a mission, I'd mix one package of cocoa with one package of coffee and a couple of packs of sugar. All the guys would crowd around—wiping the moisture off their rifles, adjusting their load-bearing equipment (LBE), pulling in their packs, and getting ready to have an LRRP ration before setting off. I'd pass the cup around, and each man would take a sip. That was our sacred communion, and that simple ritual would get us ready for the rest of the day.

Besides, if any gooks walked up, we could just tip the cup in their direction and say, "Come on over and let's work this shit out. Just you and me. Here's the plan. You don't shoot me, and I won't shoot you, fair enough? Here, have some coffee." Wouldn't that be the day!

I could hear the grunts starting to move around, making noise and talking as if they were back on the block. I handed my cup of cocoa to Saenz and headed up the hill for the morning get-together. I climbed up the old rock stairs and walked straight up to a tight cluster of officers seated in metal folding chairs, drinking hot coffee, and taking notes. Old Major Bulldog was talking to his platoon leaders and didn't acknowledge my existence. I took a seat in the rear. About the time he was giving us directives about how we were to act, an OH-6A (Loach) scout helicopter popped up over the edge of the perimeter, then sidled over to the center of the firebase, setting down in an open area next to the command bunker. The sound echoed inside the room. Everyone ran outside except me. I walked over to the open ledge and watched.

Seconds later, two officers stepped down and walked toward Major Bulldog. One was a tough looking, full-bird colonel, and the other was Maj. Gen. Melvin Zais, commander of the 101st Airborne Division.

I ran to the other side of the ledge, waved at Saenz and yelled,

"Hey, Saenz, it's your boss." Saenz flipped me the bird. He was listening to the squawk on both radios and sipping coffee at the same time. Another one of our teams was calling in its sitrep.

Meanwhile, General Zais walked inside, with everyone following like pups behind their mother. He spent about thirty minutes telling them what a great job they were all doing. I thought old Major Bulldog was going to start crying, he was so happy. As Zais walked back to his chopper, I got out my camera and yelled down, "Hey, General!" He and all the brass turned, and I snapped his picture. Zais waved; the bulldog glared.

While I was busy making friends and influencing officers, the second of our teams—call sign One-three—had inserted uneventfully. They spent the day walking around until they found a trail. Frank Anderson was the team leader.

The first time I'd met Anderson was eight months earlier when John Burford and I pulled his leg—so to speak. At the time Anderson was a fresh cherry, ready to try anything. He was the kind of guy you expected to see in a surfing magazine—lean, tan, blond hair—not the normal-looking Ranger, if there was such a thing.

That night, Burford and I pretended to go outside the wire to kill some Viet Cong. What we really did was go have coffee until we knew Anderson was asleep, then we crashed into the tent as if we had just escaped with our lives. I tossed an old AK-47 we'd borrowed from the TOC on his cot, and Burford pretended to be arguing with me about killing so many gooks. Frank was sitting up, all wide-eyed, and asked me if I killed some enemy soldiers. I took out my K-bar knife and let him run his fingers over the blade. "Blood!" he stammered, as he pulled his hand away. I just nodded. He never figured out we were bullshitting him until months later.

Anderson's senior radio operator and assistant team leader was Jim Peterson. Pete had also been there the night we goofed on Anderson, but questioned how we got out and back. Billy McCabe was their point man. William Solomon McCabe was a full-blooded Navajo Indian from Parker, Arizona. Of course, he was known to us as Chief. He was famous for his W. C. Fields imitation. A neat guy. McCabe had a sixth sense—when his ears started to ring, there were gooks around. On a number of missions, he'd be on a listening halt, and nobody would hear a thing. You could look at him, and he would point at his ears, meaning they were ringing. Without fail, gooks would be in the area. Ken Young was walking rear guard and would trade off at point.

Their mission was supposed to be a four-day operation into the Elephant Valley, so each man on the team carried the minimum LRRP rations and the customary thirteen quarts of water. They wore web gear, i.e., H-harness suspenders, and a pistol belt. Every man on the team wore camouflage fatigues. Anderson, Pete, and Young all carried CAR-15s, and McCabe had an M-79 (single-shot 40mm grenade launcher). Pete and Anderson also carried the new URC-10 radios Rangers were experimenting with. We couldn't receive on them, just transmit a beacon. The drill when in trouble was to transmit four minutes of a beacon and then one minute in the open with no code.

Anderson had strapped a strobe light (for signaling to helicopters) to his right shoulder, over which he hooked his CAR-15. The sling was attached from the front side to the sling fixture on the butt of the CAR-15. On the left shoulder of his web gear was a K-bar. On the pistol belt, he had two M-14 pouches for five M-16 ammo magazines each; four standing on end, open-end down, and one flat in the lid. A lot of guys preferred the M-14 pouch because you could carry five mags, as compared to the four that would fit in the standard-issue M-16 pouch.

On each side of the ammo pouches hung a hand grenade. On the right side, just behind the ammo pouch, a canteen cover contained five more frags. In Anderson's rucksack was a radio, an extra battery, a claymore, and two and a half pounds of C-4 in the form of two M-112 blocks. Taped onto his back were four smoke grenades—one red and the rest yellow.

Team leaders normally made an overflight before each mission, but they hadn't this time. The team was looking for a base camp that intel knew was on one of the three hills surrounding the valley.

Anderson told us later that McCabe said he had a really bad feeling about that patrol. Anderson wasn't real excited about the mission either.

As nightfall came, Anderson's team moved to a hill adjacent to the suspected enemy location. It was dark before they realized they'd made a mistake. But without an overflight and going in on the low ground, the error wasn't surprising.

McCabe's ears were ringing like crazy that night as they moved up the hill, and sure enough, they began to hear movement. What they didn't know was that they were headed directly into the enemy's base camp. McCabe switched the point position with Young. The team moved a couple of times to try to get out from the hot zone and into an area of really thick brush. They were in a first layer canopy when they spotted ten enemy soldiers coming down toward them in an inverted V formation.

I received Anderson's 2200 hours sitrep. He said he had enemy elements swinging around his position, possibly platoon size. They were not walking trails; they were breaking brush—which was unusual. It sounded to me like they were trying to flank Anderson's team and come in from below. He had been on time with his next sitrep call. It seemed they had given the NVA the slip. If his team was compromised, the bad weather would prevent the helicopters from pulling them out. All we could do was sit tight and hold their hands over the radio. By then, it was around three in the morning, and I had turned the watch over to Saenz.

What we didn't know was that the gooks had already moved in on Anderson. Young was sitting at rear security, suddenly he opened fire on the tree line. The gooks returned fire and hit him in the leg, taking a chunk of muscle out of his calf. It was pitch-black dark. McCabe was trying to use the M-79 like a mortar, firing it up, but it damn near came back down on the team—so he stopped.

The gooks then opened fire on the rest of the team. A grenade exploded, and the concussion tossed Peterson into a one-and-a-half gainer from a kneeling position. Anderson was sitting with the headset on, trying to make radio contact, when something hit the right side of his head. He told me later that it felt like somebody had slapped him with a baseball bat. He had actually taken a grenade fragment one and a half inches above his right ear. At that point, he tried to pull everybody in, get some cover, and return fire to hold the gooks back.

McCabe saw the silhouette of a gook trying to flank them. The enemy soldier appeared to be holding a canvas bag, and McCabe assumed it was a satchel charge, so he opened fire when the gook was five meters away.

By this time, Saenz had gotten word from Anderson that his team was in contact. We had three radios set up on different frequencies: one on the team, one to the artillery, and one back to base. Thankfully, Anderson and I had spent time plotting preplanned artillery fire, the idea being that if he got in trouble, he would radio me a grid or reference point. If the gooks were so close he couldn't talk, the team leader could respond by breaking squelch once, then twice to acknowledge the transmission and to signal their compliance.

All I remember was being awakened out of a solid sleep by the roar of Saenz' voice. I couldn't hear what he was saying above the rain, but I knew it was bad. "Anderson's in contact. He's on the horn, and he wants to talk to you, *now*!"

Anticipating the worst, I pulled my poncho liner over my head and crawled over to the radios. Anderson was whispering over the radio, "I got beaucoup Victor Charlies on my position and three WIAs. They got lights, and they know where we are. We need Redleg (artillery) fifty meters north from my last position."

"Can you give me your present grid?" I responded.

He answered back, "Negative. I can't turn on my flashlight."

"Roger that. I'll put a marker round of HE (high explosive) fifty meters north from your last position," I replied.

Anderson had previously reported that the enemy kept moving in and out and probing. He suspected the team had been followed since they landed that morning and had been on the move all day. It would have been easy for a trail watcher to see the team insert. It had been flat land there, with elephant grass and some shrubs but not enough near the LZ that could conceal their movement, especially from high ground. Now they were trapped on a ridge and being aggressively hunted by an NVA kill team, closing in fast. Boldly hunting for the team with flashlights, the NVA flanked our guys on two sides.

I got on the other radio and called up Captain Cardona, but I knew he couldn't fly until first light. We had to do something, but all I had to go on was a frightened team leader's last known location. I was going to have to call Anderson's artillery for him blind. I checked the direction he'd been traveling from his last sitrep. Saenz held the flashlight, and I tracked the team on the map to determine what ridge they were most likely on. We had no time to spare, but we had to be precise. If I made a wrong call, I'd wipe the team out. I tried not to think about that.

I marked where I thought they were on the map. Saenz agreed. Then I called the artillery officer and shouted commands over the mike. "Redleg Seven, Redleg Seven. Cheyenne Two-two, fire mission. Over." Static filled the space between transmissions.

"This is Redleg Seven. Go!" More static.

I gave him the preplotted coordinates. "November Victor Alpha, moving to the grape two three. One-zero-zero-zero mikes from preplotted coordinates, zero niner."

The grape was our code: two for north and three for west. I figured Anderson's team was moving northwest. "Give one round willie peter air burst, then HE full battery on the deck, fire for effect. I will adjust. On my command. Fire!"

"Shot!" came back over the radio.

"Shot out," I whispered to Anderson.

Peterson was the first to hear the roar of the 155mm artillery round and looked upward through the trees. We were right on the money. Anderson came back on the radio, "Cheyenne, add fifty right, drop five zero, fire for effect!" I repeated his adjustment to artillery exactly as he had said it.

The rounds impacted fifty meters below his position. It was

thick brush. Anderson's team stayed down because they were so near the gun–target line. A fragment was thrown off the 155 round and propelled upward. Some fallout came zinging down and landed in the brush near the team, then a small fragment tore into Anderson's right leg. He'd said he wanted the fire mission *danger close*, and that's what he got.

Peterson was now working both radios even though he had taken a piece of shrapnel underneath his right eye. The shrapnel had lodged in the root of his molar. Anderson put a bandage over his eye and mouth, and Peterson had to lift it up to talk.

We had accomplished our mission. Anderson had out his topo map and was plotting a course to the LZ. He had called a cease-fire on the artillery about the time Puff, the Magic Dragon, came on station. Puff was our nickname for a C-47 (World War II vintage DC-3, a twin-engine aircraft normally used for passengers and cargo) armed with computer controlled miniguns capable of saturating with fire an area the size of a football field in just a few seconds.

Peterson gave their call sign to the Puff pilot. The pilot radioed back, "May I help you? I've got 750,000 rounds and twenty-two hours of illumination. What's the size of your perimeter?"

The enemy had already begun to move back in again. Anderson grabbed the mike from Peterson and pulled it closer, "Five meters!"

"I copy, five zero meters," the pilot responded in an unemotional tone.

Anderson shouted back over the radio, "Negative, negative, negative. *Five* meters. I say *again*, five meters!"

If the pilot was too wide, the rounds would drive the enemy right into the team, which was not the idea. The idea was to form a tight circle around the Ranger team with the plane's radar-controlled machine guns, then slowly widen the arc of the circle. Hopefully, the team would be safe inside.

The pilot said, "Roger that. I need you to mark your location."

Anderson unfastened his strobe. Afraid that the pilot would

lose sight of the strobe in the vegetation as the plane orbited, Anderson duct-taped it near the top of the whip antenna. Then he lost his balance and fell down next to Peterson. Anderson's shirt, trousers, and the top of his right boot were soaked with blood and sweat. That was the first time Peterson realized that Anderson had been hit.

The plane circled overhead; its armament system consisting of four 7.62mm Gatling guns opened up and zeroed in on the strobe light. Anderson and Peterson watched as a ribbon of white tracers came crashing down, encircling the team in a cone of fire and lighting up the night sky.

Peterson curled into a tight ball with one hand over his neck and one covering his genitals as 7.62mm machine-gun bullets rained down at six thousand rounds a minute. Every fifth bullet was a tracer round, filled with white phosphorus powder that was designed to ignite when fired, then burn an imaginary line along its path on the way to its target.

The sound was unbearably loud, like a gigantic sewing machine, metallic and precise. As the plane flew over, it dumped hot casings out, which scared the bejeezus out of everybody. Anderson told the team that the stuff falling all around them was only the plane's brass—not live bullets—and to stay put.

The plane's guns gradually worked their way out from the team, chopping up the foliage and a few NVA in the process. But Anderson was disoriented. To him, it sounded like bombs were crashing through the trees above them.

Finally, things settled down just before dawn, and the 2/17th Cav brought in a ready reaction force platoon that landed at Anderson's original LZ. Another unit headed up by a cherry second lieutenant. This one didn't even know how to call in artillery.

Anderson radioed the Blues (code name for the Cav's reaction platoon) that he had three wounded and was unable to move. Nevertheless, the second lieutenant ordered the team to move down to its original location. So Anderson picked up the team, and they hobbled downhill roughly in the direction they had come from.

Doc Gray had been brought along with the Blues to take care of the wounded. When he had heard Anderson's initial response, he started making his way toward the team. Doc didn't have a weapon, wasn't even carrying a radio. All he had with him was his aid bag and some water. Anderson's wounded team met up with Doc, and in the dim light, he dressed their wounds.

At the LZ, since the second lieutenant was unable to call in artillery, Anderson was back on the horn to me and I relayed the call. After another artillery fire mission pushed back the last of the enemy, a helicopter landed and two Kit Carson scouts came in to search the area for bodies. They saw tracks and drag marks, but no remains. They also found some AK-47 magazines, which they policed up, but no enemy dead.

Finally a slick arrived to take the team out. On the ride back, since they were safely aboard the rescue ship, Doc tried to change the dressing on Young's leg. He pulled the field dressing and revealed a mass of meat and bone which was still bleeding profusely. Doc picked some leaves and debris out of it with his fingers and was just about to rewrap it when the right door gunner hurled.

It was a *long* flight back to a fuel point, where Young was removed to a medevac. The medics left Young's wound open but gave him multiple injections of antibiotics.

Back at Eagle, Peterson's shrapnel wound was X-rayed, and the medic decided to pull his tooth, but he ended up breaking it off at the gum line. Peterson had to go through emergency dental surgery.

That night, Saenz and I talked to Anderson over the radio, and he said, "Thanks, partners. If you guys hadn't been there, we would have been toast. We couldn't have gotten out. No way."

A few days later, Anderson heard an aviation crew member talking about some asshole who was sticking his hands into some guy's leg. He was telling how the leg was all chopped up, and it made him sick. Anderson walked over and said, "Thanks for the ride. That was my team."

The grenade frag had cut a nice little groove in Anderson's

skull, traveled down and lodged underneath his right temporal artery. It took a couple of months before the wound healed, leaving a little numbness, but the sutures were out by the time he rotated back to the States.

Big Foot Lives in Vietnam

Two weeks later, one of the Kingsmen helicopters came in, picked our relay team up, and transported us to our next location, LZ Sally, where we were given our own bunker next to the command post. Boy, were we happy. Saenz set up our radios, wired the field-expedient (i.e., make do) antenna, and I called in a commo check, when we heard the screeching sounds of an APC (armored personal carrier). Saenz walked outside to see what all the noise was about. The vehicle had impressive white dragon's teeth painted on the front of its hull. Up on top, the APC's .50-caliber machine gun was manned by a guy whose arms were covered with tattoos.

I caught up with Saenz, and we walked over together. A big mistake. The back hatch opened, and as it did, the tattooed guy yelled to us to help unload its grisly cargo. We looked through the hatch. Three M-16s and an AK-47 lay next to three body bags. We didn't waste time unloading the three bags, which smelled strongly of rubber and cordite.

The next day, a replacement member for our radio-relay team arrived. It was Jim Peterson. Boy, were we surprised! He had just been released by the medics, and had been assigned to radio relay.

We spent that day getting ready for the next mission. Pete was standing next to the poncho-covered entrance of our bunker, talking to one of the infantry guys. The guy seemed cocky as he told stories about being with the Tiger Force (the recon platoon of the 1st Battalion, 327th Infantry 101st ABN). He also claimed that he had extended twice. I thought, *Right, I bet.* His name was Jeff Paige and he had grown up just outside of Atlanta, Georgia. His father had been with the army air force. Paige had joined the army right out of high school and volunteered for Vietnam. He asked Peterson a lot of questions about joining the LRRPs. Then he told us the Tiger Force had him working as a clerk.

Peterson said, "No offense, man, but we already have some company clerks."

"No, I want to be on a team," Paige explained. A lot of people would approach us about joining the company, but with many of them it was mostly talk. Paige turned out to be the real thing; later that month, he showed up and joined our Rangers.

Later that day, we were told a big storm was about to hit I Corps and was expected to last the whole month, so the missions were canceled. Saenz, Peterson, and I caught the next helicopter back to Eagle. We were flying low, and I remember looking down, watching a water buffalo in a rice field. A boy was behind the animal, holding the reins and making deep cuts in the water-filled field. The kid was up to his knees in mud. A smaller girl was standing alongside him. She wore a brown straw Chinaman's hat, a plain light gray shirt, and black silk pajama bottoms. They both looked up and waved their arms as they saw us coming. We threw our candy bars to them, which they scooped up. We had very little contact with the locals. We mostly just flew over them.

Then we flew over the largest cemetery in the world. It seemed to stretch for miles and was just on the perimeter of Camp Eagle. The stones for each grave were arranged in horseshoe shape, with a stone wall blocking the end of the U so that no evil spirit could enter the grave straight on.

When we landed, the three of us walked straight to the company club. It was open, and Passmore was acting as bartender. Kenn Miller was petting Dixie while spinning another yarn to some of the new guys about his prowess with the local hookers. The distinctive club odor was a mix of beer, stale cigarettes, and Hai Karate.

We ordered beers. After a quick drink, and one more tale of Miller's sexual adventures, we decided to visit Missy Lee—if she was still in business. Peterson brought up the saltpeter story. Miller said, "That's bullshit about saltpeter. No one is putting anything in our food. Think about it. How could Missy Lee stay in business?"

"The story I've heard is that cooks have orders to put that shit in our food to keep us from having any sex drive," I said. But I did agree with Miller that mine hadn't changed.

Miller said, "That saltpeter story has to rank up there with the black-syphilis island story."

"I haven't heard that one." Peterson said.

"There is supposed to be an island off the coast of Vietnam where they quarantine guys who get black syphilis."

"What?" Peterson shouted.

"Supposedly, they can't send those guys back to the States because the black syph is incurable, so they live together on an island somewhere . . ."

"That's bull," Saenz piped in. I agreed.

Miller continued, undaunted, "Well, it doesn't matter. Missy Lee doesn't have it."

"How would you know?" Peterson laughed.

"Missy Lee is a clean person," Miller said seriously. "A real American patriot. She ranks up there with Lady Bird Johnson and Eleanor Roosevelt." He paused for effect. "Besides, one of the Cav MPs told me she was okay."

"Why don't we go see?" Saenz suggested.

"Not me. I'm gonna sack out. You guys just tell me all about it tomorrow." Peterson bailed out.

Dixie followed the three of us as we made our way to the company motor pool. Miller told Top Gilbert we were going to get ice for the club.

Threatening gray clouds were gathering in the west as we headed toward the ancient imperial capital of Hue and the famous home of Missy Lee. Along the way, we passed a weather-beaten bunker where an MP sat on a pile of frayed and rotten sandbags. He flashed us the peace sign. We all waved as we roared by and he choked on our dust. There was almost no other traffic on the road. We each carried our weapons. I had my CAR-15 under my seat, locked and loaded just in case, and Saenz and Miller had M-16s.

We casually watched for any surprise ambushes but let our guard down as we drove past Phu Bai. The majority of the buildings were a lot of burned-out shells.

A navy way station, where two U.S. hydrofoil boats lay in dry dock, guarded a bridge along the road. Fishermen sat mending nets in thatched-roof huts while sampans with entire families living aboard floated along the shore. Many of the boats were painted bright red on the front, with giant eyes. Vietnamese believe the eyes are the spirits of the boat and protect and guide them.

The road was full of rural life. Children were having their hair cut, and old men drank coffee and soft drinks at tiny outside cafes. On the outskirts of the city stood the "Imperial Citadel." Fortunately, the imperial palace and most of the buildings in the court weren't damaged during Tet.

Miller said it was one of the most beautiful places in Vietnam. Two miles square, the Citadel sat on the bank of the Perfume River and was surrounded by thick walls. Vegetable plots waved in the breeze.

We drove past Lich Doi school. Miller explained to us how hard it was for the South Vietnamese kids to speak conversational English. "The reason is there are more letters in the English alphabet than the Vietnamese."

"No shit, professor. Turn here . . . I think," Saenz said.

"Yeah, this is the place all right," Miller agreed.

"There's an escape route." I pointed down a side street. I started getting butterflies in my stomach.

Miller knocked on her door, and Saenz and I remained in the street next to the jeep. Motorcycles were passing by every few minutes. A warm rain began. She answered and seemed happy to see us. She looked like a peasant version of Madame Nhu. She even spoke like her—with short, choppy sentences and words left out. Miller got right to the point and negotiated the price. She smiled wide and in a singing high tone that resembled Chinese yodeling, invited, "You come in."

I grabbed my rifle and followed the guys inside. The whole house smelled like sweet rice and *nuoc mam*, a strong, evil-smelling fish sauce that was the common condiment of Vietnam. Saenz and Miller disappeared inside with two of the girls. I started talking with Missy Lee, and she led me into her room.

On Missy Lee's dresser was a small picture of her mother and father, in formal black gowns. "You want me or other girls? I know you want stay with me."

"No . . . I'm not sure," I stammered.

"You not being nice to me." Now the rain was pouring down outside. "You good GI, number one. All GI dinky dow (GI slang for crazy based on the Vietnamese phrase *dien cai dau*)." The whole affair took less than ten minutes. She counted her money.

On the ride back, while Miller negotiated the narrow streets that led out of Hue, he nearly hit a teenaged Vietnamese soldier who darted in front of the jeep. The ARVN turned and flipped us the finger. Suave as always, I yelled, "Viet Cong look-alike!"

We arrived back at the company, parked the jeep, and were walking back to the club when Miller asked Saenz if he had noticed how small the Vietnamese girls' feet were.

"What in the hell made you think of that?" Saenz asked. Miller always initiated strange conversations. As we walked along the muddy road listening to Miller and trying to figure out Miller's meaning of life, I noticed dog prints. "That's it!" I shouted. "I've got a great idea!"

Saenz was tired. "What now?"

"The gooks would freak out if they found huge footprints in the jungle. We could wear fake shoes to make footprints like Bigfoot. The VC would see these prints and go nuts. They'd tell Ho Chi Minh, and they'd all surrender."

"You're nuts, Chambers. I have no idea what the fuck you are talking about," Miller fired back.

"You guys have never heard of Bigfoot, have you?" I asked. Remember, this was thirty years ago. Bigfoot hadn't yet had his own TV show.

"Big Feet?" Clearly Saenz thought it was an Indian tribe in Montana.

"Before I joined the army, I drove a fire truck in Northern California," I said. "We'd spend all summer looking for forest fires."

Saenz shook his head.

"You've never been out of the city." Miller laughed.

"That was the summer I saw Bigfoot."

Saenz was now listening like a schoolboy. Miller tried to pay no attention. "One afternoon, my partner and I were ambushed by a group of Job Corps guys just bright enough to turn on a fire hose. They hit us broadside with 150 pounds of water pressure. So the next morning, I took a two-by-four and pounded six five-penny nails into it so it looked like a claw.

That night after supper, we told them stories about the local legend, Bigfoot. "Bigfoot is a giant half-man, half-ape monster that roots around and leaves huge footprints all over the forest. But no one can catch him."

"Anyway, I told the Job Corps dudes that Bigfoot had been seen just east of where we were." I continued, "You should have seen their eyes. Every one of those guys was from the city, and not one had ever spent a minute in the forest. They used to go in groups of three to the bathroom and carry sticks to beat off the lizards they'd find in the outhouse. The Bigfoot story really scared them, and their supervisor told me to knock it off."

"So what happened?" Miller asked, now drawn into my story.

"Later, my buddy and I pretended to head back to our camp-site. At exactly midnight we sneaked up to their tent. My buddy did a full-blown imitation cougar yell, while I came down with the wooden claw, slashing a four-foot gash in the tent's canvas roof. The first guy tore the door down to get out. Even when they found out it was a prank, they still wanted to transfer outta there."

I tried to convince Miller and Saenz we could do the same thing here. "Miller, you could wear prototype Bigfoot shoes on your next mission." He was scheduled to go out in the next few days. He told me to "bite the big one."

Later, I explained my Bigfoot plan to First Sergeant Gilmore. Top's answer to my suggestion was a simple, "Uh-huh. Chambers, did I mention I'm going to take you up on your offer to fly bellyman for a few weeks? It may do you some good."

I never understood why no one would take my Bigfoot plan to end the war seriously.

Ruong Ruong Valley

Someone once told me that flying bellyman would be a relatively safe job. Boy, was that guy wrong.

The bellyman's job was to help the team members in and out of the chopper. It, too, was a volunteer position. One of our Rangers flew bellyman with the helicopter crew on every insertion and extraction. In the old company, that job had been reserved for senior NCOs who knew everything about the aerial Ranger operation. But as more and more men rotated back to the States, the job fell on guys like me. The job seemed easy enough—I would fly in the trail ship of our two-ship formation and learn as I went.

My first day as a bellyman, I arrived early enough to rig the helicopter and watch how Jim Meiners tied the rope ladder to the floor of the Huey. He was about to show me how to deploy the McGuire rig when the ship's radio crackled. It was Kenn Miller's team. They were somewhere in the Ruong Ruong Valley, and they'd spotted a small group of enemy soldiers. They had not been seen by the enemy, but there was a nervousness in Miller's voice.

We quickly rigged both helicopters, had a short briefing in the TOC; then we each boarded a different slick. One of the Cav crew chiefs slid a wooden box full of smoke grenades across the floor to me. I took out six canisters and fastened them, one by one, to the posts on the side of the cargo bay: two red, two yellow, and two purple. I secured my rifle with a bungee cord to the structural support post and pushed my ruck under the fold-out seats. I grabbed a flight helmet as we lifted off the acid pad, and sat back, monitoring the pilots' conversations. I listened to the *slap-thump* of chopper blades between transmissions. I wasn't sure how everything worked yet, but I wasn't too worried about it. Meiners would handle the extraction of Miller's team. I was there for backup.

Off in the distance, I could see a thunderstorm rolling in. Huge clouds billowed high above the mountaintops. It was four in the afternoon, and I prayed we'd be back to Camp Eagle before the storm hit. I was still freaked out about lightning.

After a thirty-minute ride, Meiners's helicopter hovered over Miller's position and dropped the rope ladder. Our slick circled several miles behind them, and above the scout C & C (command and control) chopper. The first man on the ground had just started up the ladder when Miller's slack man heard gunfire.

That was the most vulnerable moment for any LRRP team and helicopter crew. The chopper was a fixed target. Miller's men climbed as fast as they could up into the lead chopper, but not fast enough. With five men hanging on the ladder, something went wrong.

"We're going down; we're hit!" crackled over my headset. Adrenaline rushed through my veins, and I lunged forward to try to see out.

Our pilot's voice came over the intercom radio, "Looks like our lead ship's down. Might've been hit. Jesus, look at that . . . ! It just hit the side of the mountain. It's on its back."

The five men on the rope were tossed like rag dolls down the steep embankment, barely missing a rotor blade out of control. Steve Daring, who was on the bottom of the ladder, fell down the ridge and landed flat on his back. As the helicopter flipped over, he watched it come directly down on top of him. The skids of the helicopter touched down on either side of him, then bounced off and tumbled like a kid's ball down the hill. The chopper came to rest, upside down and broken, on a sheer incline.

I looked over the shoulder of our pilot, Ken Roach. He held

our chopper in midair and waited for instructions. Whatever was going to happen next was up to us. Within minutes, we circled over the downed ship. Roach made a hard right turn. I looked straight down and could see what was left of Miller's team and the crew of the slick (Huey lift ship), scattered all over the side of the hill near the mangled chopper. All I could think was what if that sucker explodes?

Over my headset, I heard Miller's voice. He told Roach that they had one KIA, meaning one of our guys was dead, and a couple of others slightly injured. Without warning, the right side door gunner swung his M-60 machine gun around to the front and pulled back on the gun's charging handles. "One o'clock, I've got a gook. I'm on him," he called out abruptly.

The chopper dropped as our ship took a hard banking right turn to circle out over the jungle canopy. As we turned, two more enemy soldiers with automatic weapons came into full view and began firing at us. I hit the floor and looked over the edge of the wide-open door frame as rounds hit the bottom of our aircraft. I closed my eyes. When I opened them seconds later, a stream of green tracers was heading directly at us. It looked like we were going to take a direct hit. I started praying. The tracers seemed to bend up and over us at the last minute.

Our door gunners opened up again. I looked back and saw the snakelike body of a Cobra helicopter gunship silhouetted above the mountains beside us. He made a fast pass with his 40mm cannon blazing away at the enemy soldiers' position.

As the helicopter made another hard bank, my stomach went up into my mouth. I just lay on the floor and waited for the ride to smooth out, but I didn't get my wish. Roach put the chopper into an even steeper turn. The blades catching air sounded like gunfire. Over the intercom, Captain Cardona told Roach to hold back and he would bring in a medevac to remove the body of the dead Ranger. We were instructed to climb to a higher altitude and circle the area. It finally hit me that I wasn't sure what I was supposed to do.

The medevac took enemy fire, but never wavered. Medevac helicopter crews had balls the size of King Kong's. Miller and Doc Glasser loaded the body of Sgt. Keith Hammond in a cargo sling that hung below the ship. We circled over their position, and I could see the Rangers on the ground, and remembered what it felt like to be waiting to get pulled out.

Finally, we got the word to go in and extract the helicopter crew and Miller's team, but we had another problem. The jungle that covered the steep mountainside would make it nearly impossible for our pilot to keep the blades from hitting the trees. Because of the steep terrain, Roach wasn't going to be able to look forward, down, and fly the craft at the same time. The crew chief normally helped guide the pilot in, but he was busy watching for the gooks. I told Roach that I thought I could help.

I untied the sling ropes securing the ladder and moved it from the center of the cargo floor to the right side. I then refastened the snap links to the last ring. I extended the ladder all the way out the right side, kicked it out, then grabbed the doorjamb to support myself. The down blast from the rotors hit me hard as I climbed out onto the skid of the hovering chopper. My crew helmet cord pulled loose from the wall and I no longer had radio contact with the crew, but there was no time to climb back in and fix it. I had a death grip on the door handle. I noticed that, by climbing down the ladder, I could look through the lower Plexiglas window and see Roach. He would be able to see my hand signals and still observe the steep mountain in front of him.

I felt like I was helping somebody back his Oldsmobile into a parking lot. Then, *ting!* The metal ladder kicked, and I felt myself swinging as a single round hit the metal rung below my right foot. I looked down to see a lone enemy soldier in a small clearing less than a hundred meters from the team. I guess he thought it was great sport to see if he could shoot me off that ladder. Without a gun and no contact with the door gunner, I waved furiously to get anybody's attention inside. But Roach was looking straight ahead and the door gunners were busy scanning the mountainside.

The lone enemy soldier pulled his weapon back to aim, and I thought it was all over, so I just flipped him the finger. One of the Cobra gunships had also spotted him, and emptied its

Gatling guns on his location. My opponent seemed to disappear into thin air, followed by the sound of a cannon blast.

Miller and his team members waved and cheered. Then Roach pulled his chopper in tight over the downed bird. Using his peripheral vision to register my hand signals, I backed him in tight to the mountainside. Because of the Laotian mountains and high altitude, we could only carry three people per trip. It was tough to put my hand up to stop the fourth man from climbing in, but I had to play it by the book.

We flew to Camp Evans, which was about halfway back to our home base. We dropped off three of the helicopter crew members and returned for more. After two more extractions, only Miller and McCann, his senior radio man, remained on the ground, if they were still alive.

"Kingsman Leader, this is Two-five. Over." It was Miller.

"Hold on Two-five, we'll be right back." Roach added in an upbeat voice, "Need a little petrol. Over."

"Roger that," Miller came back.

I could tell by the sound of his voice that Miller was about at the end of his rope. It seemed to take forever to fly back to Camp Evans, but it was the closest base with fuel. While we were off line, Miller had gotten into it with some general who had to authorize destruction of any downed or abandoned helicopter or aircraft. The problem was, as long as Miller and McCann were still on the ground, their aircraft wasn't abandoned. A small military technicality.

I sat on the acid pad and made sure I had extra rounds for my CAR-15. Each door gunner loaded additional ammo for the M-60s and rechecked the guns. Then we got the go-ahead. The cloud cover now rolled in like a big gray blanket, filling up the valley and creeping up the sides of the mountains. We knew the area would soon be socked in, and it would be impossible to make the extraction. Miller and McCann would be trapped in the jungle, and they'd be history. After twenty minutes in the air, we again approached the Ruong Ruong Valley. By now the cloud cover was so heavy, Roach couldn't see the downed chopper until we were almost on top of it.

"There! There it is," the left side door gunner shouted.

The pilot locked the ship in hover, and I climbed back down that ladder. At the bottom of the ladder, I reached down and grabbed McCann, helping him get a start up. As I turned back for Miller, the chopper started to drift out away from his reach. It was now or never. "Jump, Miller," I yelled. He jumped and grabbed hold of the bottom rung of the ladder as the helicopter pulled away and up. I reached down and grabbed him by the back of his gear and pulled. I climbed along with him on the same rungs. When we reached the door and top rung, with adrenaline surging through my body, I gave Miller a big push. In he went, disappearing into the cabin of the chopper, and part way out the other side!

"Jesus!" I yelled when I saw his legs dangling under the chopper. Miller was hanging on for dear life, his legs pumping wildly in the air. McCann scrambled across the cargo floor and pulled Miller back in.

My arms felt like rubber, and my fingers were mashed from all the combat jungle boots that had scrambled over them. But I climbed in and scooted in tight next to Miller and McCann. I couldn't believe my luck. I had volunteered to fly bellyman so I could get *out* of the jungle action. We had just made four separate, extremely dangerous extractions. But the worst was yet to come.

The chopper pitched hard to the right. I hadn't even noticed the turbulence during all the action. The helicopter's rocking and pitching became more violent; we were right smack in the middle of that thunderstorm. It was getting very dark. I plugged in my headset and could tell from the pilot's voice that something was wrong. We were still hovering in the dark cloud cover, without moving forward. I looked out, but could no longer see the mountains. Miller grabbed my shirt and pulled me in close. "I don't know if I should kiss you or kill you," he groaned.

Then the chopper began rockin' and rollin'. First a few hard jolts; the helicopter vibrated so hard I thought we were going to be knocked out of the sky. My stomach had twisted into a permanent knot. I put my right hand on Miller's shoulder and tried to comfort him, "I know how you feel, man." I wasn't sure what words to say as we bounced around inside that storm, but it felt good to hold on to somebody.

I glanced down and saw the metal ladder still dangling outside the chopper. The bottom rung had disappeared in the thick fog. With one hand holding me inside, I tried to pull the ladder up, but it was as if someone was on the other end pulling down even harder. Then the chopper bounced and rocked so hard I lost my grip and hit the floor. By then, I was as shaken as Miller.

Back then, the G-model Hueys didn't have much instrumentation so if they got too deep in the soup, the pilots could get vertigo and turn the piece-of-flying-shit upside down. Good pilots had done worse. Over my headset, I could hear Roach telling his copilot to search for a hole in the storm. The copilot answered back, "I can't see past the nose."

"We don't have the fuel to hang here for long," Roach said.

The helicopter would lift up twenty feet, then *ka-bang*, it would fall as much as thirty feet in the uneven air.

At last, "Hey, I see a hole!" Roach called over the intercom. "There it is, right there, that small hole at your one o'clock."

I shot Miller a look of reassurance, and continued listening to the pilots. After a few more frightening moments, Roach got the helicopter out of the storm, then lowered the nose and kicked his bird into high gear. The whine of the turbine dropped to a steady drone. A cool gust of wind blew in the door of the helicopter. It felt like a cleansing rinse. Miller sat hunched over on the cargo floor. He tried to wipe the blood off his hands and looked up at me. "Shit, man, I should never have let him go; it's my fault." Miller had been breaking Hammond in, and it was his first time out in the bush. Doc Glasser and Miller had pulled Hammond's body from under the downed chopper's blades. There was no way Miller or Glasser was going to leave him behind.

I wasn't sure how to respond to Miller and for once kept my mouth shut as we flew back to our home base. I just stared at the jungle that was flowing like a green river below us. The trip seemed to take forever, and not much else was said.

We all took Hammond's death hard. He was the company clown, the kind of guy who always saw something funny about everything. We just had that sickening feeling you can't get away from. One of your friends is dead, and you know you'll never see him again.

By the time we got back to Camp Eagle, the other members of Miller's team and the chopper crew had already arrived from Camp Evans. They were on the acid pad to greet us.

Miller waited around until the pilots shut off all systems, then walked up and thanked Roach personally for saving the lives of his men. They walked off together to the debriefing. I had to jump on another helicopter and fly back to Camp Evans. There were still two more teams out in the field, and that meant we'd have to stay on call. At Evans, I followed the crew chief up to an empty tent, laid out my poncho liner on an open bunk, and ate what was left of a cold LRRP ration. I fell asleep, promising myself that I would never climb outside and underneath a helicopter again.

The next morning, I planned my new strategy. I'd take my second R & R in Hawaii. I had been awarded an extra R & R for capturing a North Vietnamese officer during Recondo School. When I returned from Hawaii, I would take a nice safe job somewhere in the rear, maybe recruiting volunteers for the company. If everything went right, my last months would be spent down south, then I'd just slip on a Freedom Bird home. Sounded like a good plan to me.

The Road to Bien Hoa

Sometime between the never-ending helicopter insertions and extractions, we got a new company commander, Capt. Robert Guy. His job was not only to take over operational command of L Company but also to implement the concept of saturation patrolling. Ranger teams were to be inserted in clusters of five or six teams to completely saturate an area.

Captain Guy had been in the 173d Airborne Brigade, the 2d of the 503d, on his first tour. He told us they never saw anywhere near the kind of contact, situations, or operations the Ranger teams did. As he explained to us, "As an infantry platoon leader, you were constantly expecting to make contact when you went out on operations, but most of the time you didn't—make contact that is."

It thunderstormed the day I was to meet with our new CO; I hoped that wasn't a bad sign. After introductions, he started in on a very short speech about staying in the army, but my look must have given me away, because he cut his speech short. I told him that I wanted to extend my tour to get an early out and finish college. He thought that was a pretty good idea and he'd see what he could do to help.

For now, his problem was the 101st Airborne's new policy. He explained, "Division wants six teams in the field at all times. It's not like we got six teams sitting around on the shelf. I'll be having people going on R & R and people getting wounded. Here's my biggest problem—no one stays together on a team anymore. We're gonna have to throw people together on different teams. The way things are going today, large groups of new personnel are arriving in country every day. This will cause a large DEROS 'hump' when they rotate out and leave the unit at a loss for trained and qualified personnel. I want a steady stream of well-qualified replacements, not a last-minute scramble for new guys when you old-timers head home."

I saw my opportunity. "Captain Guy, I'm supposed to take a leave next week. Sergeant Gilbert asked me if I wanted to be the company liaison. How about if I stay down at the replacement center and get some good recruits for you?"

He thought for a while, then said slowly, "Yeah, that's a good idea. Keep me informed, and let us know the numbers you'll be sending up."

I packed that night. There were three of us headed to the 90th Replacement Center in Bien Hoa, the division's rear area—myself, Kenn Miller, and a crusty old E-7 everyone knew as Horny Mills. Both Miller and Mills were headed home; they had put in their time.

Horny Mills was a strange guy. He looked like a milspec Captain Kangaroo with tattoos. But Mills wore Master Blaster wings (master parachutist) and had been a HALO instructor (a specialist in jumps made from a high altitude followed by free fall to a low-altitude opening). At one time in his career, he'd even been in the Golden Knights, the army's parachute team. He knew all sorts of prominent people, and when he went out to meet arriving generals, most of them already knew who he was.

No sooner had the huge C-130 taken off than the crew chief's voice came over the intercom and asked for Sergeant Mills. When Mills came back from talking to the chief, he said to Miller, "The pilot wants me to come up and fly his plane for him."

"Bullshit!" Miller said.

I felt a knot in my stomach. "Oh, great." Mills disappeared into the cockpit.

We'd been in the air about ten minutes when the air force crew chief came back and asked Miller and me to follow him to the cockpit. We went up the drop stairs to the cockpit and there was Mills sitting at the controls, flying the plane. The pilot was sitting in the navigator's chair, and Miller asked him, "Are you giving flying lessons?"

The pilot turned and said, over the roar of the props, "Nope, we're old flying buddies from up in Alaska. Mills probably has more hours in one of these boats than I do. I just happened to be making an honest living at it."

Turned out Mills had been stationed in one of those weird Airborne units up in Alaska and became a bush pilot in his off time. Our C-130 pilot had been stationed there in the air force, and the two flew together.

Suddenly the big aircraft banked hard to the left, and I grabbed hold of the compartment door frame, and Miller grabbed hold of me. Mills told us we were headed into some turbulence and we'd better go strap in. I didn't have to be told twice.

An hour later, the big cargo plane finally landed and taxied toward the parking apron. I could barely hear Miller bitching about anything and everything over the roar of the turboprop engines. "We're lucky to be short-timers," he finally said, summing up his spiel.

"We're lucky Mills didn't crash us," I responded as I extracted my legs from the cargo straps.

As the C-130 braked to a halt, allowing the four huge engines to windmill, I grinned at Miller. "You're going to show me how to do this recruitment thing, right?"

"No problem, man. You just stand up in front of a hundred new replacements and tell them how great it is to do your duty for your country. If you want to become one of us, the good, the bad, and the—"

"Okay, okay, I get it." I was sorry I'd asked him. We stood and shuffled toward the back of the plane, steadying ourselves along the metal ribs.

I was anxious to see my new home, plus I had a lot to do. Big plans. I was going to visit a Recondo School buddy. I had made contact with him back in March 1969. He was an air force pararescue guy who had been on my team. And, I had my R & R to Hawaii coming.

With a hiss of decompression, the huge tailgate jolted toward the ground. I recoiled from the blast of hot, heavy air that roared into the aircraft.

"Here, Chambers. Don't forget this." Miller tossed Mills's AWOL bag at me. He had been using it as a pillow on the flight.

I tossed it back to Miller. "You carry it, Miller. I'm too short, dude. You don't realize you're lookin' at a double-digit midget. Besides there's a tip in it for ya."

"Your mother's the tip," Miller said as he tossed the bag back at me again.

I stepped down onto the blazing tarmac. Because of the local soil—red dust actually—everything seemed to have a reddish tint to it. We caught a jeep ride down the road along the Bien Hoa airport, a permanent air base just northeast of Saigon, to Long Binh and the 90th Replacement Center, which serviced all the army units in Vietnam.

The compound had literally grown from a camp into a city, covering twenty-five square miles with over 40,000 Americans living there at the time. Our driver informed us we'd have hot water in the showers, and flush toilets in the latrines, but the colonels had air-conditioned trailers and the generals had air-conditioned houses. And *lawns*! We drove past rust-colored buildings and bunkers manned by South Vietnamese MPs.

"Glad to see the South Vietnamese Army is doing its part," Miller said sarcastically.

"Yeah, guarding the airport so our mail won't get blown up," I answered. "I sure feel safe now."

"Welcome, Chambers. You have just entered the world of spit-shines and starched military bureaucrat bullshit," Miller said.

I tossed Mills's bag on the ground and headed for the 101st reception center. "Some reception center, Miller. Where are the girls?" I had extended for a three-month tour, so I wouldn't have to do additional time back in the States, but it was beginning to dawn on me that I might have gotten the worst part of the deal. My jungle shirt was completely soaked by the time we found our new quarters.

"Let's check out our living quarters," Miller said, as we dropped our gear in the wooden barracks. "I hear that these places come with a maid."

"Look at this, Miller—concrete floors."

The first thing Miller did was ask for directions to Saigon, then we grabbed two cans of Coke at one of the few refreshment stands. Miller was contemplating the possibility of extending and transferring to Special Forces. I reminded him that he would not pass the height test, which really pissed him off. His ears locked back the way a German shepherd's do before it bites.

"Just kidding, Miller. I'm sure your head would look good stuffed in one of those glass cases reserved for heroes back at FOB-1." FOB-1 was the Special Forces forward operations base in Phu Bai. SOG teams left from there. Often they didn't come back.

"I'll play on their sense of patriotism," I told Miller later, as we sat having our Cokes.

"Patriotism is an outmoded concept, Chambers. If you want guys to volunteer, you've got to lie. Appeal to their egos."

As we searched for a ride, we walked past a group of new replacements unloading AWOL bags and clicking cameras at everything within their view. "Man, remember those days, Miller?"

With their fresh haircuts and newly issued dark green jungle fatigues, we looked like ragtag guerrillas next to the replacements. I looked at Miller. The leather on his jungle boots was worn almost through. His uniform was bleached by the sun, had been ripped by wait-a-minute vines, and patched together with pieces from other uniforms. He had two white lines of caked-on sweat under each arm. "Miller, you look like shit, man."

"FNGs," Miller said. "Your uniform is not exactly regulation, Chambers."

We both wore CIBs (Combat Infantryman's Badges) and parachutist's wings on our upper pockets. I also wore a silver belt buckle inscribed with a North Vietnamese star; definitely not per uniform regulations, but then nobody was about to ask me to remove it. "Just look at our sorry-ass replacements."

"Hey, a week or two cutting the bush, and they'll fit right in."

Anyone with a week or two longer in Vietnam automatically inherited the right to deliver sage advice, or semiserious harassment, to fuckin' new guys (FNGs). When you had been there over a year, with a CIB, people had a certain respect for you.

"Lifer at two o'clock," Miller warned and motioned with his head.

I looked up. "Shit, it's a sergeant major."

Lifers were a different breed. To our minds, they were the guys who had stayed in the army a little too long. And a sergeant major, now that was a different story entirely. That was as high an enlisted rank as a man could get.

This hard-core-looking sergeant major walked directly in front of Miller. "Young Sergeant, while you are on my base, you will get a haircut and change that ragtag piece of nonregulation uniform." He looked at me and shook his head. "Christ, if I was your XO (executive officer), I'd bust both of you before you had time to shit." Then he stormed off.

"I guess he wouldn't want to hear my Big Food idea, huh, Miller."

Miller spit and said, "A lifer even walks like a lifer. They all have a sort of corncob-up-the-butt way of walking. Kinda like the way a horse looks after it's been castrated."

Miller waited until the sergeant major was a few steps farther away before he added, "REMF," which stood for rear echelon motherfucker.

"Miller, *we're* REMFs now," I said. Miller's ears went back again, and I realized it was not a good thing to remind him of the true status of our new positions. One time I saw Miller's ears go back like that, and then he bit off a piece of Sanders's ear in a fight at the Ranger compound. I disengaged Miller by quickly changing the subject.

All my big plans needed to be well timed. After a few days in Saigon, I would finagle my way onto a jet for seven days of surfing in Hawaii. While I was gone, Miller would do the recruiting for the company, which by then was desperately short on bodies. I told him if I timed it right, I could turn my seven days into fourteen, then take over his job and spend my extension sitting on my ass. But nothing in Vietnam ever seemed to go as planned. I rubbed my Thai Buddha for luck. "I've got this all worked out, Miller," I said, trying to convince myself.

"You ain't got shit, man." Miller was in a huffy mood.

Fill the Pipeline

The good news for the day was that Hawaii wasn't going to require a short arm inspection. Miller informed me that most of the men on the plane would either be senior NCOs (noncommissioned officers, i.e., sergeants, like me), or officers taking leave to see their wives. He added, "You just might get lucky, Chambers, and end up with the wife of some general who couldn't make the flight."

I told him I didn't call that luck. However, when we landed on the island of Oahu, we were literally mobbed by a sea of women. And, they were mostly army wives in search of their husbands and fiancés.

I was seated near the back of the plane and one of the last ones off; even so I had to pass through that gauntlet of round-eyed women and was stared at by each of those who remained as if I might be the one they were looking for. They'd make eye contact, then break it as they eliminated men. Once in a while, I heard a loud shout of recognition as a woman broke the line and ran to her husband. It was really pretty sad. There were about twenty women whose men didn't make the flight. Looks of worry and disappointment quickly replaced their happy smiles. One woman started arguing with one of the attendants about why her husband was not on that flight. As I walked by, I wanted to tell her that I could fill in for the missing husband but realized my wisecracks wouldn't be appreciated just then.

I walked outside and was hit by the wonderful clean smell of

Hawaii. There was a pineapple processing plant near the airport, and the sweet smell filled my senses. After a short bus ride to Waikiki Beach, I found Kalia Road and then the Fort Derussy hotel. It was just down the sand from the more expensive hotels. I checked in for a five-night stay at the rate of fourteen dollars a day, then I changed into my trunks and headed for the beach. I spent the next few days on a rented surfboard, trying to perfect my surfing style and attempting to pick up any local chicks who even glanced my way—which never happened. I guess the Airborne haircut and farmer's tan (head, neck, and hands only) were dead giveaways. It wasn't like the forties movies of elaborate USO dances and women running up to any guy in uniform. In Waikiki, we were looked at as if we were carriers of some loathsome disease.

On the way back to the hotel one day, I was waiting at the bus stop when a young Hawaiian kid rode past me on his bicycle. I caught a glimpse of him out of the corner of my eye as he tossed something my way. Automatically, I rolled over the bench and onto the ground, assuming he had tossed a grenade. I was embarrassed when I saw an empty Coke can roll to the curb.

The highlights of my trip were buying fresh pineapples every morning and a concert ticket to see Jimi Hendrix. I couldn't wait; this was going to be great. Miller had told me Hendrix had been a paratrooper before he became famous. I thought it was just another one of Miller's stories. The concert was scheduled for the night before I was to leave. I arrived early and waited two hours for the show to begin. But Hendrix quickly smashed his guitar against the stage and walked off, clearly in a drugged-out state. He never even finished his first song. The management offered us rain checks for Sunday, but my flight was Saturday morning. I figured I'd see him when I got back to the States.

At the airport, I sure wasn't anxious to get back to Nam. I thought about having three more months in Vietnam and knew just how those guys on Alcatraz must have felt, looking across the bay at San Francisco, knowing there was no way to get there. I was very tempted to jump on a flight to California when

I saw the San Francisco flight listings. A commercial flight was leaving around the same time as our charted Arrow Air flight to Nam. I actually crawled under the rope and casually walked over to the United ticket counter. One of the MPs kept eyeing me, then he walked up and asked for my ID. I guess my new tan and surfer shirt were not much of a disguise.

The return flight was depressing. Not only did it seem to take forever but one of the guys in front of me had a flower lei around his neck. For some reason, it pissed me off.

By the time I arrived back at SERTS,* I discovered that Saenz had already departed for his leave home. The next morning, it was raining. I picked up orders for my new assignment and met with one of the cadre, who filled me in on where to meet the newbies. I was to give my first speech that night.

There were always three or four guys sitting on sandbags outside the hootch telling stories. So I spent the afternoon inside, rehearsing what I was going to say. I wrote a letter to my mom, then walked over to the latrine and practiced my speech in front of the shaving mirror.

Later that afternoon, I made my way down to our reception area. I could hear voices inside a huge military-style tent. Most of them would be "legs." A leg is someone who has not completed army jump school. He is non-Airborne, and therefore, we Airborne types considered him a bastard, ranking somewhere down around whaleshit. Anyway, that's another thing Miller told me. But by 1969, the 101st had become "Airmobile," and most paratroopers were ending up in the 173d ABN or Special Forces. I was hoping to find guys among the newbies who were jump qualified, but I'd just have to take what I could get. I stood around outside the tent nervously thinking about what I was about to say as two replacement sergeants walked past me. I looked down at their brand-new cardboard-looking black jungle boots and new jungle greens. There wasn't much leather left to shine on my boots and they were my third pair. Worn leather was a distinction reserved for guys who had been

*Screaming Eagle Replacement Training School. The 101st's training, refresher, and acclimatization course for its new arrivals in Vietnam.

in the field. For some strange reason, I wanted those cherries to notice, but they didn't even glance my way.

I had all the trappings of a guy who did his entire tour in a combat outfit—and if they wanted more proof, my collar was open just enough that they could spot my body-count rope. They could count each knot and wonder what it must have been like. One knot for each enemy kill. I was building up a good head of resentment and thought, God, I'm beginning to feel the way Miller does.

I brought my concentration back to what I was going to say. At that point, I didn't really care if any of them volunteered; I just wanted to get that first speech over. I had read somewhere once that public speaking was the one thing people feared most—even more than dying. Now I knew what that meant.

I figured most would tune me out as soon as I walked in. What they didn't know was that they needed me more than I needed them. I'd survived, and I could tell them how. It was their choice. I didn't care if they respected me or hated my guts. I had taken the same chance after listening to an old LRRP's bullshit, just the way they were about to have to do. I had listened to the stupid stories and didn't half believe them. Now I was going to tell the same stories.

Just a year earlier, I was a lemming, a sheep headed for "the line," until someone stopped me and said, "Listen to me, you dumb shit. You join the LRRPs (back then Rangers units were called LRRPs—long-range recon patrols), and we will take care of you. Just do it, man, and you'll thank me later. You'll be making the right choice."

I heard the cadre sergeant tell the group to take their seats. This was the first speech I'd ever done anywhere in front of any group, and I felt totally unprepared. After I introduced myself, I just stood there for a moment unsure of what to say next. Then I started in on my pitch. I tried to lighten them up with a joke, but no one laughed. I told them about sneaking around in the bush and finding NVA base camps, and how great we had been at doing that, and exaggerated a little.

I wasn't getting anywhere with these guys, so I read from my notes. "I had to make the same choice you're about to. I made the right choice, and now I'm here to tell you what I know. I'm not a lifer. I'm here to share my secrets of how to stay alive." They had no idea what was in store for them, what the infantry's war was going to be like. It certainly wasn't like any of the stupid movies they'd ever seen about war. Ever since the 7th Cav had been badly hurt in Ia Drang Valley, the gooks had known how to fight us—their tactics were to get close and stay there. And no place in this country was safe.

When I was finished, no hands went up. I felt like a sorry piece of shit. I realized I was going to have to get used to that. As the newbies started moving out of the tent, some wiseass in the back row yelled out, "I'm not volunteering for this shit; no way, man. That's the kind of shit that gets you killed. You guys go on and be some kind of hero. I'm going to the line." Before I could turn around and grab that stupid piece of low-life scum, he disappeared into the crowd.

For most of these guys, I was just filler—a break in their in-country training. But I hoped it would be different for some. The problem was, I just didn't know how to get it across to them.

The good news was, up north, Jeff Paige had arrived and volunteered for the Rangers. It had only been a month since Peterson and I had met him on LZ Sally. He just showed up and went to see Sergeant Gilbert. "I'd like to join your unit. I've got twenty-seven months in country with Tiger Force." Gilbert shook his hand and said, "Come on in." Gilbert gave him a few days to get oriented, then assigned him to radio relay and sent him out to firebase for the next four days. When he came back in, he would start going out on missions.

Shit-for-Brains

My main goal, I had informed Miller, was to find replacements who could point an M-16 in the right direction. I wasn't going to take all comers. I felt a responsibility to the Ranger Company not to let someone in just because he volunteered. That is, if someone did volunteer. My strategy would be to check each guy's military IQ scores to see if their scores were as good as or higher than mine. My college football coach had used that strategy to find quarterbacks, but he reviewed every player's grade-point average. I had been on the honor roll in my sophomore year, so I started the season as one of his backups. When I told him I couldn't throw a pass, he said, "I can teach you how to pass a football, I can't teach you how to think." I figured that same tactic would work in combat.

At breakfast the next morning, I ran into Kurt Hagopian—a thin, wiry, street-smart Armenian from the Bronx. He'd been in the company for over a year and had extended to work at SERTS as an instructor. I'd met Kurt when he had been in the LRRP commo platoon.

He took me over to the training field so I could get a feel for what the FNGs had to go through before I got hold of them. We walked to a stand where the new replacements listened to instructors. The replacements had already been given basic training and advanced infantry training—an eight-week course in everything the Stateside army could teach them. Most of them knew how an M-16 worked, but I was sure no one had told them what to do if it jammed. Nothing in training could prepare them for the overload of stimuli they would be facing in the upcoming months. If they became Rangers, they would have to learn their jobs with the added stress of enemy forces shooting at them.

A short, heavyset, red-faced instructor was telling one hundred fresh-faced replacements how to squeeze a claymore firing device at the right time. As he gave his demonstration, Hagopian and I caught one another up on all the news. After a year in the bush, I felt I had earned the right to stand around ghosting. Ghosting was an army term for being seen, but not by anyone who could put you to work.

"This is the clacker," he said in that army instructor's tone, with long pauses between every sentence. "This firing device is your best friend in combat. It has a wire clip that wedges under the handle to prevent misfiring. Flip back the clip, squeeze on the handle, and a jolt of electric current through the wire will set off the blasting cap. The detonation of the cap will then touch off the C-4 plastic explosive and propel a hail of seven hundred steel ball bearings, destroying everything in the kill zone. Keep your head down so the backblast won't tear it off," he continued in the same monotone.

Then the guy got a little sappy, telling them they would have to hold their own fear inside. He neglected to tell them, however, how the blast of a claymore turns gook bodies into mush—legs twisted, bodies full of holes, arms blown off. And the smell would take one's breath away—a mixture of cordite, human body chemistry, and blood. The unofficial description we used was the "sweet smell of death." I guess he was telling them what he thought they *needed* to know. I sure couldn't describe it to anyone; you just had to experience it.

Hagopian told me to watch carefully what the instructor was going to do. "This guy is a numbnut. He's got the reputation for partying all night and scaring the bejeezus out of the newbies. But watch, it's pretty cool."

As the instructor talked, he held a block of C-4 explosive. "He'll toss it over there at the end of his speech." Hagopian pointed to the open field. The guy pulled the pin on the fifteen-second-delay fuse and casually strolled back and forth, talking in front of the bleachers. Just as it seemed to me that he was going on too long, *kaboom!* The C-4 exploded in his hand.

One hundred replacements watched in horror as the explosion ripped open his body, blew off both his hands and his foot. Hagopian and I hit the ground. The recruits were jumping off the bleachers, running into the open field, not sure what to do next. Kurt got up and ran over to where the instructor lay. The guy's entire body cavity was ripped open, and Kurt watched his heart pump a couple more times before it stopped.

A group policed up what was left of the instructor, gathered his body parts from various corners of the training field, and placed all the pieces in a body bag. A medevac landed and took the body away, and Kurt took charge of the training.

He noticed one of the recruits frozen in place. The guy was staring at a piece of raw meat—a chunk of the instructor that had landed behind the bleachers. Hagopian grabbed a shovel, walked over, chopped it into smaller pieces, then covered it over with soil. He then handed the shovel to the private and turned back to continue with training. The recruit dropped the shovel and passed out.

Hagopian and I met later at the crowded EM club. He was trying to enjoy some local Vietnamese talent that was imitating the Beatles. Hearing "I want, hold your hand . . ." sung with a Vietnamese accent was almost worth the trip to Nam.

The place was buzzing about the instructor who blew himself up. Hagopian was sitting with Miller when I arrived. "Chambers, *que paso*?" Miller said. I filled Miller in on all the company news, until the gook music died down. By then Hagopian was on his sixth glass of whiskey and getting drunker. Hagopian took the opportunity to climb up on a barstool to read a poem he had written.

> I'm a combat paratrooper, that's what I am.
> Live hard, die fast, and don't give a damn.
> But I'm a special paratrooper—better than the rest,
> because I'm in the 101st, and we are the very best.

Then he lost his balance and fell on the floor.

Miller and I helped him back to his seat. "We had some good times though. Right, Chambers?" Hagopian slurred.

"Right," I answered as he fell off the stool again. Miller and I helped him back to his hootch. I guessed he had been more affected by the afternoon's incident than he had let on.

Volunteer Number One

Frank Johnson was my first volunteer. I spent the next half hour talking with him. I found out he grew up in Pomona, California, was into drag racing, and liked raising hell a whole lot. But he wanted to better himself, and that's why he wanted to join the Rangers. I told Miller that if the guy was as strong mentally as he was physically, we had us a good one.

The next day, three more guys volunteered. One was a staff sergeant just out of Ranger school—Jim Bates. Bates had just finished in-country training and was getting ready for a line-company assignment. He was walking to chow when Lieutenant Jackson spotted his Ranger tab and shouted, "Don't move, Sergeant, don't move!"

Bates froze, thinking he was in trouble again. As the lieutenant came running up, Bates came to attention.

"Where you headed, Sergeant?" Jackson asked.

"I don't have my orders, sir," Bates replied.

"You want to earn that Ranger tab, don't you? Go see Sergeant Chambers tomorrow and tell him I sent you."

"Yes, sir." Bates remained frozen at parade rest.

"Oh, yeah. Dismissed!" Jackson said, walking away.

When I first met Jim Bates, he reminded me of Lil' Abner, straight from Dog Patch. He said some Ranger lieutenant had told him to come see me. I found out he'd graduated from an NCO course, made sergeant (E-5), then went to Ranger school. After he graduated from Ranger school, he

To Tell the Truth

The next morning, Miller and I dragged Hagopian out to get breakfast. I told them I wasn't getting any volunteers and tried to solicit their suggestions.

"Look, Chambers, tell it to them straight," Miller said. "Tell them what it really means to be in our unit. Don't spend so much time trying to entertain them. This isn't the Ed Sullivan Show." Then he changed the subject. "Let's go into Saigon today. I know where we can get a plate of ham fried rice for two hundred dong."

I decided I was going to stop the bullshit and tell it just the way it was. The truth. At that night's talk, I was more serious and challenged them. I told them I was proud to be a member of one of best long-range patrol companies in Vietnam. I got them to laugh a bit when I said, "I'm better in the jungles than on this stage, for sure."

I watched my audience cling to every word I said, intent on understanding me. Good thing, too; my words could alter the course of their lives.

Then I remembered what Miller had reminded me to say. "One of the most important things you should know is that Rangers don't leave Rangers behind." I paused and let the impact of those words sink in.

A hand went up. "You mean . . . if you guys are surrounded, you bring everyone out?"

"Let me tell you a story about one of our guys, Chet

Lozenger. During his first tour, in one of the worst gunfights anyone can remember, he runs out under fire, grabs one of the wounded, and starts back to safety. An enemy bunker opens up, and a round from a .51-caliber machine gun tears a hole in his back." I held my forefinger and thumb in a circle shape. "It blows a chunk this big out the side of Chet's lower back and knocks him to the ground. He gets up and picks the other guy up again, holds him over his shoulder, and runs back to friendly lines. Chet survived and was awarded a Silver Star. But he said, 'It was nothin'. A Ranger don't leave Rangers behind.'

"Then there's the story about Riley Cox who fought with his hand almost blown off and his guts hanging out. He slapped bandage on his guts, rolled over, grabbed his M-16 again, a kept firing. By the time reinforcements arrived, Cox had go in piles all over the side of the hill. You don't often see that of behavior in line units. It's usually everyone for themsel

It was so quiet in that tent, a dropped hand-grena would have echoed.

"If I'm making sense, then here's your opportunity t teer to be in a Ranger unit. I'll check you out and you've got what we're looking for." I looked around one guy stood up. One was enough. It was a beginn one else walked out of the tent.

automatically picked up another stripe. Bates had only been in the army six months, and he was now an E-6 staff sergeant. Not bad for a guy with no combat experience—yet.

The nice thing about being a Ranger liaison was being able to sidestep the army's legendary bureaucratic paperwork. Getting orders drawn in peacetime could take months. I just walked over to operations, and they cut them for Bates that day.

When new men arrived in the LRRP company, they were immediately assigned to a team for training purposes. That kept each team fully manned and gave the new recruit a chance to bond with his teammates. A newly assigned cherry was a long way from being a vital component of any team, but the assignment gave him an immediate sense of belonging and a strong desire to contribute his part to the team effort. If the cherry did not quickly demonstrate a budding sense of loyalty, his days as a Ranger were already numbered.

Whatever I was telling the guys now was working. Johnson made the trip north on the morning flight; Bates was on the afternoon manifest. They rode with twenty other newbies out to Camp Eagle.

With vehicles revving, helicopters flying overhead, men hollering, piles of gear everywhere, and the omnipresent smell of diesel fumes mixed with burning shit, they knew they had arrived. The deuce-and-a-half dropped them in front of the L COMPANY, 75TH RANGERS sign—their new home; that is, when they weren't in the jungle. It wouldn't take long for the men to make names for themselves in the company. Johnson and Bates were assigned to the second platoon. That night, Johnson went with Burgess Wetta to see the movie. Wetta was an All-American junior college quarterback. He reminded me somewhat of Frank Johnson, only Wetta was a couple of inches taller and about fifteen pounds heavier. That night the 17th Cav outdoor screen was featuring the latest Clint Eastwood movie, *Hang 'Em High*. Frank took a seat in the front bleachers. Two REMFs a few rows back started making wisecracks about the new Rangers. Johnson turned around and told them very firmly to shut up. One of the guys yelled, "Go to hell." That was all it took. Johnson jumped and shoved the guy backward onto the person sitting behind him. They started swinging, and Johnson got in a few good punches, and the guy went down. Then Johnson turned to the other wisecracker, an even bigger guy, and grabbed him by the shirt. Soon that big old boy was flying down the bleachers, with Johnson hanging on. By then everybody was getting in on it, and it wasn't looking too good for Johnson. Until Wetta intervened on Johnson's behalf.

Now, you didn't want to fool with Wetta. He had a worse temper than Johnson. Wetta pulled a guy off Johnson's back and commenced to kick his ass. The poor bastard's nose and mouth were bleeding badly.

Just then, one of the 17th Cav's lieutenants showed up and called a halt to the free-for-all. Johnson tried to explain that he was just trying to watch the movie. The lieutenant grabbed Johnson by his shirt. Johnson pulled his arm away and accidentally smacked the lieutenant in the face. Wetta grabbed Johnson, and they took off running back to the company area.

The next morning, I was bullshitting on the landline with Top Gilbert, who related the whole story to me. At morning formation, a 17th Cav spec-4 had shown up with the lieutenant and some of their MPs. Their intention was to take Johnson to jail.

It turned out that Johnson had broken one guy's nose and knocked out a tooth. The other guy's arm was broken and in a sling. Luckily for Johnson, since it had been dark and everything had happened so fast, no one could remember what the guilty party looked like. Top Gilbert told them that a guy who sounded like the one they were looking for had just gone out on a mission. Of course, Top had confined Johnson to his hootch for his own good. Gilbert ended our phone call with, "I don't know where you got that guy, but get me a few more like him."

The next morning I told the story at my recruitment speech, and three more guys volunteered: PFC Mike Lytle, a kid by the name of John Strope, and a spec-4 named Mark Morrow. I went through the same routine: checked their records, cut their orders, and had the men on the next flight for Phu Bai. I was on a roll.

I got a report back that Jeff Paige had taken Johnson and Morrow out in the field for their first training mission—a few days on an old firebase called Helen. They set up a radio relay, and on their first night, Morrow spotted what he thought were two VC. He thought they were running up the hill toward them. He got his rifle ready, took aim, but the enemy troops turned out to be a monkey chasing a mongoose. Still, it was the first enemy monkey or mongoose Morrow had ever seen.

They spent five days getting used to living firebase style. While they were there, a Huey came in to resupply them with water, but its rotor hit one of the bunkers. The chopper crashed and flipped. The copilot whacked his leg, but no one was hurt badly. After Johnson's first "welcome" mission, they put him with Dennis Karalow on Team 2-4 for his next mission.

The night before the overflight, Johnson, Robin Christensen, and Andy Ransom went back to the 17th Cav outdoor movie to see the ending of the movie they'd missed because of the fight. Johnson was wearing an ornate Catholic cross around his neck. He was always touching it to make sure it was still there. They had just sat down when Johnson realized his cross was missing. He didn't want to make a big deal of it, so he waited until the show was over and the lights came on. Then he told the guys he couldn't find his cross.

Although he was embarrassed to tell them, he believed that if he wasn't wearing that cross, he would be killed. Johnson said, "We're gonna make contact on this mission, and I'm going to die."

Andy, who was also scheduled for that mission, just said, "Okay, so we've got to find your cross."

They backtracked the way they had come and still couldn't find it. So they went to see Dennis Karalow and told him of Johnson's concern. Karalow had been there for a year already by that time. Instead of saying something cool like "Yeah, you stinkin' cherry," he got the team together and told them, "We're gonna really play it safe this time out." Karalow was a good guy whose job was to keep the FNGs busy and learning. His team would spend all week practicing immediate-action drills, weapons zeroing, map and compass reading, radio communication, first aid, insertion/extraction techniques, and long-range patrolling.

A new patrol member had to demonstrate that he knew how to pack a rucksack, set out claymore mines, load magazines, give hand signals, recognize rendezvous points, direct artillery and airstrikes, and the myriad other survival skills critical on a long-range patrol mission. Then, and only then, was a guy ready to go out.

The only personal comforts allowed were a poncho, ground cover liner, and extra socks. No sleeping bags were carried because of their bulk and the extra weight.

Karalow instructed the men to always carry morphine inside the handles of their CAR-15s. And everyone carried it in the same place so it could be easily found. "If you have to administer morphine, always use the casualty's first, not your own; you might need your own a few minutes later."

The team carried spare batteries for patrol radios, plus extra water and food. Everything had to go with them when moving on as nothing could be left behind to compromise a position.

They loaded extra magazines. The M-16 magazine was as important as the weapon itself because if the spring didn't push the round into position, the working parts of the rifle couldn't push the round into the breech. The CAR-15 magazine normally holds thirty rounds, but Karalow told his guys to always use twenty-eight, which allowed a little extra push in the spring.

Andy Ransom, Karalow's ATL, handed Johnson a box of tracers. "If you want to see where you're shooting, put one tracer in every third round. That will help you direct your rounds to their next target."

They rechecked the detonators and tested the workings of the claymore antipersonnel mines. Karalow used a circuit tester. All weapons had to be test-fired. The whole morning would be spent at the rifle range—zeroing in weapons and testing each magazine. They'd lie down in the prone position, aim at the center of the target a hundred meters away, and fire six rounds. Then they'd adjust their sights according to how the shots hit the target. Every rifle was different, with variations in the distance between the eye and the rear sight. If you fired your buddy's rifle, the zero would be off for you, but that wasn't necessarily a problem because most of the time a firefight was within a thirty-meter range.

Next, the team rehearsed different combat scenarios. Each situation on the ground can be different, and everything happens rapidly with no time to think. Yet everything has to be preplanned. Paradoxically, the more you practice, the more flexible you can be. If a team is ambushed, for instance, the point man opens fire to break contact. Then he runs to the back of the column. Each man fires a magazine, then leapfrogs behind the next, until they are all facing the opposite direction. At first, all this is confusing, and the cherries bump into each other. But with practice they get better.

By the time that Karalow got the warning order, his team was eager to go. The mood was very upbeat when Captain Guy, Karalow, and Ed Drozd made their aerial reconnaissance of the AO. Karalow selected the insertion LZs, while Captain Guy delineated the two-klick recon zone.

The radio-relay teams were dispatched in advance of the Ranger insertion. The Ranger team packed their gear and readied themselves for the mission.

Karalow coordinated all the nitty-gritty details, went over sitreps, grid references, and escape routes. They synchronized their watches, checked radio frequencies, recited codes and codewords, and reviewed departure times. The cherries pretended not to be nervous.

The morning of the mission, Johnson's rucksack was outfitted with twelve freeze-dried meals, fourteen mags of ammo, six hand grenades, four smoke grenades, two white phosphorous grenades, a radio and spare radio battery, three pairs of socks, jungle sweater, poncho liner, poncho, twelve packs of cocoa, strobe light, two morphine syringes, blood expander, knife, map, insect repellent, camouflage stick, pen-gun flare, compass, two pounds of C-4 explosive, six quarts of water, and his M-16 rifle. Wearing over ninety pounds of gear, he was ready for his first mission. His primary job would be to keep his mouth shut and follow the old guys' lead.

As the cherries walked to the acid pad, Jim Peterson, who was still recovering from his head wound, yelled, "Hey,

Cherry! Can I borrow some of that Stateside money you brought with you? You ain't gonna be needing it where you're going."

Each man slipped into the shoulder straps of his rucksack, tightened web gear, and rechecked rifles. Then, as a group, they headed for the lead chopper and climbed aboard. The interior of the Huey was Spartan—a bare hull with just a metal nonslip floor to sit on. The seats were folded back into the firewall. No one ever used the seat belts in a Huey on a mission. The first thing the guys noticed, once on board, was the strong smell of aviation fuel.

The pilot went through his start-up procedures as the crew chief and door gunner strapped in. He turned and gave Johnson one thumb-up. The whine of the turbines picked up, and the rotor blades started a lazy rotation. Johnson sat on the floor of the helicopter with his rucksack propped against the back of the pilot's seat and his foot hooked into the door gunner's seat frame. As the rotor blades picked up speed, he removed his floppy hat and stuck it in his shirt.

The pilot pulled pitch, and the ship trembled, breaking away from the ground. They dropped the nose to pick up speed and climb up over the barbed wire that encircled Camp Eagle. The chase ship fell into formation behind the C & C helicopter and the two Cobra gunships that were off to their three o'clock. The formation headed west toward the hills and jungle.

The trip seemed long. Because of the deafening sounds of the rotor blade, not much was said. Everyone was nervous on his first mission, but that was never talked about. There was a sense of the mission's being the final exam. And there were no makeups, just pass/fail grades. If the cherry failed to measure up, he'd get a fast trip back to a line unit, or worse—become a REMF.

The chopper flew above the clouds to go over the mountains, and when they got over the AO, they popped down through the high clouds only to find dense fog. The pilots couldn't see a damn thing. The four helicopters began to lose airspeed as the pilots tried to find a hole through the soup. The Cobras went into a wide orbit a mile or two behind. Finally, the pilots of the two slicks, with only fifty meters between them, slowly began to inch their ships into the fog. A hundred meters inside, they broke through into a gauzy pocket of dim light.

Only the tops of tall trees jutting up through a thick blanket of ground fog enabled the pilots to tell up from down without relying entirely on their instruments—perhaps a good thing because in those days army Huey pilots didn't get much—if any—instrument flight training. Complicating the situation was the fact that somewhere ahead of them in the clouds was a pretty tall mountaintop.

The side of a mountain suddenly appeared dead ahead, and the pilots scrambled to pull up as hard as they could, and those choppers practically nosed straight up in the air. They were almost touching the side of the mountain when they pulled up.

Johnson noticed the rice paddies below had bomb craters in them. It was his first ride in a helicopter, and he told me later that he'd been praying all the way, "God, I just don't want to be a baby. If I don't die right away, don't let me be a baby."

They inserted at 1000 hours into a clump of elephant grass. Five meters off the LZ was a high-speed trail, so the team moved especially slow. They walked on the trail for about three hundred meters. Ed Drozd was walking point. As point man, he selected the route through the jungle. Eventually they set up behind a tree about five meters off the trail and took a chow and water break.

John Strope, Ransom, and Lytle were sitting in bushes so thick they couldn't see Johnson. Twenty minutes later, they heard *gunkies* talking. Gunkies was Johnson's name for NVA, as opposed to Viet Cong; myself, I just called everyone gooks.

Johnson and Karalow got on their hands and knees and could make out three enemy soldiers less than twenty meters away, up the trail. It was Johnson's first good look at the enemy. The NVA stopped, sat down to the side of the trail, and opened a food pouch.

Karalow decided that the conditions were favorable for them to try to capture a POW, but while he and Johnson decided what to do next, the enemy started moving. One enemy soldier walked about ten meters ahead of the others and made a big mistake: he stepped off the trail and walked right into Drodz. Lytle and Ransom were sitting in the bush behind Drodz and couldn't see what happened next.

Drodz stared at the pair of frightened Oriental eyes looking back at him. Without thinking, Drodz shouldered his rifle, shifted the front sight onto the center of the man's head and squeezed the trigger. The steel-jacketed M-16 round snapped the man's head back violently, and he collapsed into the brush.

Karalow and Johnson immediately started taking fire from the other two enemy. Johnson was still on his hands and knees when an AK-47 round went right under his chin. Karalow still didn't know if one of his team had been shot, so he called out to Drodz who yelled back that he was all right and that he "got one." Apparently realizing they were outgunned, the other two enemy soldiers ran off down the trail. The team gathered around the dead NVA. He'd been carrying an AK-47, two fifty-pound sacks of rice, and a bag containing payroll and a packet of orders in Vietnamese. Karalow policed up the rifle and papers and pulled the team off the trail.

Since they didn't know if there were more NVA on the trail or if there might be a base camp up ahead, Karalow called in a fast mover (jet fighter-bomber) for a napalm drop in the direction the other enemy soldiers had run.

Meanwhile, the team backtracked to the LZ and waited for the 17th Cav Blue reaction team to reinforce them.

Johnson always kept a little notebook with him. He'd take notes on everything that happened to him, then every couple of weeks or so, he'd add the pages to a big binder under his cot back at base. On this mission, Karalow was watching as Johnson was writing, and he noticed that Johnson's arm was dripping blood. When he pointed it out, Johnson casually put away his pencil and put a field dressing on the wound.

Later that day the team was extracted. They got a night's rest at Eagle and were sent back in the next day, this time with a Kit Carson scout. Johnson noticed the air had a putrid, sweet-sour smell this time around. The napalm had devastated everything. The trees didn't have any leaves or branches on them. But they didn't find any other gunkies.

Johnson did find a huge green iguana on the side of a tree at about eye level, right in the napalm impact area. The Kit Carson scout with them had wanted to whack it in the noodle and said he would be great eating. But Johnson just petted the lizard and let him go.

When they returned to base camp, Ransom went off to Recondo School, and Lytle and Bates went over to Dave Bennett's team.

Pararescue

I didn't have another group of replacements scheduled in for another few days, so I decided to hitch a ride to the Bien Hoa airbase. A buddy in air force pararescue, whom I'd met in Recondo School, had invited me to the base for a few beers.

Bien Hoa was one of eight air force bases scattered around Vietnam. It was the showplace, complete with a ten-thousand-foot concrete runway, a parallel taxiway, tens of thousands of square yards of apron for parking, hangars, repair shops, offices, buildings, barracks, movie theaters, service clubs, and even a swimming pool. What really got my goat was the gym, complete with Stateside weights, a bench, and a sit-up board.

At Bien Hoa, air force guys were scurrying around like ants guarding a birthday cake. I asked an AP (air police, universally called apes, probably because of their relaxed and friendly manner) where the pararescue hootch was. He looked at me as if I were speaking a foreign language, then pointed down a paved road along the runway. I walked past a Kaman Huskie helicopter that looked very odd because it had two long intermeshing rotors and no tail rotor at all.

Eventually I reached and entered a nearly empty hangar and asked if anyone knew Sgt. Dave Rhody. "Sure," an airman replied, "Rhody's in the briefing room. Down the hall. Go right in." I opened the door and was hit by a blast of cool air. Air-conditioning! Six air force enlisted men were sitting around in their shorts, reading *Mad* magazines, and listening to a tape of Credence Clearwater's "Proud Mary."

"Hey, Chambers, is that you?" Rhody yelled, walking toward me. He was wearing green coveralls and carrying a camouflage-painted flight helmet.

"It be me."

"Hey you guys, this is the crazy army LRRP I met at Recondo School. He single-handedly captured six NVA officers." A couple of heads looked up and nodded approval. Damn, the air force was good! They had air-conditioning, and they knew the properly worshipful way to greet their betters. I decided to overlook Rhody's inability to count.

"Come on in, man, you want a drink?" Rhody set the helmet on the table.

"Yes, sure do."

Rhody was a wiry-looking guy with arms like tree stumps. He'd just gotten back from rescuing a downed F-4 pilot up in North Vietnam. He shook my hand with a bear grip, then opened a small refrigerator and grabbed a beer. "Here you go, friend."

As I looked around the surroundings, I said, "You guys really know how to live. Now I know why my dad told me to join the air force." That got a laugh all around.

"You gonna stay for steaks? Some of the REMFs are barbecuing up a pile, and you're invited," one guy offered.

"Wouldn't miss it." I smacked my lips.

After an afternoon of swapping war stories, I was starting to feel the beers. In fact, I realized that I wasn't sure how I'd found my way to the bunker Rhody and I were sitting on. I looked down at the giant pile of Lucky Lager cans we had tossed down over the side. The rest of the night played like a bad dream. From atop that bunker, I was watching the air force guys lining up, piling their plates high with grilled steaks, baked potatoes, and fresh salad.

Pausing in his story, Rhody opened a bottle of mescal, stared briefly at the worm on the bottom, then took a big gulp and passed the bottle to me. But my attention was on a group of guys gathered around the barbecue pit. "Rhody, this really gives me a case of the ass. Our guys are on the tail end of the food chain, and these guys are eating steaks."

The party was getting louder, and I was getting madder. I couldn't explain it, but I wanted to push over their barbecue pit and weight machines, and shoot holes in their portable swimming pool. But I could smell the steaks cooking, and hunger was dampening my cause.

Rhody and I jumped off the bunker and walked over to the fifty-five-gallon-drum barbecue pit. I guess it was the beers, or maybe the tequila. I really have no good excuse for my lack of manners, but I started urinating all over the three dozen steaks cooking on an open flame. Rhody almost fell on the ground laughing, tears in his eyes. But one of the cooks grabbed me and pushed me back against the bunker. I was laughing so hard, I didn't even notice when my head hit the PSP steel roof. I just grabbed my bleeding head and scrambled back up on the bunker with Rhody, who handed me the bottle of tequila.

"That was the funniest thing I've ever seen in my life! Did you see the look on those cooks' faces? I guess we'll be having a new kind of A-1 sauce tonight! Go for the worm."

I held the tequila bottle upside down and took a long swig. As I lowered the bottle, I saw a crowd of angry guys forming. One of them pointed in our direction. Then they looked to me like an anthill moving in unison toward us. I stopped laughing.

Someone yelled, "That army asshole pissed all over our steaks!" I hopped off the bunker and landed in front of the biggest air force single-striper I'd ever seen.

Rhody was egging me on in the background, "Kick his ass, 101!"

The guy looked up at Rhody, then grabbed my shirt and said, "I'm going to knock the shit out of you." The guy had hands like a Neanderthal and towered over me like King Kong. His eyebrows went up and down like two angry caterpillars. I pushed him in the chest, but he didn't budge. *"Shit!"* I knew I was in trouble now. I couldn't back down now in any case, so I gave this guy my deadliest stare and said, "It's gonna take twenty more guys your size to kick my one ass."

"Are you threatening me, you piece of shit?"

"No threat, asshole. Let go of me, so I can cream ya."

He pulled back to swing, but I ducked and came up with a punch to his stomach. He caught me with a blow to the head, and just then I felt an AP's nightstick hit my arm. They pulled us apart.

Rhody, who could not stop laughing, dragged me back to the bunker, and the big boy disappeared into the crowd. I was reviving myself with another gulp of tequila as the pack regrouped and headed our way. I looked behind me for an E & E route, but the only way off the bunker was in front of the pack. Rhody jumped to his feet and shouted, "We're over here, assholes."

"Good, Rhody!" I said. "Give away our position!"

By the time they reached us, it looked like about a hundred hungry wolves moving in for the kill. But Rhody stood up and taunted the group, yelling, "Pussies!"

A hand grabbed at my legs in an attempt to pull me off the bunker, but I kicked the guy in the head. Rhody was smiling like it was the happiest day of his life.

"Let me take 'em; he's mine," he shouted and took one last swig of tequila.

"Well, under any other circumstance I wouldn't, but these *are* your guys," I replied.

Rhody leaped off the bunker, fists out straight, landing on top of the pack, yelling, "The worm has turned!"

"Kick his ass," I shouted. Then I have no idea why, but I jumped off the bunker, too. Being totally drunk, I missed my target and landed on my hands and knees just to the right of the brawl.

All I could see was a swirl of combat boots and dust. I waited for someone to grab me and pull me into the rumble, but no one even noticed I was there. Now I'm not saying I'm proud of what I did, but one tactic I had learned in combat was that when you're outnumbered, discretion is the better part of valor. So I started low crawling and continued right past the human pile-on, shooting a beeline into the darkened street.

Once I felt safe, I got to my feet and looked around for an escape route. I removed my army fatigue shirt, leaving on only a black undershirt for camouflage. Feeling invisible, I casually walked down a long row of hootches until I found an empty barrack. Once inside, I found a vacant bunk, pulled back the mosquito netting, and crawled inside. Luckily for me, no one claimed the empty space that night.

I could hear pissed off air force guys running back and forth yelling "I'm going to kill that son of a bitch," like cheers at a football game. About every twenty minutes, a few guys would run through the barracks, but I just closed my eyes and slept off the drunken stupor.

I had the granddaddy of all hangovers when I awoke just before dawn, the perfect time to make my escape. I grabbed an airman's shirt that was hanging over a chair and pulled it on, then peeked out the door. All clear. I retraced my steps along rows of quiet barracks until I saw the gate. I walked right past the guard, gave him a high sign, and out the gate. I turned the corner on the main road and soon hitched a ride in the back of an army deuce-and-a-half, back to our side of the base and safety. I never saw or heard from my pararescue friend, Rhody, again, but he saved my life that night, and I still owe him.

The next day I ran into Joe Bielesch. He was on his way back to the company for the night. He'd just extended and was leaving the next morning for Camp Eagle. I showed him around my "war room." It had everything a recruiting office could ever need—a bed, a fan, a radio, a couple of prowar posters. Bielesch walked in and inspected my workplace. "Wouldn't be a bad job for a lifer." He asked me what was going on up north.

"Our AO stretches from the DMZ, north to Ruong Ruong Valley, and to Thua Thien Province in the south. The gooks are building up their troops and supplies, so you know we'll be going back into the A Shau Valley."

"No way," said Bielesch.

"Yeah. I talked to a guy from the First of the 327 who said they had actually seen gook tanks and vehicles moving during daylight hours." I flicked off the fan.

Rain started banging on the roof. Bielesch looked at his watch then said, "It's almost chow call. Let's hit it."

"One of my buddies was in the 327 back in '65," I said as we walked to the chow hall. "When we were in college, Kranig told stories about some guys he met in the 101st who later joined Special Forces. He made me feel that what we were doing in Nam was really important."

"Had you fooled." Bielesch wiped the rain off his face.

"He told me some schoolkids who didn't show up for class had their fingers cut off by the local Viet Cong."

"Keep them stupid and out in the fields, out of trouble," said Bielesch.

"Kranig got nailed in his third month."

"Ah, man."

"Yeah, he got shot point-blank with an AK-47 thirteen times—in the chest, stomach, back, fingers, legs, and arms. And lived to tell about it. Luckily not his head or his face, then he'd have really been pissed off.

"So I go to the hospital in San Francisco and meet him in what was called the 'Pus Ward.' " That's how they talk about the infection ward. He opened his shirt and showed me some impressive wounds.

"He walked into some gooks and one of them nailed him good. Shot Kranig in the arm, and the impact spun him around. He fell to the ground and looked up and saw the gook running at him, with his rifle. Kranig watched as the guy pointed the rifle and opened up on him. The first bullet hit him in the ankle. Then the guy shot him up the leg, right to his nuts. Figuring the GI was done for, the gook turned and ran away."

"Your friend never got to return fire?" Bielesch asked.

"No. Well, so, I was talking to Kranig when an orderly wheeled in some guy from the First Infantry Division. I didn't want to look, but I had to. The patient's head was completely bandaged, and I could see his body stopped at the torso. He'd stepped on a land mine, and army medics field dressed what was left of his legs. No one ever checked him until days later when he landed back in the States.

"When they unwrapped those field bandages, Kranig looked over and saw that underneath the gauze covering the guy's legs were about a million maggots. Then the stench hit him. Kranig said he got right out of his own bed and pushed it way down to the other end himself." I finished the story just as we opened the mess hall door.

Joe Bielesch left the next morning for Phu Bai.

On-the-Job Training

Joe Bielesch arrived back at the company compound. He thought he'd have a little free time, maybe even get a night's rest. But he was wrong. He was told that Captain Guy was under pressure to keep a minimum of six teams in the field, and that would be a struggle. Captain Guy not only had to worry about the weather, the enemy, and the equipment; he had to maintain his men's physical condition. When men continuously go out in the field, it takes its toll.

Joe Bielesch would find out there was a problem with being good at LRRPing—you're in constant demand, and people have high expectations.

Most of the training by then was on-the-job. After the first couple of missions, everyone knew if they could cut it or not.

Dave Bennett had stopped by to see me on his way back north. He was just beginning a six-month extension after having served a full year with L Company.

The next day, two newbies, John Kiefel and David Antonelli, had picked up their official orders to the 101st, and they'd be at my presentation that night. When I finished my talk, both Kiefel and Antonelli volunteered. Kiefel had a smile on his face; Antonelli was more reserved and harder to read. Kiefel said that during infantry training, he told his drill sergeant that he wanted to be an LRRP. The drill sergeant told him he must be crazy.

"Anyway, you're going to get more training than the line

doggies. You'll work, but it's a million times better than being in the line, I promise you," I said.

Kiefel told me later our talk had marked a real crossroads in his life. I did some research and found both Antonelli and Kiefel had high IQ scores so, based on that, I took them. Two days later, Kiefel was standing in formation, and the SERTS cadre shouted out his name. "Kiefel, you got your wish, 75th Rangers."

The following afternoon, both men boarded the C-130 flight north. Two hours later, the tailgate of the cargo plane lowered, and they were hit with the jungle rotting-leaf smell that permeated the air around Phu Bai airport. It was hot that day, and sweat was dripping off them before they even stepped on the tarmac. The runway was so hot, Kiefel could feel it burning through the molded soles of his issue-fresh jungle boots.

Inside the open terminal building, they and the other disgruntled passengers stood stalled in the long line that extended to the restroom door. Kiefel gave up waiting and dragged his duffel bag over to the crowded gook drink concession, which consisted of two mamma-sans squatting behind a wooden box of warm Cokes. The older mamma-san's teeth were shiny black from chewing betel nut, and the other woman was pregnant. Both wore the traditional black silk pajamas and straw hat.

The old-timers waiting to board the C-130 walked slowly around, like they were in a daze. A soldier dressed in an OD green T-shirt, ripped pants, and worn-out jungle boots looked exhausted. He had a far-off stare.

Antonelli nudged Kiefel. "Did you see that guy? That's what happens after a year in the line." That made Kiefel feel even better about his instinct to become a Ranger.

Kiefel looked like a professor and was built close to the ground. David Antonelli, in contrast, was tall and thin. They joined eight other cherries in the back of a deuce-and-a-half headed to Camp Eagle. The driver wasn't sure where the Ranger company area was so he drove around the base twice before he stopped to ask the MPs.

After he'd been assigned to a team, Kiefel was lying on his cot when someone tossed a fake hand grenade into the hootch.

He didn't even jump; he was cool. He and Antonelli were both put on Joe Bielesch's team; Chief McCabe was their ATL. They liked McCabe, the Navajo who had been on Frank Anderson's team. He had big cheeks and was wearing a black baseball cap with the Recondo patch. Joe Bielesch grabbed bags of claymores, some extra grenades from the ammo bunker, two strobe lights and pen-gun flares, a compass or two, some "lifer bars" (GI chocolate), and two handfuls of Stateside snacks. He stuffed all this in the new guys' pockets and packs. They each carried two quarts of water on their LBE. They also carried poncho liners for protection from the elements. With the heavy moisture in the air and the dense cloud cover, temperatures in the jungle at night could plummet into the fifties or sixties, and that posed a very real threat of hypothermia.

The team grabbed their weapons and their web gear, and headed for the company chopper pad. As soon as the chopper sat down on the acid pad, the team boarded immediately. The pilot turned in his seat and looked back at the Rangers, his own face hidden by the dark visor of his helmet. Kiefel and Antonelli were anxious to get going.

The flight took only twenty minutes. Because of the open terrain, the chopper and the chase ship engaged in a series of false insertions and leapfrog tactics to confuse the enemy about the real landing site. Suddenly, the insertion aircraft flared over a stretch of open ground, fifty feet from the tree line that bordered a river. Their Huey dropped its nose to pick up forward momentum.

When the pilot of the lead aircraft gave the green light to begin the insertion, Bielesch stepped out onto the left skid of the helicopter. He took one look down at the vegetation being whipped into a froth by the chopper's downdraft, then stepped off, quickly followed by his men. Once on the ground, the team ran to a jungle-covered opening, dropped, and lay panting in a tight circle facing out.

Kiefel was fighting to get his breathing under control. The noise of his own heartbeat was pounding in his ears. Sprinting twenty meters with a hundred pounds of gear on his back had drained the wind from his lungs.

Bielesch established radio contact with the TOC back at Camp Eagle, then quickly double-checked his map to make sure that their position was where they were supposed to be. His patrol had to cover three hundred meters of single-canopy cover choked with thick clusters of bamboo to reach a little knob of high ground overlooking the river. Three hundred meters in thirty minutes doesn't sound like a difficult task, but if you're trying to accomplish it without walking into an ambush or making noise that might alert the enemy to your presence, it's extremely demanding.

Kiefel was waiting to move out when he spotted something. He looked closer—a booby-trapped mortar round. He tapped McCabe on the shoulder. McCabe hand-signaled Bielesch, and every one of them completely backtracked every step.

Bielesch decided the AO was booby-trapped, and called for an extraction. The choppers turned around and came back, but would not touch down because of the good chance of hitting a mine. Finally the bellyman tossed down the metal rope ladder, and they all climbed aboard. After they were in the chopper, McCabe grabbed Kiefel. "You saved our lives. You're a natural." McCabe never said a lot, but when he did, he meant it. From that point on, Kiefel walked point. He was good enough that other team leaders asked him to walk point for them, but he wanted to stay on Bielesch's team.

Meanwhile, down south I was doing good and had five more guys volunteer over the next few days: PFC Joe Kennedy, Mark Martin (assigned to the 2d platoon), Randall Stein, and privates first class John Strope and Randall Stice.

Military Payment Certificates (MPCs)

It was early morning, July 15, 1969, and Miller was almost excited. He finally had a seat assignment on a "going home" flight out of Bien Hoa the following Monday, which meant we still had the weekend to get into some trouble. It was also the morning he told us about his big plans.

Kenn Miller had different exit plans than most of us. He wasn't going to be heading back to the States, intent on joining a peace march, or getting a job with Dad's company. He was already planning to head for Taiwan. He loved the Taiwanese. He'd been there on one of his R & Rs, and his goal was to attend the University of Taipei. He'd have to go back to the States first, however. At that time, overseas discharges were not allowed. Even so, Miller was anxious to leave Vietnam, and was trying to make his last few days pass as quickly as he could. I knew we'd find some trouble to get into.

That morning at breakfast, I met up with Miller. He was reading *Stars and Stripes*. "It says here that Saigon has over fifty-six thousand *registered* prostitutes, and that figure doesn't include the amateurs." Miller was a connoisseur of Saigon and felt that the bar girls formed the elite among the prostitutes. They received a percentage from drinks of colored water, called "Saigon Tea." You would buy it just to enjoy their company and dance together to blaring rock 'n' roll music. In Vietnam, unlike most bar girls of the time in European GI hangouts, after bar hours, sex was available but cost extra. In Germany at the time, bar girls were available for talk and dancing—and the sharing of high-priced "champagne"—but not usually for sex. That was more easily available from streetwalkers.

The bar girls and their less fortunate sisters who worked the brothels and the streets were pathetic looking. They would flaunt themselves in makeup and clothes they did not know how to wear. Some had their eyelids "westernized" by cosmetic surgery, an operation that had become popular among young upper-class Saigon women and, more recently, throughout Southeast Asia.

I had a hundred dollars in American twenty-dollar bills. Miller told me that on the black market in Saigon, we could exchange them at five-to-one, whereas the PX—the post exchange—would give the equivalent of the face amount. Of course, it was illegal to trade on the black market, and if we got caught, we'd be busted. On the other hand, we decided, "What can they do to us—send us to Vietnam?" We had nothing to lose. The next morning we caught a jeep ride to Saigon.

The refugee slums that lined the roads in and out of town consisted of shacks constructed of scavenged materials. The most distinctive were made of empty beer and soda cans discarded by the camps. The Vietnamese cut the cans open, pounded them flat, and nailed them to strips of wood to make metal sheets for walls. Everyone living there depended on what others discarded.

Our ride let us off near the center of town—Saigon's Rue Catinat. Old and young women, dressed in traditional black silk, bustled past and haggled with each other. The street was filled with what sounded like geese cackling. Peasants lined sidewalks holding an assortment of montagnard bracelets, pins of all kinds, army badges, Coca-Cola, water-buffalo-hide watchbands, and baskets full of colorful fish. Two Iranian shopkeepers leaned against an open shop door, smoking slim brown cigarettes. Inside their shop, Persian rugs of all kinds lined the walls; in the window were ivory elephant tusks carved intricately to create people walking up mountains. I stopped to examine the tusks. I remember the smell of sweet curry and rice cooking. One of the Iranians asked me in perfect English to come in.

"Look around," he said, pointing to the walls.

"Yeah, like I can carry a rug in the jungle."

"We'll ship to any place in the world."

"No thanks, I have a poncho," I said and moved on.

Miller tipped his black hat to a pretty young Vietnamese girl on a motor scooter as she passed between us. We started across the street. Crossing the streets was like a ballet dance through the maze of humanity on wheels.

A kid with sores covering his legs came up to me and shouted, "Hey, you GI!"

When I didn't respond by giving him any money, he shouted a few obscenities my way. We passed two White Mice, the slang term for Saigon's police. They stared at us for a while, and I almost chickened out, but then they turned down a side street and I let out a sigh of relief.

Kenn and I crossed a second congested street and found the LeLoi hotel, then checked in and headed out to make our big scores. Miller headed for the local massage parlor while I scouted out the local black market. It didn't take me long to find a money changer. A few streets from the hotel looked safe—no MPs. I was more scared about making the exchange than going out in the field. My mom had once made me return a few pennies that our local grocers had undercharged us. She told me that if nothing else, we were honest. And here I was about to deal in the black market.

There were lots of street kids running around, and one young Vietnamese kid, about eleven years old, approached me. "You want girl? I got Cambodian girl for you, GI."

"You exchange U.S. dollars for Vietnamese piasters?" I asked him.

He nodded and told me to follow him down a side street. We passed shops, people talking, doors open, fish on the corner, people walking back and forth. "Wait here," he instructed.

I nervously waited outside an old, French-looking courtyard. A few minutes later, the boy returned holding a thick wad of

Vietnamese money. I was thinking, Wow, five-to-one. I can get laid, have dinner, and still have money left over.

The kid unraveled the large roll. On the outside of the roll were the smaller bills, maybe the equivalent of about fifty cents U.S. He handed it to me and let me count it. "Five hundred dollars!" I said, feeling smug.

He nodded. Then he took the money back, rolled it up, put the rubber band back around it, and stuck it in his pocket. As I handed him my American twenties, I began to get a bad feeling. While he was counting my money, I nervously looked around for MPs, or the Vietnamese equivalent.

Then he said, "Okay, number one. I be right back. Have to show mamma-san. She give you number one rate."

"Oh no, no. We make the exchange here, now! I wasn't born yesterday."

"Okay, GI, you too smart for me." The kid let out a big laugh, as he reached back into his back pocket and handed me the roll of Vietnamese money.

"Hey, I'm no sucker," I said seriously.

We shook hands, and with a wide smile, he turned and walked back into the old building. I stuck my black market roll of hot money in my front pocket and headed south on my way back to the hotel. I thought maybe he just wanted to exchange the money in the privacy of the building. Maybe he wasn't a bad kid.

I got back to our room, feeling on top of the world. Then I laid the roll of money on the table, thinking about what a great time I'd have with it. I'd buy everybody drinks, the whole thing. I popped that little rubber band off and opened the roll, but didn't see any large bills. I must have counted it five times before it sunk in. I had about the equivalent of a dollar in small Vietnamese bills. Gook pennies printed on paper. The kid had done the ol' switcheroo with two rolls of money in his back pocket. Boy, did I feel like a sucker.

I grabbed my K-bar and attempted to retrace my steps. After an hour of looking, I found the street—but, of course, nobody was there. The shops were closed, windows bolted, doors shut, not a person around—no kids, nothin'! It just looked like an alley. I walked up and down and thought it must not be the same street. I went to the next street, nobody there either. I banged on a few doors where I thought the incident had happened. Then I gave up, thinking, okay, the sons of bitches got me. I was broke.

Later, when Miller showed up, I told him the story, and he almost split a gut.

"Shit, you do need me to show you around."

I borrowed five dollars from Miller and spent that night trying to convince a pretty bar girl that she should take me home. Once she discovered that five dollars minus the cost of drinks was all the money I had, she moved on, and I returned alone to my hotel.

After my Saigon escapade, I got down to work. I finished the month by sending twelve more guys to the company: John Manderberg, Gary Baker, Don Bochman, Jerry Bowman, Calvin Duncle, William Gordon, Kevin Henry, Charles Keogh, Jarvis Dale, Robert Kelley, Alfred Lee Littlon, and James Bowers.

When it was time for Miller to out process, he got in trouble on one of his last stops. A leg, noncombatant, spec-4 clerk took his records, glanced down at them, then said, "You're a sergeant. If you want any medals, just let me know. I can give you whatever you want."

Miller always had a weird thing about medals, and the closer he got to going home, the more he began to regard them as bad luck emblems. He also had a thing about REMFs, and this REMF offering him medals was such an outrage, he flipped the table over on the guy, told him to get fucked, and stomped out, leaving his paperwork in rubble. Miller hadn't gone far before a redheaded major from division "P" school caught up with him and calmed him down. The major promised to look into the awarding of unearned medals but advised Miller to watch his behavior. He was still in the army, still subject to Uniform Code of Military Justice.

An hour later, the major came around to the hootch with Miller's paperwork, and his out processing was complete. Miller went to Long Binh the next day, him and Hagopian. The day after that, they flew back to the States; Hagopian to New York City, and Miller to Reno, Nevada. Only problem was when Miller got his separation papers in the mail, the "Awards and Decorations" section was blank—not even as much as a National Defense Service medal. He still hates REMFs.

Swimming Behind Nui Khe

S.Sgt. James "Lobo" Bates was assigned as assistant team leader to Sgt. Dave Bennett's team. He was just out of Ranger school and knew his status as a new shake 'n' bake E-6 might be resented. Bennett had never been offered the opportunity of attending Ranger school, yet he was to train Bates so that Bates could have his own team. Bennett also picked up two privates I had recruited, Robert Kelley and Mike Lytle. He picked the team name Excalibur, since he figured there was no word for Excalibur in the Vietnamese dictionary.

Bates and Bennett walked from their NCO hootch down to the tactical operations center (TOC) for the mission briefing. Along the way they picked up Robert Kelley and Mike Lytle. As they walked, Bennett looked back at the two men and began giving instructions. "Tomorrow I'll take you guys down to fire your weapons a few times. We've got a fifty-five-gallon drum filled with sand for test-firing weapons before we go out." Bates glanced down at a helicopter sitting on the acid pad.

"You gotta keep 'em oiled every day; the humidity is a bitch." Bennett continued, "Try to find a towel to take out. You'll carry it around your neck and use it to wipe everything down, including the sweat off your face." Kelley laughed nervously, as Bennett went on, "Bates and I will go over equipment tonight. Bring an extra canteen of water. Lytle, you'll carry the radio." Lytle nodded.

They were walking faster as Bennett rattled off the list of

what they would need. "I'll show you where to keep your poncho liner."

They turned and climbed up the berm toward the TOC. The helicopter below them started up. The noise of the rotors winding up stopped Bennett's talking. When they entered the TOC, a handful of men was sitting in the back row on folding chairs. They were the radio-relay team.

At the front of the room, Captain Guy was talking to First Sergeant Gilbert. Behind them hung an acetate-covered map, which took up most of the wall. The map was a composite of several smaller topo maps that made up the entire area of operations. Bennett and Bates took seats in the front; Lytle and Kelley sat behind them.

Bates studied the map. At the top was the DMZ, and to the west of the DMZ the Laotian border was marked in red. The right side of the map bordered on the South China Sea. Jungle areas were in light and dark green, with the lowlands and swamps in white. Firebases were red triangles drawn with a grease pencil. The map was covered with tightly packed contour lines showing steep mountains and deep valleys. Bennett pointed to a small group of tight lines. "That's Nui Khe."

Ellis, one of the radio-relay guys sitting in the back row, cleared his throat. Captain Guy turned around. "I guess that means let's get started!" The group broke into laughter.

"Okay, settle down," Sergeant Gilbert called the group to order.

Everyone got quiet as Captain Guy began, "Division G-2 wants a reconnaissance mission into the mountains behind Nui Khe. Your team will be patrolling six klicks west of Nui Khe.

"We've had teams around Nui Khe extensively for the past eighteen months. It's known as the rocket belt. The NVA have been launching 122mm rockets at Hue, Phu Bai, and here, at Eagle. And we have new intelligence indicating an enemy buildup. Sergeant Bennett, we're still short men; can you handle this with only a four-man patrol?"

Bennett looked up. "Yes, sir." Then after a short breath, added, "I guess it will be quieter." Everyone laughed, except

Bates. He still didn't have his feet wet, and they had to go in short.

"We're going to keep the Blues on standby and two Cobras in case the shit hits the fan." Captain Guy looked straight at Bates. "The insertion will be at last light on the twenty-fifth."

Bates shifted in his seat under Captain Guy's gaze. He knew that going in just before dark was riskier than first-light insertions. If the team was compromised, that would mean a night extraction under fire, or at the very least, escape and evasion through pitch-black jungle.

Guy finished the weather report about the time the division intelligence officer arrived, a tall, skinny captain who spoke with a Texas drawl. Bates liked the guy right off since he himself was from Texas. "Good evening, men. The 5th NVA Regiment has been working this area." He pointed to a location on the wall map. "In the next few months, they will be building up for a possible Tet offensive."

Bates glanced quizzically at Bennett, who said quietly, "It's the gooks' New Year celebration."

"We've had a number of positive 'sniffer' contacts that substantiate that someone is out there." The Texas captain continued, "This probably means an enemy offensive is in the making. Your mission will be to conduct a long-range patrol into the area to determine just what is causing all the positive readings on the sensors."

After the mission plans were finalized and everyone briefed, Bennett decided to walk point himself during the patrol. He assigned PFC Mike Lytle to walk his slack (i.e., second man in the marching order) carrying the primary radio on his back. Kelley would occupy the third slot with the artillery radio, and Bates would bring up the rear. In addition to the two main PRC-25s, Bennett and Bates would each carry small squad radios. That way everyone on the small team would be able to communicate with someone if they became separated during E & E (escape and evasion).

On the morning of the twenty-fourth, Bennett and Bates went on the overflight of the AO. The entire area consisted of heavily vegetated, steep, mountainous terrain. Thick double canopy opened up into a fifty-meter-wide belt of sparse scrub vegetation along both sides of the Khe Dau River that ran through the middle of the recon zone (RZ).

Bates and Bennett agreed that the river could be a plus. It meant that water wouldn't be a problem during the patrol, so they could leave behind the larger collapsible canteens they usually carried in their rucks. Without the added weight of all that extra water, the four-man team would be able to hump more ammo, which certainly could come in handy if they made contact with an enemy unit.

Bennett pointed to a small clearing as the team's primary LZ. It was located on a narrow secondary ridge that rose slowly away from the river until it connected with a major ridgeline that crossed the team's RZ. Bennett explained to Bates that the dense vegetation covering the high ground would make it harder for the gooks to observe their insertion. The Huey turned and headed back to base.

The next morning, Bennett ran an equipment check and test-fired weapons with his team. Bennett made sure everyone had everything they'd need—weapons, web gear, an extra bandolier, strobe lights, a pen-gun flare, a compass. Bates grabbed some lifer bars and a handful or two of Stateside snacks and stuffed them in the cargo pockets of his pants.

The men changed into cammies and applied camouflage face paint. Finally all SOP safeguards and premission rituals had been followed; they were ready. Bates didn't have enough time to get nervous.

The evening of the twenty-fifth came fast. Bates met the rest of the team on the chopper pad. As he adjusted his pack and equipment, he looked across the valley. Perched on the ridge across from the company area sat two deadly looking Cobra gunships with their rotors windmilling. Every fifty feet were two rows of sandbags piled six high and stretching for twenty feet. Between them sat the gunships. At the end of the ridgeline sat a tear-shaped helicopter Loach, short for LOH—light observation helicopter. Bates watched as the Loach lifted and flew over to the company tarmac, where Captain Guy boarded. It rose again, the sideways lift blowing up a cloud of dirt that

Author Larry Chambers shortly after his swearing-in.

Sgt. Bill Marcy, killed in action, May 20, 1969.

Frank Anderson,
July 1969.

John K. Kiefel
moments before
a mission.

Sgt. Joe Bielesch in the field, October or November 1969.
(Courtesy Robert Guy)

S.Sgt. James A. Bates prepared for deployment into Khe Sanh, February 1970. Note the LAW mounted vertically on his rucksack.

Capt. Robert A. Guy in communication with a team after inserting it, October 1969. (Courtesy Robert Guy)

Bill Young (left) and Jim Peterson with their CAR-15s in the test-fire pit at Camp Eagle.

Larry Saenz
at Camp Eagle.

Larry Saenz
happy to be back
at the office.

Sp4. James Rodarte about to deploy on a mission from
Camp Eagle, March 1970.

Sgt. Ron "Mother" Rucker, Swedish-K around his neck, returning with shrimp from the market at Phu Bai.

Mother Rucker on the chopper ride into the A Shau Valley three days before the lightning strike.

Larry Chambers (left) and Gary Linderer just before the
mission into the A Shau that would be ended by the
lightning strike.

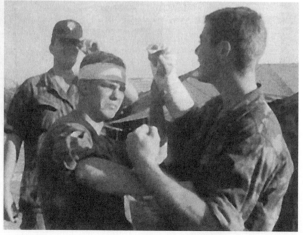

Gary Linderer (left) watches as Kenn Miller (center) and author
Larry Chambers mix it up in Vietnam, a tradition the two have
continued into the present.

almost obscured it. The swift, agile Loach would serve as the command-and-control bird.

Finally, two Cav Hueys landed on the tarmac, and Bates joined the other three members of the team Excalibur aboard the first slick. Both slicks lifted and leaned off in the direction of the AO, timed precisely for insertion during that brief few minutes between dusk and full darkness. The Cobra gunships stayed in a wide orbit a mile or two behind the team's helicopters.

As usual, the insertion slick and the chase ship engaged in a series of false insertions and leapfrog tactics designed to confuse the enemy. Finally, Bates saw the proper stretch of open ground flare fifty feet from the tree line that bordered the river. Their slick hovered briefly over the LZ, and the four Rangers dropped from the skids, then it disappeared over the trees at the edge of the clearing.

On the ground, the team lay in a tight circle facing out, expecting an enemy reception. The noise of Bates's heart was still pounding in his ears as they rose in unison and sprinted twenty yards to the heavy cover off the LZ. They remained frozen there for another fifteen minutes while the jungle slowly forgave, then forgot their rude interruption. The team established radio contact with the TOC back at Camp Eagle, and Bates quickly double-checked his map to make sure that their present position was where they were supposed to be.

Finally, satisfied that the insertion was cold and they were alone on the small ridge, Bennett took the handset from Lytle's radio. He called in a negative situation report and released the gunships circling in the distance. Then he got a commo check from the relay team set up on Firebase Birmingham, seven long klicks to the north.

Though it had grown dark, just to play it safe, Bennett waited until the regular nocturnal birds and insects began their normal evening chatter. It was a good indication that no alien creatures were in the vicinity. Bennett signaled Bates that it was time for the team to move. Silently they crossed over the end of the ridge, skirting a shallow depression just inside the bamboo.

Under full darkness, heading down to the river below, the

team moved cautiously away from the LZ. Bates knew that if there were any major trails in their recon zone, they would most likely be on the level, more open ground, near the water. It was dangerous breaking brush and covering ground at night, but it was even more dangerous to remain too long in the vicinity of an LZ.

Bennett stopped every twenty meters to wait and listen. When they had covered a hundred meters, they located some dense cover just off their line of movement. Lytle and Kelley moved into the center of it and took the opportunity to drink from their canteens. Bennett stopped and called in the team's location. Bates caught up after sterilizing their backtrail, putting leaves and branches back in place where the team had walked.

The Rangers sat down, slipped off their rucksacks, and undid their web gear. Bates and Kelley removed their claymores, and quietly moved outside the thicket to set them to cover their tiny perimeter. In the darkness, to ensure that the curvature would be facing away from the team and the mines would be pointing in the right direction, Bates held each claymore to his chest before setting it.

With that accomplished, Bates and Kelley pulled back into the heavy brush. The team leader whispered that everyone would be on full alert until midnight, then each man would stand a one-and-a-half-hour guard shift until 0600 hours.

The early part of the evening proved uneventful, and the normal sounds of the night returned to reassure them. Bates took the first guard shift while everyone else pulled poncho liners over their heads to hide from the mosquitos. Bates quickly felt the bump of a leech that had attached under his armpit. He reached in and dabbed it with insect repellent, then pulled the slimy, black bastard off and tossed it into the darkness.

Bates passed the watch over to Lytle at 0130. After another quiet hour and a half, Lytle gave the watch to Kelley. It was 0330 hours when Kelley shook Bennett awake, whispering that they had movement on the ridge above them and more below, near the river. Bates also could hear the hushed sounds of voices from below.

Bennett got on the radio to the relay team at Birmingham to report that they had enemy movement. The information was relayed back to the company TOC, which promised the team air support at first light. From that point on, no one slept and rifles were kept on laps, grenades were kept within close reach, beside the claymore clackers.

Dawn finally began to break, and they sat, shivering, until the sun warmed the air. They spent the time reapplying camouflage and covering any exposed skin with insect repellent.

As promised, a Loach (LOH—light observation helicopter) and a pair of Cobra gunships arrived, and circled in the distance. Bennett established contact while Bates hurriedly disarmed and brought in the claymores. The enemy sounds had quieted just before daylight, and Bennett decided to continue the mission. They picked up and moved out cautiously in patrol file, five meters apart, south, in the direction of the river.

Trying to be invisible, they took their time coming down the ridge. Fifty meters later, they walked out of the underbrush and found themselves looking down on a six-foot-wide, enemy high-speed trail. Bates could clearly see muddy footprints, and the overhead canopy had been pulled together and tied off to conceal the trail from the air. Bennett called in the trail's location, condition, and direction. Captain Guy radioed back that the patrol should lay dog and monitor the trail while the air support went back to Firebase Birmingham to refuel.

As soon as the choppers had departed, Bates once again heard sounds of enemy movement above and behind the team. He also thought he heard dogs, and the NVA were talking openly, even shouting back and forth. They were obviously maneuvering to flush the Rangers from hiding before the helicopters could return. Bates exchanged glances with Bennett, who signaled the team to stay close together. Bates took up his position in the rear, and they moved away from the sounds of the enemy. Bates realized that the NVA were close enough to observe the patrol and probably were making a lot of unnecessary noise to drive the Rangers out into the open.

Bennett halted the team and switched rucksacks with Lytle, so that Bennett could handle the radio as they moved. Bates kept his CAR-15 pointed in the direction of the sounds and waited for Bennett to move out.

The team continued traversing the hillside through the brush, sacrificing noise discipline for speed. It was important that they put more distance between themselves and the pursuing NVA; if they failed to outdistance the NVA, the enemy would quickly overrun them.

Finally, as tail-end Charlie, Bates stepped aside and waited. He raised his CAR-15, slid the selector switch to semiauto, aiming down at the spot where the noise indicated the gooks should emerge. It seemed liked an eternity until the first enemy soldier materialized. Looking over his front sight, Bates squeezed the trigger. He could feel the adrenaline rush. AK-47 fire erupted, and the rounds whistled through the trees overhead. Bates reacted; he took cover.

Bennett radioed relay that Excalibur was in contact, and he called for an extraction. Captain Guy, back on the net again, radioed for the team to "hang in there," promising them that help was on the way.

But with only four men, it was time to cut and run; the gooks controlled the high ground. Bennett took up point and broke brush heading down to the high-speed trail along the edge of the river. Captain Guy radioed the team for its grid coordinates so he could direct the gunships but Bennett didn't have time to stop to get a fix on their position. With no response, Captain Guy instructed his pilot to fly low over the valley until he caught a glimpse of his Rangers scrambling down the hillside.

Though slowed down by his miniambush, Bates caught up with the team when Bennett halted the team to make contact with the Loach. He spoke into the handset, "Six, this is Excalibur. You just passed over my position."

"I've got you, Excalibur," Guy replied.

The Loach came around again, and the hillside opened up on it with enemy fire. The pilot screamed over the radio, "Jesus Christ, they're everywhere!" The gunner seated behind Guy opened up with the M-60 as the pilot made a hard evasive right. Guy called for the first Cobra to make a run on the ridgetop.

Bates hung back to cover the team as the men sprinted down

the trail. Through the noise of the miniguns, he could hear the shouts of the enemy soldiers. Bates knew they were trying to re-organize their forces and continue their pursuit.

Captain Guy had his map in his lap and radioed Bennett that he had just located a suitable LZ two hundred meters ahead. The only problem was that the team would have to cross the river. Guy tossed out a red smoke grenade as one of the Cobras took heavy ground fire from just ahead of the team's direction. Bennett knew there were gooks in front of them. Bates moved in closer to the body of the team while firing at enemy behind him. Surrounded by gooks on three sides, there was no place left to move but down to the river.

Bennett stopped at the edge of the water; it was foaming on his side of the bank and looked more like white-water rapids than a jungle stream. The recent rains had swollen the creek and had increased the speed of the normally sluggish current. The four men stood next to the water's edge. Crossing it was their only chance for survival, but they couldn't tell how deep the water was.

Since the gunship runs were pushing the enemy soldiers faster and closer to the Ranger team, Bennett yelled for Bates to get the team across the river, then turned back to cover them. Bates stood waist-deep in the water and gave him the thumbs-up. He and the other two Rangers lunged forward against the current. They were heavy with rucks and web gear and tried to hold their weapons above the surface, but Bates was immedi-ately pulled under, and he lost his grip on his weapon. The cur-rent and his gear dragged him to the bottom, and he struggled to remove his weapon sling, before he could dump his pack and web gear, then fought to get to the surface.

By then, Kelley had also dropped his gear and was swim-ming hard for the opposite bank. The current had moved them almost twenty meters down the river. Bates and Kelley finally banged against the rocks on the other side and dragged up onto the bank. Exhausted, Bates turned and looked for Lytle. There was no sign of him. Bates scanned the torrent, then saw the dark form of Lytle as he swept past. Lytle's head popped up, then he was dragged back under.

Bates jumped into the water and struggled to get to Lytle, reaching within four or five feet of him. Lytle was flailing his arms about wildly, struggling to stay on the surface. Bates tried to toss him one end of an empty ammo bandolier, but then the Ranger just disappeared. Lytle was gone. Bates barely made it back to the rocks, and Kelley had to help pull him out. They stared at the river; there was no sign of Lytle. Neither of them spoke. Across the river they could hear the muffled sounds of Bennett's firing.

NVA rounds kicked up dirt at Bennett's feet as he turned to follow his team across the water. He leaped in, and the current immediately grabbed him and dragged him around a bend in the river, then shoved him ten meters, back to the shore he had just left! Bennett crawled up the bank and removed his gear then jumped back into the water. He had grown up along the California coast and was used to rough surf; he knew not to fight the current.

Bates watched as Bennett tried to make his way across, reaching a large tree stump jutting just above the surface of the river, then striking out for the shore again. With the last of his strength, Bennett reached the shore and pulled himself out onto a sandbar. Waiting several minutes until he had recovered enough strength, Bennett stood up and looked for the rest of his team. When he spotted Bates and Kelley, he yelled, "Where's Lytle?"

"We lost him!" Bates yelled back.

Eventually, the gunships turned the enemy away. Captain Guy sat in the back of his OD green, command-and-control chopper, monitoring a bank of radios intently. The pilot flew the ship at some two hundred feet in a northeasterly direction, then back in the opposite direction, trying to reestablish radio contact with the team. Below, the jungle canopy flowed uninterrupted in all directions, most of the trees seventy to one hundred feet high were an even deep green. The pilot took the LOH down close to treetop level so they could peer through the jungle canopy. He used his prop wash to blow an opening in the canopy and spotted a Ranger standing on a sandbar.

It was Bennett, looking up, waving his arms wildly. The Loach sat down on the sandbar, and Captain Guy jumped out. He ran over to Bennett and yelled over the rotor noise, "Blues are on the way!"

Above, two helicopters raced in from the east, circled overhead, then landed, and ten members of the aerorifle platoon (the Blues) debarked onto the sandbar. They quickly set up a half-moon perimeter around the LOH. Then Captain Guy had the LOH's pilot fly down the river to try to locate Lytle's body.

The scout ship immediately swung far out over the river and began to make slow, deliberate passes back and forth across the stream. Almost thirty meters downstream, the door gunner pointed straight down. Lytle's body was visible where it was pinned by tree roots and flood debris.

The LOH pilot moved back up the river, landed on the sandbar, and shut down his engine. The Cobras continued patrolling the hills above the river, but were no longer firing their weapons systems as the enemy was either dead or in hiding. Bennett and Bates had a quick conference with Captain Guy, the LOH pilot, and the platoon sergeant of the Blues to determine how they could best recover Lytle's body.

One of the Cav troopers stripped off his gear and entered the river above the spot where Lytle's body lay wedged in the current. He made a valiant effort to swim out to the snag, but the current was too swift for him to make it. The soldier quickly turned around and struggled back. Then Bennett grabbed a coil of rappelling rope from Captain Guy's C & C ship, tossed the loose end to the LOH pilot, and asked him to fly it over to the opposite shore. When the aircraft reached the far side, the ship's gunner got out and secured the rope to a large boulder. Then the LOH returned to the sandbar where Bennett and Bates quickly fastened the other end of the rope to the skid of the C & C ship. One of the slick's door gunners then fastened another section of rope to himself and secured it to the lifeline spanning the river.

Hauling himself hand over hand to where Lytle's body lay submerged, he dove beneath the water. Thirty seconds later he returned to the surface, but without Lytle's body. Several more times the gallant crewman dove, but he was still unable to recover the body. Gasping for breath, he shouted that the current was too strong and had pinned the body tight against the debris.

Next, Bennett stripped and dove into the river and swam across to the crewman. Between the two of them, they managed to dive down and pry Lytle's body away from the debris. Gasping for air, the two soldiers brought it to the surface and swam it back across the river to the sandbar.

When they got Lytle's body up on the rocks, Bennett dropped to his knees and tried desperately to revive him with mouth to mouth resuscitation, even though he knew it was too late. Captain Guy finally draped his arm around the young team leader's shoulders and said, "It's over, Dave." Bennett could no longer hold back his emotions . . .

Captain Guy stepped back and ordered several of the Blues to put Lytle's body aboard his C & C ship. One of the men grabbed Lytle's body around the shoulders, while another grabbed his boots. They began dragging him across the sandbar toward the waiting helicopter. Handling the body like a piece of luggage, the two soldiers banged Lytle's head along the rocks.

Bennett went ballistic. Still naked, he sprinted across the sandbar and shoved the two surprised troopers roughly to one side. He squatted down in the sand and lifted Lytle's body in his arms and carried him the rest of the way to the waiting helicopter, then slid his dead teammate across the floor of the cabin, feetfirst, taking special care that Lytle's head took no more abuse.

Bates handed Bennett his clothes, then climbed silently into the waiting slick. The Huey rose from the sandbar and returned to Camp Eagle.

Back at the company area, Bennett was off the chopper as soon as the skids hit the pad. He didn't say a word and walked away with his hand shielding his eyes. Bates understood Bennett's emotional reaction and left him alone. Bates kept replaying the incident in his mind, especially the part about not being able to reach Lytle in time. Later, Bennett told him he had gone directly to Lytle's cot and wrote a letter to Mike's parents, telling them what had happened. But Bates knew that he couldn't dwell on the incident; he was learning what came with the responsibility of being a Ranger team leader.

Ammo Bunker Blowup

I got word of Lytle's death and the bad news about Bennett's team a few days later when I returned to the company to pick up my paycheck. I was hoping to see some of the new guys, but when I walked into the company area, the only one there to greet me was Dixie Dog. She walked past me, stopped, squatted, and took a piss. Welcome home, Chambers.

Later that night, I was sitting around the club drinking Cokes with some of the guys I hadn't seen in months: Joe Bielesch, Chief McCabe, Pete Peterson, and Doc Glasser. We were talking about old times, as we watched a couple of new guys head to the ammo bunker. Dixie was running along beside them. I couldn't resist telling them about the day Dixie Dog saved my life.

Dave Biedron and I were on bunker guard the night after Tet. Dixie Dog was sleeping in the sun on top of the ammo bunker when I went to draw equipment. In those days, our underground bunker was constructed so that we had to enter by crawling through a canvas-covered doorway.

Inside, it was dark, musty, and crammed to overflowing with tons of stored explosives. The bunker was our company's catchall for every type of munition, and was piled six feet high with boxes of grenades, claymore mines, trip flares, white phosphorus grenades, M-60 and M-16 ammo. I remember standing behind a pile of crates, gathering up supplies. The place was a mess. A pile of claymore mines hastily wrapped in their detonator wires sat next to a small box of blasting caps near the edge of a shelf. I looked down at my foot and could make out the outline of a pile of det cord on the floor. My eyes hadn't quite adjusted to the dark as I reached over the claymores, feeling for a pouch of hand grenades. The pouch seemed to be stuck on something, so I yanked, but it wouldn't break free. I pulled again and heard a popping sound just behind the pouch. The hissing of the fuse echoed inside the enclosure as it started its cook off before exploding. I didn't have time to think. My blood turned ice-cold, and my instincts took over.

The only way out was the way I came in. Now the small flash had turned into a full burn. I let go of the grenade pouch and moved quickly back the way I'd come, tripping over a loose belt of M-60 machine-gun ammo and knocking over another crate of ammo. It became clear to me, the way things come to men just before they die, that this wasn't the way it was supposed to happen. No way was I supposed to blow myself up. I pushed a crate out of the way. I wasn't going to die because some lazy asshole didn't take the time to stack his gear properly.

Dixie was barking at the entrance. I ran toward the sound, found the opening, pulled back the canvas flap, and scrambled skyward. I yelled at the top of my lungs, "Fire in the hole!" As I cleared the doorway, I smashed my knee on the metal frame and fell over Dixie Dog. Then—*ka-blam!*

I crawled behind a pile of sandbags next to the bunker. I reached over, grabbed the little dog, and pulled her in close to me. I thought I heard someone shouting, "Get the hell away from there!" Next, rounds of M-60 machine-gun ammo started firing off. I could hear them ricocheting in every direction inside the bunker. I pushed myself up. My eyes still adjusting to the outside light, I looked around for a safe place to run. We had to get out of there, *now*. A bunker covered with steel PSP (perforated steel planking used for constructing runways) and sandbags was about sixty feet away. That became my target. I grabbed Dixie by the collar and ran, crouched, in the direction of the bunker.

At the time, I was more embarrassed than scared. I was thinking, Shit! Everyone is going to blame me. Then I heard a sizzling sound, like a willy peter cooking off. I knew spears of phosphorus would soon come flying out after the detonation. Once that shit gets on your skin, there's no way to put it out. The bunker was only a few meters away. The opening was a horizontal affair with a slit just large enough for me and Dixie to flop through. Dixie tried to pull away, but I held on and jumped in with her. We both fell to the floor. I smashed my arm on something metal, rolled to my side, and held on tight to the little dog. I closed my eyes and waited.

Then the whole world seemed to blow apart. The earth shook, and a dust cloud rose where the ammo bunker once sat. I put my right hand over the back of my neck and held Dixie with my left, waiting for the fireworks to end. It sounded like an explosive pinball machine had gone berserk. More secondary explosions, hand grenades cooking off, then a second, even louder explosion sent huge plates of PSP mixed with sandbags and ordnance into the air. Pieces of grenade shrapnel smashed into the steel just above my head. Dixie was now clawing at me with her back feet, like a wild animal, trying to get away. Sandbags, rocks, and dirt rose in a geyser and showered down over the bunkers.

Then a tracer round hit directly above my head and buried into a sandbag. That's when Dixie pulled out of her collar and disappeared, yelping, out the back of the bunker. I rolled onto my side and pushed up on my elbow, trying to see if the coast was clear. Smaller explosions were still going off just outside the bunker. I ducked back down. The buzzing in my ears became an ominous hum. It seemed like an hour, but all this happened in a matter of a few seconds. Finally, the last of the ammo cooked off.

I lay there, my head ringing like I had just gone eleven rounds with Muhammad Ali. Once I regained some composure and got to my feet, I peered out the opening and planned my escape. I couldn't believe what I saw. It looked like a scene from an army nuclear training film. A crater the size of a house had replaced the bunker. Twisted metal, broken M-60 links, and all kinds of unexploded ammunition lay along the road. Exploded

CS gas canisters had mixed in with the smoke from the blast, and I could feel the chemicals stinging my eyes.

I ducked back down and waited for the gas to pass over the bunker. Then as I got up, I dug out the tracer round that hit above my head and grabbed a piece of exploded wrappings from a hand grenade; I stuck them in my pocket as keepsakes. The metal was still hot.

I figured it was safe to move out, so I climbed out of the hole and started down the road. Through the thick smoke, I could hear men shouting. "Anyone down there?" I yelled something back, straightened myself up, and tiptoed between piles of still unexploded ammo, hand grenades with their tops broken off, and belts of expended M-60 ammo. I was still choking on the CS and wiping my eyes. It was like a nightmare.

I tried to walk casually. I could see a small group of Rangers about a hundred meters up the hill—some standing, some kneeling behind anything that offered some cover. It was quite a scene. I must have looked like an apparition from hell.

I called out, "Hi guys! Sorry about the bunker. I'll clean it up later." Captain Eklund—the CO at the time—told me later that he'd called division headquarters to see if enemy MIG fighters had attacked the camp.

We resumed guard duty, and Biedron handed me a Dex to keep me awake the rest of the night. About the time I gulped down the pill, the landline rang. It was Eklund. He wanted Biedron and me to come down to TOC and explain to G-4 exactly what had happened in that bunker.

I felt like it was all my fault and asked Biedron what he thought I should say. "Just tell them you think the gooks booby-trapped the place, and you crawled out just in time."

We arrived at the TOC. Inside, two captains and a major started demanding an explanation. I told them I wasn't sure. That I reached down and heard a click, like a fuse cooking off. The major asked me if I thought it had been booby-trapped. I responded by asking him, "How could they have gotten in there?"

Then one of the captains asked me what color the first explosion was. But about that time, the effects of the Dex kicked in. I started talking fast and grinding my teeth. "It was an orange light. No, red. No, it was blue. I mean, orange, red, and blue. It was very cool. I mean it was bright."

Biedron kicked me under the table, trying to get me to shut up. The brass looked at each other, then told us to follow them down to the acid pad. They were going to blow some incendiaries to see if I could recognize one of them.

It seemed like the entire officer corps of the 17th Cav was standing around us. An engineer placed three explosive charges for us to observe. The first test was a trip flare laid sideways on the tarmac. The second was a fifteen-second delay fuse in an oblong piece of C-4. As each explosion went off, the officers would turn, look at Biedron and me shaking our heads 'no,' and write in notebooks. The last charge was an incendiary grenade. As that cooked off, I felt like I was back inside that bunker. As the device burned itself out, the major, by that time more than a little impatient, asked, "Well, which one, Sergeant?"

I told him that the last one was so beautiful, I'd like to do it again. The officers left, mad.

I finished my story and held up Dixie's dog tags. "See, I still have her tags. I'm going to keep them and give them to my kids, if I ever have kids."

A New Year

During that fall, L Company had begun using Kit Carson scouts. The Kit Carson Scout program was another one of the brilliant schemes the Pentagon came up with to give us the advantage on the ground. The idea was to take captured North Vietnamese or Viet Cong and use them as scouts. I once witnessed the way the South Vietnamese treated a POW. They beat the shit out of him, then twisted his nuts until he told them what they wanted to know. I always figured the Kit Carson Scout program was a way for the gooks to comfortably evade similar beatings but tell us nothing. The whole thing seemed stupid to me—kind of like using ex-Nazi storm troopers for road guards to Berlin, just because they had been there. I figured if push came to shove, the gooks would shoot us in a second and rejoin their enemy units. After all, this was war, and they were not on our side. But no one ever asked for my opinion.

Dixie Dog didn't like the Kit Carson scouts either. She barked at them every time they came around. Everybody figured she barked simply because gooks like to eat dog, but I think she had dog intuition.

This was the first time our company had used the Kit Carson scouts to go with our guys on missions. Unfortunately, any advantage they might have afforded us on that mission was offset by the poor weather. In November, our guys conducted thirty-eight patrols, but made only sixteen sightings. In December, the Rangers conducted thirty-one patrols and spotted enemy troops on only seven occasions. Rainstorms, low cloud ceilings, and dense fog eventually caused operations to be suspended altogether in the A Shau Valley through the monsoon season. Then during January, L Company was told to concentrate its patrols up in the Khe Sanh plains in the Da Krong River Valley. The 3d brigade had pulled out, leaving it wide open and vulnerable. Division commanders wanted an eye kept on enemy movement in the area.

The worst part of going to Khe Sanh was that it was a forty-five minute flight to get there. At one time, Khe Sanh had been an intensely green and beautiful area. With the Marines and army gone, the area had turned lush again. The arriving teams could barely see it, but the original airstrip still had the large 1st Cav patch painted on it.

During January, Captain Guy inserted two six-man teams, which were ambushed by an NVA squad then immediately engaged by a larger enemy force, resulting in a fierce firefight. The patrol leader and assistant patrol leader were killed, but the other LRRPs managed to fight their way through the dense jungle to the emergency jungle pickup point. Still, it took over an hour to get to them. It was a remote area, and to get there, you had to fly over a mountain, then drop into a huge valley. Anyone who ever worked there felt dangerously isolated.

By the time our teams were ready to go north, the powers-that-be had decided to close all the U.S. firebases and refueling stops. Our teams wouldn't have any friendly contact the whole flight, which would make a long fifty-minute flight seem even longer. Especially sitting on the metal floor in the back of the chopper.

Captain Guy told me that on one of his overflights into the A Shau Valley, he had raised his sun visor, looked straight down, and saw two burned-out shells of UH-1 Hueys, left over from the big battle the 1st Cav Division got into back in 1966. He said, "It was eerie to look down and see two American helicopters on the floor." The lack of available emergency assistance was a haunting thought on the flights out there: How the hell do we get out of here if we crash?

How to get his teams out of both remote areas if they got into trouble was constantly on Captain Guy's mind. The problem was more than just distance; the clouds frequently hung so low that his pilot had to fly the scout ship right down the roads. The gooks could literally shoot bullets in through the door. Upon entering that valley, for even the toughest guys, the fear was overpowering. The place had a reputation.

The 7th Cav had spent time in the A Shau. They were one of the first airmobile units in Vietnam. Early on in the war, they brought in over five hundred helicopters, and soldiers joked that every guy in the Cav had his own helicopter. The NVA, however, didn't think it was very funny. But they had many years to prepare for the 7th Cav's arrival, so when the Cav choppers entered the valley in 1966, the choppers got clobbered. The NVA had posted antiaircraft guns on practically every mountaintop—12.7mm (51 cal.) heavy machine guns and 37mm guns, with seven-man crews. They could bring down choppers, and jets flying as high as twenty thousand feet. When our choppers flew down the center of the valley, they were running a gauntlet of NVA heavy machine-gun fire. Like Custer's 7th Cav, history replayed itself, and our pilots were bombarded from all directions, from every mountaintop. Ten choppers were shot down, and twenty-three had serious damage.

Now that it was the monsoon season, Guy was even more concerned. If a team was stranded in that water for a couple of weeks, they'd have immersion foot, and black leeches all over their armpits and crotches and everything else. Guy was also really worried about his directives. The radio batteries would only last a day or two each, and the teams in the jungle would have to keep the radio on all the time. The batteries were big and really heavy, and teams would take as many as they could, but still, there was a limit to how many they could carry. They didn't have the benefit of today's sophisticated miniaturization.

To conserve batteries, it was decided that team leaders would prearrange check-in times, and Rangers were assigned to twenty-four-hour duty to monitor the radios. The teams in the field would turn theirs off and conserve juice. A liaison between the Airborne Command and Control Center in Thailand was established. If they were lucky, they'd get an air force C-130 in the area to act as their aerial relay, passing messages and information to and from teams on the ground.

By early 1970, L Company found itself working sometimes fifty kilometers from Camp Eagle. For support, they had to depend on 175mm guns firing at maximum range out of Camp Evans, with fair to poor—and sometimes no—communications. We also got a new first lieutenant, David Ohle, who'd have to learn Ranger operations fast.

Hiding in Plain Sight

January 22, 1970

Intelligence had reports of heavy enemy activity in the mountains east of the Ruong Ruong Valley. Because of this, someone higher up decided it would be a good idea to not make overflights on some of the missions, reasoning that they would alert the enemy. As a result, two Rangers teams were to go in without making a visual recon of the area. We called it going in blind; a very stupid idea.

Of course, my guys would be the guinea pigs. Each of the team members had averaged over six months in country, except Jeff Paige. He had been there for thirty months and would be the overall team leader. Jim Bates would be the other team leader. The idea was to insert the two teams in two separate LZs, then have them link up once on the ground. Leroy Suko was ATL on Paige's team. Paige's point man was Joel Conrad and Britton Buehrig would carry the radio. David Antonelli would bring up the rear as tail gunner. Jim Bates selected Mark Martin to walk his point. Jim Sheppard would carry the radio, Larry Fout was junior scout, and David Hazelton would pull tail gun.

The primary mission was to monitor enemy activity, and a secondary mission was to capture a POW. The plan called for the helicopters to deliver the teams to an obscure hillside landing zone. First Lieutenant David Ohle had chosen that LZ because the helicopter could make a concealed approach up the valley and then a sudden hard right turn to the target. He believed that this concealed approach would allow the Rangers to surprise the enemy. Intelligence reports indicated that two elite North Vietnamese sapper battalions occupied the area. The mission was to recon their bases and capture prisoners.

In order to cover the most ground, the two teams would land in separate places and move toward one another to link up. Paige prepared the mission overlay, depicting primary and alternate infiltration/exfiltration LZs, overnight halts, artillery plots, directional plots, call signs, frequencies, and E & E routes. The plan called for only one infiltration LZ. The overlay was approved, and Paige's briefback was presented according to his overlay.

The policy was for the team going in to plan the mission with assistance from the assigned mission-control officer, intelligence personnel, and others they might require. Once approved, that was the way the mission would go, unless a helicopter was downed or contact was made on the LZ. But from the time the choppers took off, things started to go wrong.

First, the insertion slicks lost sight of one another during the approach up the valley. The lead crew had landed Paige's team and lifted off before the second chopper arrived. With only seconds to go before Bates was to set down, the pilot of the second helicopter radioed for help, asking where he should land. No one replied, so he set down in the area where he thought Paige's team had landed.

It was 1615 hours by the time Bates was inserted. Both team leaders called in and reported they had not been able to contact or link up with the other team. Paige was told that the teams should be approximately a hundred meters apart and to flash a panel to identify his position. But Bates had been inserted in tall elephant grass, while Paige was in a small clearing in a wooded area two hundred meters away.

Paige got on the horn to Bates and told him to start moving south toward him. The direction was provided by the C & C, Captain Guy's helicopter, which had a visual on both teams from the initial panel flash. Then Paige heard loud noise in the wooded area, and thought it was Bates. Then he heard noise coming from the other side, as well. He got Bates on the radio and told him to halt his team and listen for enemy movement. Bates reported back that his team also had movement around them.

While Bates and Paige tried to evaluate what was going on, the noise became distinguishable as bamboo sticks clacking together, coming from three different directions. This tactic, much like natives flushing out wild game for the kill, was known throughout Vietnam, so it didn't have the effect the enemy thought it would.

It was apparent that Paige's team was being surrounded; he told his men not to fire until they made eye-to-eye contact. As he was positioning the team in a tight circle, he saw Buehrig raise his M-16 and take aim. Paige could see an NVA approximately fifteen meters away; luckily, the enemy soldier was looking in a different direction. Paige put his hand on Buehrig's shoulder and signaled to him to hold his fire to avoid detection. If the NVA passed on by, the team might be able to exfiltrate through their lines.

Paige directed his team to move toward a finger on higher ground; doing so might enable him to cover Bates—but that was not to be. The finger was about forty meters from their LZ, and there hadn't been any noise detected from that direction. But as they climbed, his ATL detected more movement above the team. The enemy encirclement was getting tighter.

Bates had his team pulled in tight. The NVA crossed the narrow stream twenty-five meters in front of the team and opened up on them. Hazelton, rear security, returned fire as Bates attempted to move the team, but they were pinned down. He called in their contact and asked for extraction. Only half an hour had passed since they'd inserted.

The Cobra gunships had been on station, flying orbits several miles from the LZ, but they were quickly on station. When Bates held up his marker panel, the gunships started making runs parallel to his side and across his front and rear, called a "box-in" movement. They almost ran the chopper over them. Their rounds hit the trees, and a frag went right through Hazelton's serum albumin pouch.

By this time the LRRPs were losing daylight fast, and only one slick was available to extract the teams. Bates's team had to be extracted first since they already had contact. Bates moved his team near the LZ; he could hear the noise of the rotors and the high-pitch whine of its turbine engine. When the chopper was close, Bates stood in the middle of the LZ and provided cover fire as his team started loading. Both Bates and the chopper door gunner were firing on enemy coming out of the woods. Lieutenant Ohle, who was acting as the bellyman, reached out and grabbed Bates by his old mountain-style rucksack and set him on the skid. From there, Ohle pulled Bates inside the chopper.

The Cobras made very attractive targets, and the NVA blasted away at them. The pilots spotted increased numbers of NVA, and the Rangers witnessed tracers firing up from all directions. Bates counted seventeen AK hits to their extraction slick, but luckily no one was injured before they were safely out of range and headed back to base.

The NVAs attention then shifted to Jeff Paige's team. There was still about an hour of light left, and Paige called for the two Cobras, Banshee 26 and 27, to make several gun runs on the hill closest to the team. But after each run, there was more enemy movement, and the stick banging increased.

The Cobra pilots radioed to Paige that they were almost out of ammo and had to return to Phu Bai for rearming. Paige was worried that the NVA would build up around them again. He asked if one pilot would stay and make dry runs until a replacement gunship could get to them.

The NVA began firing all around the team, trying to get them to make a move or to give away their positions. That lasted just a matter of minutes, and all the Rangers kept their cool. None fired back, and all stayed in their positions. Finally, the Banshee gunships were back on station and resumed working the area. But it was quickly getting dark, so a flare ship was sent out to provide visibility for the team and the gunships. The helicopters rotated on and off station and stayed in the area just in case something burst loose. By then, the NVA were shooting at the flare parachutes, yelling and banging sticks and playing psychological games.

By 2100 hours, there had been no decrease in enemy activity, and Paige told the team they had to move west or divide the team into two- or three-man elements and follow the E & E plan. The E & E plan had been formulated during mission planning and called for them to move east to a corridor. If they E & E'd successfully, in the morning they would use the URC-10 radios to enable the birds to track them and, it was hoped, pick them up.

Paige called in a sitrep and informed the TOC of his intention to move west. He used an M-79 to probe the area to the west, then, Paige and Antonelli made a crawling recon into the area while Suko, Conrad, and Buehrig stayed in a tight perimeter, monitoring the radio. Paige and Antonelli returned ten minutes later and said things seemed to be quiet. For a few minutes, Paige actually had the thought, hell, things aren't so bad. That thought only lasted a few minutes, then new sounds of enemy activity from the west brought him back to reality. Paige radioed their plan was canceled due to activity in the direction they were to move.

The team remained pinned down, while the scout helicopter tried to get an update on the enemy's status. The flare ships dropped more flares, and a gunship flew low and fast over the area and drew heavy fire.

Shortly after the fly by, they were contacted by Captain Guy in the C & C ship. He told them that, due to intensive ground fire and the low ceiling, his higher-up was aborting any extraction attempt and calling all aircraft back to Phu Bai, until first light. The higher-up was G3—the division operations officer—he had already designated the Rangers as a *lost team*. In Ranger talk that meant they weren't getting out. In short—they were being left behind. Paige informed the rest of the team, and they seemed to take it pretty damn cool.

At 2315 hours the team made the decision to divide and follow the E & E plan. Suko, Conrad, and Antonelli would move out first. Buehrig and Paige would stay behind to provide cover and follow thirty minutes later. Then, Banshee 54, the

C & C bird on station, burst on the radio. "I'm going to get you out!" the pilot said. Banshee 54 was ordered to abort the attempt, but he ignored it and got a fix on Paige's team.

Paige put a strobe light into the chamber end of his M-79 and wrapped a scarf around the chamber area to prevent light escaping. He moved approximately seventy-five meters to a very small open area and used the system as a flashlight to orient the pilot's approach. The pilot came on the radio again, "Point it at me, point it at me." Paige heard the blacked-out helicopter coming in slowly, directly at him. The pilot radioed Paige one more time. "Have your men get ready."

Paige heard gunfire from below his position. A flare was dropped from the chopper, and he could see he was on the side of a hill with trees in three different directions—a pilot's nightmare at night.

The pilot came back on the radio and said, "I thought you were trying to get to an LZ."

"Can't, sir; we're surrounded and taking fire," Paige told him.

"Okay, hang in there." Banshee 54 was still committed to the extraction.

Paige crawled back to his teammates and prepared them for the extraction. "We're going to load from one side only—there's no time to get hung up getting in. Suko, you stay with me, we'll provide cover. Conrad, you, Buehrig, and Antonelli go first. We have to board at one-second intervals and don't crowd the skids. Got it?" Everyone nodded.

Then Paige turned to Suko. "We may have to jump to the skids and pull up. You ready?" Suko gave him a thumbs-up.

The Banshee pilot aligned his approach and radioed Paige, "You can load into the transmission well." Paige had never heard a door gunner slot called the transmission well. He figured he'd ask the pilot what that meant later. Paige yelled at his team, "This is it. Go for it!"

The two Cobras circled overhead and started firing rockets, patting down fifteen meters on each side of the LZ with burning white phosphorus. While the Cobra gunships circled and prepared for a second run, the Banshee hovered, and the men ran to the open doors.

An NVA grenade plopped in front of Buehrig and exploded. He was hit with grenade shrapnel but he kept running—the wound was superficial and didn't slow him down or stop him from pulling himself up into the waiting aircraft. Antonelli and Conrad made it to the hovering aircraft without a scratch.

Once the three Rangers were safely inside, Suko and Paige rose from their cover and started sprinting. The chopper was lifting by the time they reached the skids. Paige interlaced his hands for Suko to step up for the waiting hands of Antonelli and Conrad. With a hard pull, he was inside. Then Paige slung his weapon over his shoulder and leaped for the skids. Antonelli and Conrad pulled him aboard. Paige lay sprawled on his stomach on the floor of the helicopter as they lifted straight up.

By then it was midnight. Paige's team had been detected, searched for, surrounded, and shot at for nearly eight hours. Had they remained overnight, Paige was positive that they wouldn't have seen the sunrise.

The chopper had barely cleared the trees when it turned slightly, and dropped it's nose to gain speed. Once they were at a safe altitude, the two Cobra gunships began systematically pounding the hell out of the area. Over the balance of the night and all the next morning, artillery 155s created a parking lot where the teams had been trapped.

Back at Camp Eagle, John Kiefel greeted Sergeant Paige with a grin and a handshake. "We monitored your transmission. You guys were really in the shit last night. You don't think any of the bad guys followed you home, do you?"

"I hope the hell they didn't," Paige said, gulping water from his canteen.

Break Contact,
Then Run Like Hell

To keep pace with division's request that the company always have teams in the field, a heavy team of eleven Rangers had been organized for insertion the following day in an AO where previous teams had been shot out within hours of inserting. Since they already knew the AO was hot, this mission was to hunt and kill.

John Kiefel and David Antonelli had bunker guard duty that night, and they walked past Frank Johnson's hootch on the way. Kiefel stuck his head in, but no one was home. Johnson, Bowland, and Gary Sands were two hootches away throwing down scotch and Cokes. Eventually, Johnson got so wasted that he had to be carried to his hootch. His hangover the next morning almost kept him from making it to formation, but he had just regained his sergeant's stripes and wanted to keep them. By then, he already had twenty-five missions under his belt.

Kiefel and Antonelli had just started to pull in their claymores as the first helicopters took off for the next day's missions. During the overflight, Sgt. Bernie Zentner sat on the floor of the slick, taking notes and orienting himself to the terrain. His main point of interest was a wide high-speed trail running the length of the ridgeline, with lots of little trails shooting off down the hillsides.

The next day his team members met for breakfast. By then,

some of the Rangers were best friends, and they had all worked together at one time or another on previous missions. Then Zentner, Sp. Mike "Gringo" Blinston, Rob McSorley, Frank "Buff" Johnson, Bruce Bowland, Brenner, Steijen, Gary Sands, Sp4. Paul "Blinky" Morgucz, McFillery, Lee, and Ut, the Kit Carson scout, gathered their gear and assembled down on the acid pad.

The men had rehearsed several different scenarios. Any situation on the ground can change rapidly, so you have to be prepared to expect anything. The more you practice, the more flexible your team can be. Rangers constantly planned, prepared, and did walk-through after walk-through. We'd practice immediate-action drills, where we'd react to supposed enemy contact from the front, the side, or the rear. If it was from the front, the idea was to lay down, suppress fire, and the first man leapfrog back to the rear, each man behind him in turn firing a magazine, then leapfrogging over the next one so the slack man became rear security, the team leader was still in the center, and the point man ended up back on point but moving in the opposite direction.

It would take about an hour to go through all the details of the operation: coordinate instruction, get the nitty-gritty down, grid coordinates, E & E locations, hand out the maps, and secure equipment. That way everybody knew what they had to do. Every LRRP knew what was expected of him.

The team was inserted at 1330 hours on a finger off the ridge-line inside the Laotian border. They came in with four slicks, the last two empty, to give anyone watching the idea that this was more than just a recon patrol.

The first chopper came in low to the LZ. Johnson always had to get off the slick first. It was just his thing; no matter what position he walked, he was first off the bird. Ut, the team's Kit Carson scout, was second to hit the ground. He had been with the VC for seven years before he "expatriated." Ut would be walking point with Steijen, who dropped to the ground right behind him.

Ut immediately spotted a bunch of gooks running downhill, away from the LZ. By the time the entire team was assembled, the C & C LOH helicopter also radioed the team that it had spotted two enemy on a trail *above* their position.

Zentner halted the team for ten minutes and sent Ut, Steijen, and Johnson to recon the trail. They had moved about a hundred meters when they caught up with a group of ten or fifteen gooks running downhill on the south side of the trail. Ut decided there had to be a very large base camp nearby, so they regrouped with the team and moved down the trail together.

Sergeant Zentner moved the team about five hundred meters from the LZ, pulled his men into some dense cover nearby, then waited. By that time, it was nearly 1630 hours, and they had been on the ground for three hours with no contact. Zentner radioed quietly for the slicks to return to the LZ and fake an extraction, hoping that the NVA would believe the Americans had departed.

As the first slick touched down then climbed for altitude and the second slick was just lifting off the LZ, an NVA .51-caliber heavy machine gun opened up on the extraction aircraft from a position less than seventy-five meters below the team. As the large caliber weapon pounded the helicopters, the Rangers could hear enemy soldiers laughing as they moved up the hill toward the hidden Rangers—obviously not realizing that the team was still there. Green tracer rounds were ricocheting off the rocks, and fragments were flying in all directions. One of the gunships made a turn and scattered cannon fire into the draws and ravines.

Blinston got the first visual and opened fire, killing one enemy soldier. The remaining NVA responded by rushing the team's perimeter. Blinston, Johnson, Zentner, and Sgt. Rob "Mac" McSorley were in the rear, in the direct line of the initial enemy assault.

McSorley was a Canadian citizen who, unlike the rest of Lima Company, did not have to serve in Vietnam. He reacted instantly, grabbed the M-60 from Zentner and began firing on the enemy soldiers. McSorley killed two outright and wounded several others. At one point Mac had the balls to yell at Johnson, "Hey, Buff—just like John Wayne!"

The gooks tried to flank the team. Johnson used the M-79

grenade launcher and started popping rounds into the trees to increase the bursting radius. That seemed to deter the gooks. They tried to go around the other side, but Blinston and Brenner were there, pouring on the fire.

The firefight lasted twenty minutes before the team was able to reestablish commo and contact a Cobra. The Cobra relayed news of the team's contact and started laying down fire on the enemy.

When in contact with the enemy, Johnson always had to be standing or on his knees shooting so he could see. When the Cobra came in, he got down. He looked around and saw Steijen behind him up on his knees, too, firing the M-60 machine gun. Johnson signaled Steijen to get down just as an RPG hit about ten meters in front of them. Fragments flew right over Johnson, and one caught Steijen in his left forearm. Blinston took an AK-47 "bee" in his left bicep, but McSorley spotted and killed the gook who had fired the round.

They were engaged for an hour like that exchanging fire and frags back and forth, and nightfall was only an hour or so away when the Rangers grabbed all their gear and moved back toward the LZ.

Johnson stayed behind to set up a claymore and a willie peter while Ut and Sands covered his rear. As the gooks ran up the trail in pursuit of the team, Johnson saw about a dozen of them about twenty meters away. Sands urged Johnson to hit the detonator, but Johnson let three or four of them pass the claymore before he actually blew the thing. There was nothing left but dirt, dust, and some smoke from the willie peter. The rest of the patrol had already moved nearly a hundred meters closer to the LZ. McSorley was walking point about ten meters ahead of Zentner and ran headlong into a second enemy force maneuvering down on the Rangers from the high ground.

McSorley killed three NVA before his CAR-15 jammed. He attempted to clear the jam, but the remaining NVA opened up, and he took four rounds across the chest before the impact knocked him to the ground. Lee took a hit that shattered his elbow. Then Zentner reacted and took out two more NVA with the M-60.

When Sands, Ut, and Johnson caught up with the team they learned that McSorley was shot and out in the open, and Johnson immediately started forward to get his buddy, but Sands grabbed him and told Johnson to watch the rear with Morgucz. Then Sands crawled forward under fire, grabbed McSorley, and dragged him back to the perimeter. Johnson heard McSorley screaming and again started to go to him, but Ut begged Johnson not to. Rob McSorley died fifteen minutes later.

Sands later said Lee and Zentner were behind a tree, exchanging shots with the enemy, and the battle was like a circus: everybody on both sides was going up and down like pop-up targets, trying to shoot each other.

Johnson, still in the rear, crawled out about twenty meters and set up another claymore. Twenty minutes later, the NVA reapproached from the rear. Johnson waited again until the enemy soldiers were directly in front of the claymore. When he saw at least five, he smiled and blew the claymore. Unfortunately, Johnson had wanted to watch, so he didn't get down fast enough and got debris all over his face. He spent the next few seconds spitting out dirt and scraps of vegetation, and trying to clear his eyes. When he could see again, enemy movement had disappeared.

Meanwhile the Cobras worked all around the team's perimeter, and enemy fire gradually died out. When it got dark, a C-130 Spooky put down flares for about an hour, and kept the area around the LZ lit up like an airport parking lot.

The team had to return to where they first made contact, since that was the clearest area for extraction. A slick came in and dropped his rope, but it was short. The pilot tried to chop his way down through the trees so someone could grab the rope, but ended up destroying the ends of the rotor blades instead as branches, leaves, and bark rained down on the team. Finally it became clear that the chopper was losing pitch and had to pull out. It limped off and crash-landed just before reaching the base camp across the border.

The medevac came in for the wounded and dropped a jungle penetrator, a steel device heavy enough to push its way through the jungle foliage. When deployed, its bottom unfolded like the petals of a flower, each "petal" providing a seat which could then be reeled back up to the helicopter.

Sands strapped McSorley's already stiff body onto the penetrator, and they put Lee, who was the worst wounded, on with him to hold on to McSorley's body. But when they were eight or ten feet off the ground, the medevac began taking .51-caliber machine-gun fire and the crew cut the cable. The penetrator dropped to the ground and the impact broke Lee's ankle. The pilot was killed, and the copilot was wounded, but he managed to fly the medevac out.

Just after midnight, a Stinger gunship arrived to lay down fire around the perimeter to make the enemy move back so the team could be extracted. Once the Stinger got the coordinates on points all the way around the team, he locked them into the bird's fire-control computer and set the four miniguns. When the team radioed movement from any point, the Stinger would push the gun locked on that point, and the whole sky would light up with tracers.

But even the best weapons technology can go astray. At one point Johnson watched the line of tracers waver as it crashed down on the jungle. His eyes followed the arc, and he realized something was not right. He yelled out, "Look out, we're going to get hit!" then rolled into the smallest ball he could as an errant stream of tracers ripped right through the team's position. The rounds hit so close and with such impact that they bounced Johnson right off the ground. Amazingly, no one was hit. Johnson looked over at Ut, whose eyes had grown huge like golfballs. Ut couldn't even speak a word. Johnson just started laughing.

When it was quiet again, a second medevac hovered over the LZ and dropped its jungle penetrator. This time McSorley and Lee made it out. Then another slick flew over with a pair of McGuire rigs, pulling out Steijen and Blinston, the last two wounded team members.

At 0205 hours, while a pair of Cobras worked over the surrounding area, another slick arrived with a rope ladder to extract the remaining seven men. They had to leave their rucks behind, so Johnson booby-trapped his with a couple of frags.

The fastmovers (fighter-bombers) worked the area over that night, and a grunt team came in the next day to sweep the AO.

Bowland was the last man up the rope ladder, and he had the PRC-25 radio on his back and his CAR-15 across his shoulder. Even so, he grabbed the M-60 and was trying to hold it and climb at the same time but the gooks opened up on him and green tracers were hitting the helicopter, so the pilot lifted off with Bowland wrapped around the rungs of the ladder. Bowland dropped the M-60 as the chopper pulled away. The lift pulled the chopper off to one side and the bottom of the ladder hit the tops of the trees and spun Bowland around when he was still six or seven feet below the strut. The bellyman tied himself to the side of the ship and stood out on the strut. He was just a little guy, looked like he weighed about 130 pounds soaking wet, but he leaned way out, reached down with one hand and grabbed the rope ladder, with the other hand he latched onto Bowland's pistol belt and yanked him inside the bird. The adrenaline was just pumping that morning.

Bowland thought he had been hit. Just as they pulled him into the chopper, he told the crew chief, "I've been hit in the butt or something, somewhere. I can't feel my legs, and something's burning down there." He took off his web gear and stripped down, but he didn't see any blood. After a bit of searching around he realized that a tracer had gone through the bottom of the radio and pierced the battery. Acid was running out the battery down his behind! The circulation had been cut off in his legs because they were wrapped around the ladder. When he had been spun around by a treetop, he thought he had been hit. They washed the acid off with water from his canteen.

By the time the last of the team was extracted, it had been in contact with the enemy for over ten hours straight, and the men were physically and emotionally spent. At 0315 hours, when they finally arrived back at base camp, every Ranger at the base met them on the acid pad.

"*Dung Lai*, Gook!"

The most dangerous part of any mission is the moment you step off the helicopter. The enemy could be firing at you and you'd never know it because the noise of the chopper engine and of the rotors whipping the vegetation in every direction obscures any sign of enemy fire. When the helicopter hovers a few feet above the elephant grass, you jump, hoping that you're going to make contact with the ground and not keep falling. The height of the elephant grass can be deceiving, and some Ranger teams had unknowingly jumped from higher then ten feet, which resulted in sprained ankles. Captain Guy frequently mentioned that to replacement helicopter pilots who might not be aware of the jungle's false floor.

It's hard enough knowing what to do next when everything goes roughly as planned, but unfortunately, nothing ever goes as planned. And a lot of times, it doesn't even come close. Ranger team leader Jim Bates was about to learn the true meaning of the word "improvisation." To be good at improvising, you have to be prepared, and Bates was nothing if not prepared. He carried extra batteries, two watches, and a navy SEAL survival knife that Tim Boyd had given him. He always carried the knife in a scabbard, upside down on his web gear.

It was mid-February and Bates had a recon mission up in Quang Tri Province. He assembled a strong, five-man team: Jim Rodarte would walk point, Bates would pull slack, a new spec-4 would carry the radio, Joe Stauffer would guard rear security, and Sp4. Mark Martin filled out the team.

Captain Guy was on an R & R, so one of the new lieutenants coordinated the flight with the replacement Kingsmen pilots. They went by the book. The day before the mission, Rodarte and Bates went on an overflight. The night before the mission, they got a good sleep. The Ranger bellyman arrived on time, was briefed by the pilots, and plugged his helmet in the intercom system. After the preflight checklist by the pilots and after the fuel tank had been topped off, the Huey's turbine engine started to come alive, and the Rangers climbed aboard. The helicopter lifted off, climbing out over the Vietnamese graves that surrounded the western perimeter of Eagle. Moments later, it was headed north to Quang Tri. The flight was escorted by a pair of Cobra gunships. As they got close to their destination, the whole place became socked in with thick clouds. They had only enough time for one pass at it before the weather would deny them entry.

The Cobra gunships stayed high as the insertion ship lowered onto the LZ. Bates shouted to his team, "Get ready!" Then, as the chopper touched down, "Go!" He waved them out, patting each man on the shoulder. What Bates didn't know was that the pilot inserted them twelve kilometers from where they had planned to put in. From above, the terrain around Quang Tri all looks the same.

Dirt and debris from the hundred-knot downwash filled Bates's eyes as he jumped from the helicopter. On the ground, Bates wiped his eyes and gathered the team in a tight circle. He waited until the noise of the disappearing chopper died away, then moved the team into the brush at the base of a steep, jungle-covered hill. Bates studied his map. Nothing looked right. Bates noticed a creek where there shouldn't have been water. He figured he just wasn't reading the landmarks right, so he moved away from the LZ and higher onto the ridge for a better view. Eventually, Bates established radio contact with the TOC and told them he was having trouble marking his position. He asked the chopper to return, so he could mark his location, but it couldn't get back because of the bad weather. He decided the team would spend the night on the high ground and get a handle on their location in the morning.

At dawn, Bates sent Rodarte on a recon. When Rodarte returned, unable to see a way up the hill, Bates sent him in another direction. But Rodarte quickly stopped and crouched low as he spotted the back-lit silhouettes of three NVA soldiers about fifty meters down the hill. It looked as if they were preparing an ambush. Rodarte motioned for Bates to crawl down next to him and Bates confirmed his suspicion. The enemy knew they were in the area, and the mission was compromised.

Bates called in a sitrep and reported what had happened. He also said he had spotted what looked like a usable LZ on the other side of a small stream that separated the ridge he was on from the next valley. The team's biggest problem would be avoiding the enemy until the gunships could get back on station.

Rodarte and Bates had another short conference. Bates would move the team in on the enemy's backside and get to high ground. Then he'd use hand signals to direct Rodarte down to the creek so Rodarte could cross it and scout the other side. Bates set up the team members three meters apart and above Rodarte. Rodarte made it to the streambed and started across. Visibility was limited to a few feet in any direction. On the other side, he pushed palm leaves away and slowly walked five meters, searching for a place to extract the team.

Bates moved back for cover behind a large palm; then he heard the crack of Rodarte's CAR-15, and an AK-47 returning fire. Bates's left flank also started taking fire.

A burst of enemy machine-gun fire slashed through the elephant grass. Stauffer opened up, firing a magazine into the wood line. The team now had gooks on two sides and a man out in the open on the other side of a creek. Bates released the safety and squeezed the trigger on his CAR-15, laying down suppressive fire while Rodarte sprinted for cover. Bates fired a long automatic burst into the tree line when his CAR-15 made a sickening "click" sound, then wouldn't respond. A double feed.

Bates started to tear off the cleaning rod he had taped to the barrel for just such emergencies, when he heard movement on his side of the creek. An NVA soldier had stepped out of the brush holding an AK-47 aimed in Rodarte's direction. The enemy soldier was less than five meters away and didn't see Bates. Rodarte was a dead man if Bates didn't do something fast. With no time to clear the rifle jam now, Bates took off running for the enemy soldier, screaming at the top of his lungs. He let his CAR-15 drop and swing from its sling as he popped a survival knife loose from its scabbard. He grabbed it tightly in his right hand and reached out with his left.

The NVA soldier momentarily panicked upon seeing a crazy American in camouflage paint running at him, hollering. Before he could pull his rifle around, Bates was on top of him and stuck the knife in his ribs. The soldier let out a primal scream and tried to fight Bates off. Bates, also screaming, pounded the NVA soldier with the knife for a full twenty seconds. Neither man could escape. Bates could feel the rapid beating of the man's heart, and the strong stench of sweat and body odor filled his senses. The dying soldier continued to yell and fight back until Bates heard the soldier's collarbone crunch.

But not until the enemy soldier had completely collapsed, eyes rolled back, blood spurting everywhere, did Bates release his grip. The dead soldier dropped out of Bates's grasp to the ground.

Trying to regain his composure, Bates picked up the dead man's rifle and rejoined his teammates. Bates was fighting the feelings of shock of what he had just done. He looked around for his teammates. Unless they got out of there fast, Bates knew he could count on an NVA company-size reaction force arriving soon. Once a Ranger team was located by the NVA, the enemy's next step was always the same: Bring in as many troops as they could, as fast they could, and saturate the team's area. Bates yelled to Rodarte. "Come on back."

Rodarte got up and made his way across the creek. As Rodarte rejoined the team, he grabbed the newest guy on the back, and said, "Just like in the movies, isn't it, big boy!"

Bates heard him but was too busy clearing the barrel of his CAR-15 to understand what had just happened. When the expended round fell to the ground, Bates pulled the charging handle back and slammed another round into the chamber. They then heard the sound of more AK-47 fire coming from below them.

"Rodarte, I'm going to take the team back up the finger. You pull tail gun." Rodarte nodded, then took up position to cover the men as they struggled back up the ridge.

As they neared the top of the ridge, Bates instructed his men to take a defensive position, then wait for Rodarte to join them. In minutes, Rodarte rejoined the team, panting heavily from the climb. Bates spread his men out, then lay on a flat limestone rock overlooking the north ridgeline and creek below. The firing had stopped.

Bates used the lull to take his map out and study it again. He then called in his contact over the radio. Nothing was making any sense on the map. Bates knew seasoned NVA were close by. Once they knew his location, they'd fan out and sweep the hills and jungle-covered valleys. They'd hunt them the way tribesmen hunted a tiger.

Bates was about to tell his team to prepare for E & E when they heard the holy *whopp, whopp* sounds of a helicopter. He looked up to see a slick and a pair of Cobra gunships close behind. Bates got back on the radio and relayed that six or more gooks were in the valley below, and to "work the creek below the ridge."

The first Snake started its run, tearing up the terrain with concentrated rocket fire. Bates could still partly see the creek. As the second Snake made its pass, three green-clad NVA broke cover just ahead of the exploding rockets, attempting to run up the same finger Bates's team was on. Then the NVA soldiers turned and headed south, disappearing in the tree line.

While the gunships made rocket runs, Bates tossed out a purple smoke grenade from the ridgetop. The slick hovered over an LZ just big enough for a rope ladder. The right side door gunner waved his arms, and Bates headed for the bird, running in a crouch. Dave Bennett, in the slick, riding bellyman, kicked out the ladders and motioned to the men below. The ship flared up over the LZ. Bates grabbed the bottom of the ladder, steadying it for his men to climb up. Rodarte covered them.

When the other Rangers climbed on the ladder, the ship began to rise. Bates and Rodarte snapped their rucksacks to the bottom of the ladder, and Bates clipped himself in with a D ring. Rodarte's ruck fell to the ground. He jumped down, grabbed the ruck, then snapped it in just as the ship began to lift again. Rodarte had just enough time to clip himself in, too, and grab hold of the bottom rung, then weave his arms around the rungs. The helicopter continued up, turned, then raced off into the overcast sky.

Bates and Rodarte swung on the bottom of the ladder all the way back to Quang Tri where the chopper hovered low while the two men unhooked their D rings and jumped to the ground. Rodarte pulled the ladder out from under the chopper as the bird landed. The rest of the team jumped out.

Rodarte studied Bates carefully. The strain of the past six hours showed on Bates's face, and his shirt and pants were completely covered in blood. "You're bleeding!" Rodarte called out over the high-pitched whine of the helicopter. Bates looked at Rodarte and said, "You're messed up, too!" The cargo pockets on Rodarte's pants were full of bullet holes. Bates's clothes, canteen, and ammo pouches were all shot up. The face on his watch was even shot out and hanging off its nylon band. Bates held up a full M-16 magazine. "Look at this," Bates said. "Right through the magazine." They both forced a laugh, letting go of the tension. Miraculously, considering the state of their clothes and equipment, neither of the men had taken a hit on their bodies.

The extremely violent event had left both men emotionally drained and exhausted. At the scene of the action, they hadn't had time to feel the fear. Each burst of intense action was over in a matter of seconds. A quick adrenaline rush, then intense activity. In between, a constant state of tension. When Bates got back to Camp Eagle, he slept for twenty-four hours straight. Later that week, he put in for an award for bravery for every man on his team. Bates also received a Bronze Star with V device for his valor.

Deep in Indian Country

While Bates and Rodarte spent the day rummaging around in the supply tent putting together new sets of fatigues, a platoon of the 17th Cav reaction force had executed a successful stay-behind ambush and killed twelve NVA at an old abandoned firebase. It had worked so well, they planned another one—same MO (method of operation), same everything.

Joe Kline was a Jimmy Stewart look-alike surfer from the east coast. He was another shake 'n' bake E-6 straight out of Ranger school. His team went in just before dark with the 2/17th Cav and set up its ambush site. The Cav spent the night, and you could smell their cooking and smell them all around. They left the next morning, and the six-man Ranger team remained behind, setting up its defensive position at the far end of the two-level firebase. It was straight down all the way around, and they positioned a one-man watch at the top level on the back side. The rear watch reported that he thought he had been spotted by an NVA scout, who disappeared.

The next morning, the team began taking mortar rounds from the NVA positioned in the valley below. The rounds were all dropping behind the team, and Ut, the Kit Carson scout, was freaking out, certain that the NVA were "gonna come and kill us all tonight." Johnson said Ut had totally lost control, knowing what the NVA would do to him if he was caught.

Johnson called in the activity and told the radio relay that their position was definitely compromised. The Rangers' CO,

155

Captain Guy, was on R & R so the Cav's CO was in charge of the mission. He sent in a chopper, but was on the horn arguing with Joe Kline, telling the team leader they would have to move rather than just pull out. Kline was explaining that the team was most likely surrounded and that it was straight down all the way around their perimeter. Plus, they still had all their equipment with extra explosives and claymores that they'd have to haul along. They couldn't "just move."

The Cav CO said it was SOP that any 101st unit in the field must move at least a klick a day and repeated his order to move. He said he would send in the chopper and the team should dump all their excess ammo on it; then move. Joe Kline flatly refused, saying that if a chopper landed, they would all be getting on, plain and simple. The CO actually told Kline he would give orders to his men to shoot anyone who tried to board the chopper.

At this stalemate, Kline insisted the CO call someone higher up, stressing that once a team's position was compromised, it was SOP that it be removed from the field. Joe was adamant. The CO finally acquiesced, but told Joe he wanted him to report to his office immediately upon return.

The team packed up, and the choppers came in and pulled them out. When they returned to base, Joe strode into the CO's office with all his gear still on. He slammed his CAR-15 down on the desk and demanded, "Now what the fuck do you want?" The CO responded sternly, "End of conversation. We'll deal with this later." But there was never another word about the incident!

Enemy Tunnel System

The Kingsmen (originally 17th Assault Helicopter Company, later B Company, 101st Aviation Battalion) pilots were our main lifelines for survival. Those guys routinely flew their slicks and the Cobra gunships through enemy small-arms and, many times, antiaircraft fire to support our six-man recon teams trapped deep in enemy territory.

When the weather was bad, they had to fly low level along roads and just above the jungle treetops. Talk about scary—good God, it was unbelievable. Pilots knew the NVA might easily shoot them out of the sky at any moment. They fully expected to pop out of a cloud and see the enemy walking along the road right underneath them.

On one mission, one of my recruits, John Kiefel, was leading the mission, walking point. His team leader, Joe Kline, was walking slack, a few steps behind Kiefel. An E-6, Dick Fobert, and two cherries brought up the rear.

Kline turned around for a moment, and when he looked forward again, Kiefel had simply disappeared. After a moment's confusion, he saw that Kiefel had fallen, full body, into an enemy tunnel system. After exploring some side tunnels, they determined that the underground passageways had been abandoned.

On the second to last day of the uneventful mission, they crossed over their pickup point and came upon what looked like an abandoned infantry NDP with a couple of foxholes. They continued up the hillside and checked out the trail. The weather was bad and lightning had struck nearby, so they moved back down to the NDP and set up for the night; extraction was to take place the next day.

While Kline was placing claymore mines for protection, he took small-weapons fire and rocket-propelled grenades. The Ranger team responded with a barrage of gunfire.

One of the cherries was shot right through the chest—one of those weird sucking chest wounds—and the round came out his armpit. Kline crawled out of the NDP and carried him back to the foxhole. As Kiefel, who had the first-aid kit on that mission, tended to the cherry's wounds, he felt a thud; a hand grenade had landed right next to them. Kiefel quickly lunged for it, picked it up, and tossed it downhill; it exploded in midair.

A second enemy attack commenced. Now there was so much blood on the cherry and Kiefel that it looked like maybe Kiefel was wounded, too. The kid was going into shock, so Kiefel set up a plasma IV and had the cherry lay across his own legs, on the cherry's bad side, to protect the guy's good lung. Kiefel scanned the area to see if anyone else was harmed and saw the other cherry was right in the line of fire, about fifteen yards in front of him, while an NVA was maneuvering toward him up the hill. Kiefel quickly picked up his CAR-15 and fired; the NVA took the 5.56 mm rounds in the chest and fell back down the hill. Kiefel yelled at the cherry to crawl back inside the perimeter. It was a miracle the kid hadn't been shot by one of his own team.

There was no more gunfire; it was silent. Joe signaled to the team that the medevac chopper was coming in. Joe had instructed the medevac pilot to approach from the north, but he came from the south. The chopper was about a hundred meters away when the whole ridgeline to the pilot's left lit up with gunfire. The medevac was shot down and made a very hard landing, but the pilot and the door gunner survived.

The team was advised that a reaction force was coming in, and Kline advised them to fly in from the opposite direction. He would put the wounded on the first chopper that touched down.

Soon a single Huey came racing in. The red cross on the

white border painted on its nose marked it as the Dustoff flight out of Evans. The Huey slowed, then flared. Its forward momentum forced the pilot to slam down onto the LZ on the back of its skids, and one of the skid supports snapped, causing the aircraft to list as it settled in. The pilot immediately brought it back light on the skids and held it there while Kiefel picked up the cherry in a fireman's carry and ran over to the open cabin. The Dustoff medic and crew chief quickly pulled the wounded Ranger into the aircraft, and the pilot nosed the ship forward and away from the LZ. Then it banked hard to the left as it gained forward airspeed. The medevac turned out over the river and headed back downstream toward the field hospital at Camp Evans.

John Kiefel popped a purple smoke grenade and tossed it out along the edge of the gravel bar to mark the LZ, then scrambled out into the open to guide the first aircraft in.

After a contact, a team normally was pulled out of the area, but some higher-ups decided the team should spend the night with the reaction force and see if anything else happened.

Daylight finally arrived, and when Kiefel picked up his rucksack, he saw that it had bullet holes right through it. Normally, he used the rucksack for cover, but he'd been in one of the foxholes that night. It really hit him hard when he realized that if he had been using his normal cover, he would have been killed. After the team was extracted, Kiefel got off the chopper, went to his hootch, and lay down. But he started shaking and sweating.

After the extraction, G3 had decided to call in a B-52 Arc Light strike and later determined that the team had encountered an enemy force of company strength or larger.

But the next mission was so hairy that Fobert wouldn't take it, so Kline asked Kiefel to take Fobert's team out. It would have been Kiefel's first mission as a team leader, but he didn't feel confident enough to do it. The next morning Kiefel sat staring at his breakfast thinking over the choices he had. Fortunately, by the time he got back to the company, the mission had been canceled. Kiefel wanted desperately to live to see his family again—but he also felt terribly guilty about the way he was feeling. He had no idea that soon he would be called on for a much worse mission.

Mac came up with a way of letting off some steam, so to speak. McDonald and Kiefel blew up the company shithouse and became known as the Outhouse Bandits.

A few nights later, Kiefel and McDonald sneaked down to the Ranger company's wooden outhouse. McDonald walked behind the shitter, while Kiefel opened the door to see if anyone was inside. "The coast's clear," Kiefel whispered.

"Clear," Mac said after checking around to ensure no one was around to get hurt.

Next Mac held his breath, lifted the hinged lid on the back of the shitter, pulled the pin on a fifteen-second fuse, then tossed a stick of C-4 in one of the fifty-five-gallon barrels. He closed the lid, and they both took off running up the hill, counting to themselves as they ran. It took them less than ten seconds to make it back to Mac's hootch.

Ka-boom! The explosion rocked the company area and tore the roof and walls off the outhouse. The doors and splinters of wood scattered across the company area.

The new company commander, Capt. James Stowers, ran outside his hootch and yelled, "Incoming!" Everyone ran for a bunker then—realizing they were not under attack—slowly gathered along the company road to find out what happened.

All that was left of the crapper was a large hole and a shaving mirror, covered with a thin spray of human waste. When Captain Stowers realized what had happened, he was madder than a passed-over lifer. He called a formation the next morning and vowed to find the assailants and bring them to justice. But fortunately for Kiefel and Mac, Captain Stowers had more pressing things on his mind than the capture of the two Outhouse Bandits.

Buff "Brings Smoke" on the Gunkies

In the army, once things are running smoothly, the higher-ups stir up the pot by sending you a new commander. The 101st Airborne Division got theirs—Maj. Gen. John Hennessey. The good general assumed command, and like all good generals, his plan was to increase the tempo of military operations. With the usual unwavering ideal of eliminating the NVA forces buildup in Vietnam, he gave the Rangers' new commander, Captain Stowers, orders for heightened surveillance.

This was going to require that Ranger teams infiltrate nearby suspected enemy encampments. Teams were going to be sent back into the jungles of the Ruong Ruong Valley, and patrols would be dispatched throughout the Khe Sanh plains near the DMZ. The personnel situation was about to become a nightmare because many of the new Rangers were going to be sent into high-risk areas without the benefit of break-in missions. It was even necessary for some of the radio-relay teams to provide their own security.

Of course, while American units were being sent home, more North Vietnamese were infiltrating south. That meant the gooks would keep the Ho Chi Minh trail humming. NVA engineers and soldiers had constructed a number of ammo dumps that Rangers would be hunting for over the next months.

In the early part of May 1970, Frank Johnson completed his

twenty-ninth mission. His next would be centered around an abandoned firebase named Whip. The team's code name would be Montana, and Sgt. Gary Sands was appointed team leader. This would be SFC Troy Roche's first mission. Sgt. Larry Dalton and Frank Johnson would join them. Johnson would walk point for the team.

They staged out of Quang Tri and were inserted south of Highway QL9. Within minutes on the ground, the team heard movement around them. After thirty minutes, things settled down, and Johnson moved the team about fifty meters from the LZ. They immediately set up an ambush.

The following morning, after a cold breakfast of LRP rations, the team picked up their poncho liners, claymores, and packed up. They moved down a trail that led into a gully. About halfway to the bottom, Johnson halted the team. Sands then took Johnson with him to recon the gully. They had gone only a hundred meters when they came upon a high-speed trail that intersected a small creek. Johnson counted six sets of fresh tracks in the mud up to the water. The tracks continued on the other side of the creek and disappeared into the jungle. Johnson and Sands decided to follow the trail.

After only a short distance, Johnson spotted an X on the trail, made with leaves. An X normally meant there was an NVA rest area ahead, so Johnson signaled Sands to move forward slowly. They continued up the trail until they heard noise, and then quickly stepped off to one side. Johnson had just raised his CAR-15 and slipped his safety switch to auto when a small deer crashed through the brush. He remained still and listened for more noise. It was possible that something had startled the animal. Johnson and Sands both heard splashing in the stream.

Johnson motioned Sands to follow him. They headed very slowly through the brush alongside the trail. Nearing the creek, Johnson pushed aside a large palm leaf and came face-to-face with an NVA soldier. The enemy soldier began to unsling his AK-47, but Johnson raised his weapon and fired at the gook's legs to wound him. The guy started to run. Johnson raised his weapon higher and shot again, hitting the face that time, but the tough NVA ran another ten meters before he fell into the creek.

Johnson chased after him, with Sands covering. Johnson rolled him over. The round had hit the left cheek and blown out the back of his head.

Johnson pulled security while Sands searched the dead enemy soldier. He opened the guy's rucksack and pulled out two pairs of black pajamas, a girl's hanky and bra, rice, two sandwich bags of heroin, a poncho, and two poncho liners. Sands finished the search while Johnson grabbed the guy's AK-47 and scouted the area. Then Sands and Johnson rejoined their team.

Roche, concerned when he heard the gunfire, had gotten on the horn and told the radio-relay team his men were in contact. Helicopters with the 17th Cav Blues, the reaction force, were on their way by the time the Rangers got back to the LZ. A few minutes later, a platoon of Blues and a reaction force of our own Rangers lead by Sergeant Rodarte unloaded from the choppers. The Kit Carson scout, Ut, came with Rodarte. Johnson grinned big as he handed Ut the AK-47. Ut smiled, but was reluctant to show his familiarity with the weapon. Then Johnson, with Ut walking slack, led Rodarte's team and the Blues back down to the creek and toward the rest camp, dugout fighting positions under jungle cover where men could eat and sleep undetected by overhead surveillance.

A couple of men from the Blues buried the body of the NVA soldier off the trail, and they all returned as a group to the LZ. Then the Blues' lieutenant decided they would pull out. Rodarte's team remained in the AO with Roche's, and the two teams positioned themselves in a stand of thick bamboo to monitor the trail fifteen meters away. They spent the night on 50-percent alert. They had no idea what was about to happen next.

May 11, 1970—Tragedy

Ranger team Kansas was providing radio relay and reconnaissance. Sergeant Ellis's last communications check was at 0430. It was negative.

Less than a klick away, Frank Johnson was on his second watch when he heard the faint sound of automatic weapons fire echoing down the canyon from the direction of Ray Ellis's radio-relay team. He listened intently, and a few minutes later heard what sounded like six single pistol shots spaced about ten seconds apart.

Johnson tried to raise Ellis's radio operator, but got no answer. Johnson suspected something was seriously wrong and woke the rest of his team. After several more unsuccessful attempts to call Ellis, their transmission was picked up by the TOC. Johnson informed the TOC about the shots and that he couldn't raise Ellis's team. Back at Camp Eagle, SFC Jim "Popeye" Taylor, 1st Platoon, was awakened and informed of the situation. He ran down to the TOC and immediately dispatched a Loach to establish contact with the missing radio-relay team.

The Loach pilot reported that he'd spotted what appeared to be six bodies sprawled along a trail. Popeye walked over to the 2d Platoon hootch and asked for volunteers from the Rangers remaining in the compound to mount a recovery team. George "Mac" McDonald and John Kiefel came forward, grabbed their gear, and followed Taylor back to the TOC. Within the hour, a slick was landing on the acid pad, and with a pair of 17th Cav gunships, set out for Ellis's last known position.

Ellis's mission had been to serve as radio-relay link for four Ranger patrols operating in the bush around them. The radio-relay team had been in the same location for two days, and the men had packed up that night to be ready for extraction the following morning. Nothing that day seemed out of the ordinary, and there were no unusual sightings noted by the radio-relay team.

The first slick reached the patrol area shortly after daylight. On board, McDonald, Kiefel, and Taylor nervously awaited their turn to rappel to the ground and onto the high-speed trail. They were going in light, with only their CAR-15s, ammo, and web gear. As the pilot locked his ship in a hover, the bellyman signaled Kiefel to stand in the door. He stood, adjusted his Swiss seat, then grabbed hold of the nylon rappelling rope and went out the door. The downdraft from the main rotor blade was almost unbearable, but that wasn't on his mind. The Rangers did a fast slide into double canopy, landing on a ridgeline. They were expecting immediate contact.

On the ground, Kiefel pulled his remaining rope through the D ring and then raised his rifle to his shoulder. Once Taylor and Mac had joined him, they moved off the trail into a small, open space, then cautiously ventured farther up the ridgeline. Kiefel was walking point as the helicopter hovered overhead.

No one will ever know exactly what happened to Ellis and his team, but "whatever happened, they went fast," Kiefel told us later. The three Rangers quickly reached the site where Ellis's team had set up their night defense perimeter. The first thing Kiefel noticed was a strong odor. As he searched through the cover near the crest of the hill, an ominous stillness hung in the morning air.

He reached the team's position and then reluctantly looked down. Each man had been shot in the head; then, as if by someone enraged, each Ranger's skull had been crushed with a rifle butt. Their bodies were in various states of disarray. Ellis's body was lying face up, just outside the perimeter, as if he had attempted to get away during the shooting. His eyes were wide open, staring into the sky. S.Sgt. Robert O'Conner, Sgt. Gary Baker, Sgt. David Muñoz, Cpl. George Fogleman, and PFC Bryan Knight were all lying on their backs in a circle.

From the signs around their perimeter, it appeared that a small number of NVA had simply walked right up and killed them instantly. The gooks had probably been watching the team for days, waiting for the right moment to make their move. The team's claymore mine wires had even been cut. In a rage, Kiefel and Mac started up the trail to look for the NVA, but Taylor said, "Wait! The reaction team is right behind us." The sounds of a helicopter were audible off in the distance.

Kiefel searched the area around the bodies. He was hit by the sickeningly sweet odor; smells of urine, excrement, and cordite. He picked up an M-16 magazine, but he found only three piles of empty brass around the bodies, indicating only three enemy soldiers had carried out the shooting. They couldn't find any American weapons. The casualties' rucks, web gear, and a radio were still lying next to O'Conner's body, but his pockets were inside out, as if someone had searched him in a hurry. Kiefel found his SOI (booklet containing all radio frequencies and call signs) in the brush.

It was a long time before twenty men from B Troop, 17th Cav, inserted to help in the recovery of bodies and equipment. The three Rangers went about the gruesome task of securing the bodies and gear of their six slain comrades. Then one of the helicopters hovered over the site and dropped a large net. By 1000 hours, the six dead men were placed in the net and the chopper headed back home.

Outraged by the news of the radio-relay team, Ut, Sands, Vestal, and Johnson went out on a recon, starting at the exact place they'd made contact the day before. That afternoon, while Ut was walking point, they made contact with three NVA who were setting up an ambush. He and one of the NVA spotted each other at the same time. The NVA hesitated because he didn't see Sands behind Ut. Although Ut fired first, the NVA's return fire hit Ut in the calf. Another AK-47 round went through Sands's right pant leg. Johnson immediately ran forward and opened up. Johnson grabbed Ut and pulled him back. The team then called for gunships to work over the AO with rockets, and for a medevac for Ut.

This time, three chopper loads of Blues came to search the AO, and all the teams were pulled. Taylor, McDonald, and Kiefel were met at the tarmac by First Sergeant Gilbert, who escorted the three men down to the TOC for a short debriefing. After the meeting, Kiefel walked back to his hootch and collapsed onto his cot, but he had a hard time falling asleep. He just lay there, listening to the rain beat on the corrugated metal roof.

The details of the radio-relay team's journey home was something most of the men in the company never had to deal with. The six dead Rangers were loaded onto a truck and driven to Graves Registration, where their bodies were cleaned up. A medical officer identified the cause of death, then filled out multiple forms for each, and signed the six death certificates. John Sontag drove to Phu Bai to identify the bodies.

It was agreed that they should hold a service for the dead men, and the Rangers marched as a unit to the chapel. Along the way, some REMFs shouted remarks at the passing unit, and Johnson, Kiefel, and McDonald all broke formation to chase after them. A pointless exercise, it was the only retaliation available to the men.

Meanwhile, the bodies had been evacuated to the army's embalming facility. From there, they were sent to Da Nang to be placed in metal traveling caskets and loaded on C-141s to be flown back to the United States. Once back on American soil, each casket was escorted home by an army cadre assigned to the hometown of the dead man, where a fitting military funeral would be arranged. Now the fallen Rangers were just boys their mothers and fathers had loved and would miss.

For a while, it was pretty eerie around the company area. The incident spooked a lot of the guys and had a devastating effect on the company as a whole. Sands had to go into the empty hootch where the six men had once lived and help pack their gear to send back home. That's when Sands realized that the same fate could have happened to his team. He decided he'd had enough and that he was going back to the 502d. When he left, Johnson shook Sands's hand and wished him well.

Johnson got a couple of days break during which Ut, his brother, and his brother's wife came by the company area. Johnson was glad to see Ut again. Ut showed him his wound and told Johnson he'd be back at the company in a couple of weeks. They all went to the 17th Cav NCO club together where a pretty Vietnamese girl was working. Johnson had seen her before and wanted to get to know her. He asked Ut to tell him something very complimentary that he could say to her in Vietnamese. Thinking he was well supplied with a pickup artist's infallible line, Johnson approached her and smiled but mispronounced the Vietnamese saying terribly.

Insulted, the girl grabbed an empty beer bottle and flung it at Johnson. He ducked, and she picked up more bottles, throwing them at him as he ran out the back door. Ut laughed and took off. Johnson never did know what he'd said to the girl, but he promised to get even with Ut the next time he saw him. It just goes to show, you never could trust those NVA turncoats!

A week later Johnson, Krause, Bruce Bowland, and Nelson, a replacement tracker from the 17th Cav, found themselves inserted back in the same AO. They had settled in for the night, but were awakened when two artillery rounds smashed to the ground just two hundred meters from their NDP.

Johnson immediately got on the PRC-25 and relayed back to the TOC. "Cease fire; there are artillery rounds in the AO." Finally the shelling stopped, and Johnson took the opportunity to do a leech search. He found a black leech that had crawled into his shirt, forming a ball under his armpit. He took out a plastic bottle of insect repellent and dabbed some on the leech. When it released its grip, he pulled it off and tossed it down the hill. Johnson tried to get back to sleep, but swarms of mosquitoes made that impossible. The next morning, the four Rangers were to fly out to the site of the abandoned Firebase Whip.

At the briefing, Johnson was told that the firebase had no cover except for scrub brush on the slopes. When they flew out to look it over, Johnson noticed that the firebase was shaped like a shoe—or more accurately, a high boot—with two levels. On the east side of the firebase was a steep drop. At one time, a quad-.50 machine gun proudly sat guarding the approach from the west. But by the time of that mission, only the metal ring remained. The place looked like a firebase ghost town.

Johnson and Bowland set up in dilapidated bunkers that were missing their PSP metal covers, while Nelson and Krause explored the other side of the firebase. Johnson received a radio transmission from the TOC that instructed them to make the best 360-degree perimeter they could. Bowland was taking things pretty seriously, so Johnson started clowning around and making jokes about it being their last mission, but Bowland was wound *very* tight. He said, "It's not funny anymore, you know."

They were interrupted when Johnson monitored a call from a team leader out in the field. It was Sergeant Vestal calling in a negative sitrep. Vestal read his location in code.

Still holding the radio, Johnson stood up and was about to take an azimuth to get a fix on Vestal's team, when he heard laughter coming from the lower shelf of the firebase. Johnson hit the ground, and Bowland ducked out of sight as two witless NVA regulars walked toward them in the open less than forty meters away. Johnson squeezed the handset, gave his call sign and quietly said, "We got two NVA walking into us. They might be point for a larger team. I'm going to initiate contact—*now!*"

Johnson flipped the CAR-15 safety to semiautomatic and rose in one motion. The first NVA saw him and froze in his tracks; the second guy took off running. Johnson fired. The hillside echoed with the noise of semiautomatic fire. His first rounds were tracers, and he watched as the rounds met his targets. Then Johnson switched to full auto. The first gook fell like a rock. The second gook dove to the ground.

"I've got one down. I don't know if I got the other one or not. He's behind a stack of logs."

Krause ran back to join Johnson and tossed a grenade in the direction of the logs. Johnson yelled out, *"Chieu hoi!"*, meaning "surrender." But the enemy soldier jumped to his feet and started running. He was near the crest of the hill when Johnson stood, still holding his CAR-15 in his right hand and the radio handset in his left, squeezed the trigger, putting three tracers right through the man's back. This time, the gook was knocked onto his face.

Johnson stayed on the radio and Nelson and Krause leap-frogged down to the bodies. The tracker followed. Krause rolled one of the dead soldiers onto his back. Johnson's bullets had blasted a hole in the guy where his heart used to be.

Johnson called in the contact, and the 17th Cav helicopters were immediately on their way to help. Meanwhile, Vestal's recon team was getting enemy movement around his positions, so two more 17th Cav helicopters were dispatched to extract the teams.

Back at Whip, Krause walked toward Johnson, holding a handwritten notebook he'd found on one of the gooks. He was looking at one of the last entries—a crude drawing. "Hey, Buff look at this!" Krause said, holding up the notebook. The drawing looked like a wide trail and above it, five *X*s forming a circle, and another *X* outside the circle. There were some notes in Vietnamese under the drawing.

Johnson and Krause studied the diary and the date written over the notes. It read May 11—the same date Ellis's team was wiped out. Johnson's face turned pale. "This guy was there. These marks are our guys. Ellis's team! It's the same date!" The other gook's diary had similar writing but no dates. The diary covers were white and inscribed with the year 1970, alongside a color picture of an NVA soldier in pith helmet and green khakis.

Later that night, Johnson's team arrived back home, and everyone gathered round to examine the captured notebook. Johnson told the debriefing officer, "The gunkies were wearing fresh clothes, had brand-new clothes in their rucks, and carried American money in their pockets." Then he handed the note-book to the officer.

In the dead guy's own handwriting, the diary had told of his returning from a week-long R & R to Hue city as a reward for killing an American Ranger team.

This fortuitous retaliation was a psychological victory for the Rangers.

For two more years, the company was responsible for gathering intelligence and finding the enemy in his own sanctuaries.

It was not until 1971 that the company was closed down and the remaining Rangers sent home or reassigned to different units. No parades, no final formation. There was no graceful way to exit Vietnam. We just left.

Epilogue

I never really had the opportunity to get to know any of them; we had only a brief meeting, but it was a meeting that those who raised their hands and volunteered would never forget. I had been their official reception committee. My last job with the company was to weed out the obviously weak ones before they got to the field, to check their personnel records, and use my gut to determine if the guys could cut the mustard. I wish I could have told them that if they did get out alive, their bravery and courage would go unacknowledged for years to come.

Back then, I couldn't keep up with what happened to any of them and didn't give it much thought. Occasionally, much later, when I was safely at home, I'd remember a name, a face, an expression, and pray that they had made it; they were a part of my history, but it wasn't until I sat around a table shooting the bull at our second Ranger reunion that I wanted to know their stories.

I wanted to find a single voice for them, to tell their stories, those who became U.S. Army Rangers because I asked them to do it. That was the strongest memory of my extended tour. Not the combat, but the curiosity.

Like us, they walked in the heat of the Asian sun, moving in, around, and through the same dense jungle growth, assaulted by the same insects, leeches, and snakes. The enemy wanted to kill us, many South Vietnamese people resented us, the ARVN couldn't defend their own country, and our commissioned officers often treated us as if we were cartridges to be used once, discarded, then replaced.

In the end, it would be up to us to tell each other the truth. To say how it had been and how we survived. Moments of boredom that turned into seconds of terror. And of course, I can still close my eyes and smell the pungent odor of burning, diesel-soaked excrement.

Appendixes

1. Patrol Techniques and Patrol Tips, Patrol Planning Steps
2. Patrol Techniques and Patrol Tips
3. Patrol Techniques and Patrol Tips, Tracking and Use of Human Senses in Obtaining Combat Intelligence
4. Patrol Preparation, Backward Planning
5. Patrol Preparation, Briefback Overlay
6. Patrol Techniques and Patrol Tips, Debriefing Overlay
7. Special Patrol Equipment, Student Uniform and Equipment
8. Special Medical Drugs, Descriptions and Dosages
9. Arm and Hand Signals (in English, Thai, and Vietnamese)
10. Communications Procedures, Prowords and Their Meanings
11. SOI and Message Writing
12. Field-Expedient Antennae
13. Forward Observer Procedures and Artillery Adjustment, Binocular Reticle
14. Forward Observer Procedures and Artillery Adjustment, Mil Relation
15. Company L (Ranger) 75th Infantry, 101st Airborne Division (AMBL), Definition and SOPs
16. NVA Trail Marking and Field-Expedient Mess Facilities
17. Nine Rules for Personnel of U.S. Military Assistance Command, Vietnam

Appendix 1

MACV RECONDO SCHOOL
5TH SPECIAL FORCES GROUP (AIRBORNE),
1ST SPECIAL FORCES
APO SAN FRANCISCO 96240

PATROL TECHNIQUES AND PATROL TIPS
HANDOUT 707-1 PATROL PLANNING STEPS

1. PLAN USE OF TIME
2. STUDY SITUATION
3. MAKE MAP STUDY
4. COORDINATE (CONTINUOUS THROUGHOUT)
5. SELECT MEN, WEAPONS, AND EQUIPMENT
6. ISSUE WARNING ORDER
7. MAKE RECONNAISSANCE
8. COMPLETE DETAIL PLANS
9. ISSUE PATROL ORDER
10. INSPECT AND REHEARSE
11. BRIEFBACK

Appendix 2

MACV RECONDO SCHOOL
5TH SPECIAL FORCES GROUP (AIRBORNE),
1ST SPECIAL FORCES
APO SAN FRANCISCO 96240

PATROL TECHNIQUES AND PATROL TIPS
HANDOUT 704-1

1. Make thorough map study.
2. Use difficult terrain in planning your route.
3. "Offset" method should be employed in route of march.
4. Always select an alternate rallying point.
5. Consider the use of special equipment, depending on your mission, the terrain through which you plan to travel, etc.
6. Test-fire your weapon prior to going on any mission. Once you have test-fired it, DO NOT TEAR IT APART TO CLEAN IT AGAIN.
7. Always carry a cleaning rod with you.
8. Use silent hand signals to the maximum.
9. Practice all hand and arm signals prior to departing on a mission.
10. Tape emergency frequencies and artillery-request format to headset of radio.
11. Each night put up field-expedient antenna.
12. Preset artillery frequency on your radio.
13. Occasionally, change point man and compass man on long patrols.
14. Always carry your weapon pointed in the direction in which you are looking.
15. Insure weapon is taped to prevent all noise.
16. Avoid trails, streams, and roads.
17. Don't forget to check trees as you move through the jungle.
18. Avoid human habitations.
19. Sterilize your trail.

20. If men have difficulty in staying awake, have them kneel rather than sit.
21. Sleep close enough to touch each other.
22. If you snore, put handkerchief around your mouth.
23. Do not remove equipment while sleeping.
24. Dead foliage may be old camouflage.
25. Tied-down or cut-down brush may be a firing lane.
26. Avoid streams and moats in an inhabited area; they may contain punji stakes.
27. Unoccupied houses may contain booby traps.
28. Be cautious of all civilians.
29. Do not set a pattern.
30. Always expect an ambush.
31. If ambushed, pick a single point and attack.
32. Take advantage of inclement weather; however, be careful because you cannot call an air strike or call for extraction.
33. Never return over the same route.
34. In sudden engagement, fire low. A ricochet is better than no hit at all.
35. In selection of LZs, avoid overuse or "likely" LZs.
36. Do not smoke while on patrol.
37. Men who cough need to take medicine for it.
38. Be sure to muffle sneezes, coughs, etc.
39. Make sure you observe noise discipline.
40. On hard ground, walk toe to heel; on soft ground walk flat-footed.
41. At meal times, only one man eat at a time; the rest observe security.
42. Keep one ration prepared at all times.
43. MENTAL ALERTNESS—MENTAL ALERTNESS

Appendix 3

MACV RECONDO SCHOOL
5TH SPECIAL FORCES GROUP (AIRBORNE),
1ST SPECIAL FORCES
APO SAN FRANCISCO 96240

PATROL TECHNIQUES AND PATROL TIPS
HANDOUT 704-2 TRACKING AND USE OF HUMAN
SENSES IN OBTAINING COMBAT INTELLIGENCE

I. HUMAN SENSE:

The use of the human sense in obtaining and developing combat intelligence is very important, especially in a guerrilla-type environment such as exists in Vietnam. Valuable information can be gained about the enemy, just by smelling, touching, and/or listening.

A. SMELL:

(1) Smell is very important in that it can be employed to detect the enemy before he sees you; it is also used to determine what he is doing now, or has been doing in the past.

Cigarette smoke can be detected up to one-quarter mile if wind conditions are right. You can also smell fish, garlic, and other foods being cooked for several hundred meters. You may even be able to detect a person who has been eating garlic, or other specific food, from a considerable distance, thus discovering a guerrilla ambush before your patrol walks into it.

Here in Vietnam, there are many types of wood used for fuel. Being able to identify the smell of some of these types of wood, you may be able to determine the purpose and the general location of the fire, or guerrilla camp, or patrol base.

(2) For the man who seldom or never uses soap, after-shave lotion, or other such toiletry articles, it is easy for him to detect a person using these items for a considerable distance.

In some areas of the world, the best way to prevent detection is not to use these items.

The British discovered this in Malaya. Once they set an ambush on a known guerrilla trail. The guerrillas avoided and bypassed the ambush. Later, one of those guerrillas was captured, and he told the British that he was in the guerrilla patrol that they were trying to ambush. He said they smelled the bath soap which had been used by the ambushing party.

In other cases, the guerrillas smelled the food that had been previously eaten by the ambushing parties and were alerted. Insect repellent is another item that you can smell for a distance.

If the local indigenous population doesn't use it, your recon team shouldn't either.

(3) Another item emitting a distinctive odor is explosives. You can tell that someone has been working with them just by the smell of the hands or clothes.

B. **TOUCH:**

(1) You may find yourself having to search buildings, tunnels, or enemy dead at night with no means for lighting the area; or lights cannot be used for security reasons. When this happens, you rely principally on touch, hearing, and smell.

(2) To use the sense of touch to identify an object, you consider four factors: shape, moisture, temperature, and texture.

    a. By shape we mean the general outline of the object.

    b. Moisture refers to the moisture content of the object (wet or dry).

    c. Temperature is the heat or lack of heat of an object.

    d. Texture is the smoothness or roughness of the object.

You will be able to basically identify the object. Your ability to determine what, by considering all of these aspects, an object is by touch may save your life.

A good example of this is the timely detection of trip wires by using the exposed portion of your arm for feeling. Another method of searching for trip wires is the use of a very fine branch. Hold it in front of you, and you can feel it strike anything.

Another method is the use of a piece of wire with a small weight on one end that you hold in front of you as you walk. This method has proven to be quite effective.

During the Korean War, on occasion, the Turks would remove all their clothing prior to departing on patrol. If while in no-man's-land they came in contact with someone, they merely felt or touched them; if they felt clothing they killed them. This, too, has proven effective.

C. HEARING:

(1) The sound of a safety latch being released on a rifle or machine gun could warn of an ambush or a sniper. The sound of sudden flight of wild birds may indicate enemy movement. The sounds of dogs barking could warn others of your approach to a village.

You must be able to determine whether you have been discovered or whether the dogs are barking for another reason.

Sudden cessation of normal wildlife noises may indicate passage of the enemy, or the animal's or bird's detection of you. Thus, it is important that you become familiar with distress or warning cries of birds and wild animals of the area of operation. The sound of a man talking, running, or crawling are important sounds to recognize.

In reconnaissance work, the team should always move cautiously enough to hear sounds made by the enemy before the enemy hears or sees the recon team.

Another very important sound is the striker of a hand grenade and the sound of the handle flying off. Sound can also assist you in determining range to an explosion or blast.

If you can see the flash of the explosion and can determine the number of seconds from the flash to the time you hear the sound, you can determine the approximate range.

To use this method you must be able to see the flash of the explosion. Sound travels at approximately 1100 feet per second; for all practical purposes we can say sound travels at 400 meters per second.

With a little practice, you can learn to determine range of enemy weapons using flash/bang method of range determination. It is also important that you be able to identify the type and caliber of various types of weapons by the sound of the report of the weapons.

Whenever you hear a noise, if you will rotate the upper body, with your hands cupped over your ears, until the noise is the loudest, the direction you are facing will usually be the source of the noise. When there is no wind, air currents generally flow downhill at night, and uphill in daylight.

These elements can also be a disadvantage; for example, if following a trail that leads into a guerrilla village, and the wind is to your back, dogs may bark warning of your approach. A good tracker constantly considers all these factors.

II. **TRACKING:**

Tracking, combined with the use of the basic human senses, is another important source of combat intelligence, as evidenced by the following examples:

As the recon team moved through the jungle, it came upon a crest, which had recently been evacuated by the enemy. The crest was pocketed with rifle pits. In the spoil around the pits were blurred footprints. The holes were deep but not as wide as American GIs dig them. It was concluded from these signs that the hill had recently been held by the Vietnamese.

Several men prowled the jungle below and found numerous piles of elephant dung; enough to suggest that upward of twenty of the animals had been picketed there. The dung was still fairly fresh, about two days they figured.

In one area there was a small frame house, carefully camouflaged and well bunkered, that looked like a command post. There were a dozen or so split gourds strewn about the room. Bits of cooked rice—perhaps 15 or 20 grains in all—still clung to the sides. They were still soft to the touch. Adding these things together, it was speculated that an enemy force of approximately battalion strength had held the same ground not more than 48 hours before.

A. **DISPLACEMENT:** The disturbance of soil, vegetation, or wildlife from its natural state.

(1) Footprints: Footprints can indicate several things: the number of personnel in a party, direction of movement, sex, and in some cases the type of load being borne by the person in the group.

By studying a set of prints for worn or unworn heels, cuts in the heels, tread pattern of the soles, one may be able to recognize them again. Also note the angle of the impression from the direction of movement.

Prints normally spaced with exceptionally deep toe prints indicate that the person leaving the prints was probably carrying a heavy load. If you follow the tracks you may find where the load was placed on the ground during a rest break. Then, by studying those prints and the surrounding area, you may get some idea of what the load consisted of.

(2) Vegetation: When vegetation is stepped on, dragged out of place, or when branches are broken, the lighter colored undersides will show unnaturally. This will be easier to see by looking into the sun at the trail.

a. Vines will be broken and dragged parallel to or toward the direction of movement.

b. Grass, when stepped on, will usually be bent toward the direction of movement. When the bark on a log or root is scuffed, the lighter inner wood will show, leaving an easily detected sign.

(3) Shreds of clothing: The jungle environment is very hard on clothing. It is not uncommon to find threads or bits of cloth clinging to the underbrush, particularly if movement was hurried.

(4) Birds and animals: Another type of displacement may occur when wild birds and animals are suddenly flushed from their hiding places.

a. Birds, in particular, usually emit cries of alarm when disturbed. Animals will also run away from man. You should definitely be familiar with the distress signals of the wild animals and birds of your area of operation.

B. **STAINING:** The deposition of liquids or soil not natural to a specific location.

(1) Bloodstains: Look for bloodstains on the ground, on leaves, and underbrush to the average height of a man. Examine stains for color and consistency.

(2) Soil: Observe logs, grass, and stones for signs of soil displacement from footgear. The color and composition of the soil may indicate a previous location or route over which a party has been moving.

The muddying of clear water is a sign of very recent movement which can be picked out by the most untrained eye. If the water in footprints is clear, this may indicate the trail is an hour or more old.

C. **LITTERING:** Littering is a direct result of ignorance, poor discipline, or both. If the enemy should litter the trail, take full advantage of his carelessness. Some examples of littering are cigarette butts, scraps of paper and cloth, match sticks, ration cans, and abandoned equipment.

Observe along the trail and to the flanks for these items. Uncovered human feces is another example of littering.

D. **WEATHERING:** The effect of rain, wind, and sun on the appearance of trail signs.

(1) Rain.

a. On footprints: A light rain will "round out" footprints and give the appearance that they are old. A heavy rain will completely obliterate footprints in a very short time.

b. On litter: Rain will flatten paper scraps and other litter such as ammunition bandoliers and cloth scraps. By close examination you can determine whether the litter was discarded before or after the last rain. It is very important that you always remember the day of the last significant rainfall.

(2) Sunlight.

   a. On footprints: Footprints, when first made, will have a ridge of moist dirt pushed up around the sides. Sunlight and air will dry this ridge of dirt, causing a slow crumbling effect. If actual crumbling is observed by the tracker, this is an indication that the prints were made very recently, and increased stealth should be employed.

   b. On litter: Sunlight bleaches and discolors light-colored paper and cloth. Such litter will first go through a yellowing stage and then, eventually, turn completely white. Of most interest to us is the yellowing stage.

   After one night, yellow spots will begin to form; it takes about three days for such litter to become completely yellow. On dark-colored paper or cloth, you must determine how much the paper has faded. The only guideline for this is experience.

(3) Wind.

   a. On footprints: Wind may blow grass, leaves, sand, and other light litter into the prints. Examine the litter to determine whether it had been crushed. If not, it will be important to remember when the wind was last blowing.

   b. Litter: Litter may be blown away from the trail; therefore, it may be necessary to search back and forth along the trail to locate it.

(4) Combination of all the above. All of the elements of the weather will cause metal to rust. Check recently exposed portions of metal. For example, closely examine the rim of ration cans where the opener stripped the paint. Rust will form in these places within 12 hours or less.

(5) Effects of wind and air currents while tracking. Be aware that wind and air currents carry sound and odor. This knowledge can be used to your advantage when attempting to locate the enemy.

Appendix 4

MACV RECONDO SCHOOL
5TH SPECIAL FORCES GROUP (AIRBORNE), 1ST SPECIAL FORCES
APO SAN FRANCISCO 96240

PATROL PREPARATION
HANDOUT 707-2 BACKWARD PLANNING

Make a time schedule based on time available. Use the "Backward Planning Technique." Start your schedule from the time you infiltrate, then work backward to the time you received the order.

Example:

1945–	Infiltrate
1930–1945	Move to Helicopter
1845–1915	Final Inspection
1800–1845	Rehearsal
1745–1800	Inspection
1700–1745	Supper Meal
1630–1700	Briefback
1600–1630	Issue Patrol Order
1500–1600	Complete Detailed Plans
1400–1500	Make Recon
1330–1400	Issue Warning Order
1130–1330	Preliminary Planning
1130–	Operations Order Issued

Appendix 5

MACV RECONDO SCHOOL
5TH SPECIAL FORCES GROUP (AIRBORNE),
1ST SPECIAL FORCES
APO SAN FRANCISCO 96240

PATROL PREPARATION
HANDOUT 707-4 BRIEFBACK OVERLAY

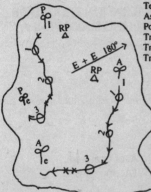

Team Leader	SANDUL	MSG
Asst Tm Ldr	ALLEE	SFC
Point Man	MORRIS	SFC
Tm Member 3	ZUMBRUN	SSG
Tm Member 4	LIGHTNER	SSG
Tm Member 5	MRSICH	SSG

MAP INFORMATION

Map Name: NHA TRANG
Map Scale: 1:50,000
Map Sheet: 6833 III

LEGEND

Primary/Alternate Infil LZ's

Primary/Alternate Exfil LZ's

Initial Rally Points   RP

Proposed Route of March → → →

Proposed Overnight Halts With Nights Numbered   1 2 3

Special Points of Interest — ✕ ✕ —

Escape and Evasion Route With Azimuth   E&E 180

Appendix 6

**MACV RECONDO SCHOOL
5TH SPECIAL FORCES GROUP (AIRBORNE),
1ST SPECIAL FORCES
APO SAN FRANCISCO 96240**

PATROL TECHNIQUES AND PATROL TIPS
HANDOUT 707-8 DEBRIEFING OVERLAY

THE FOLLOWING INFORMATION SHOULD BE
PLACED ON THE DEBRIEFING MAP OVERLAY:

1. Infiltration/exfiltration LZs.
2. Route of movement.
3. Overnight halts.
4. Enemy contacted by hearing, seeing, and actual firing contacts.
5. Called artillery strikes.
6. Called air strikes.
7. Location of enemy KIA, WIA, or captured.
8. Location of friendly KIA, WIA, or captured.
9. Team number or designation.
10. Team member by name and rank and position.
11. Legend.
12. Map tick marks.

MACV RECONDO SCHOOL
5TH SPECIAL FORCES GROUP (AIRBORNE),
1ST SPECIAL FORCES
APO SAN FRANCISCO 96240

HANDOUT 707-7 DEBRIEFING MAP OVERLAY
EXAMPLE

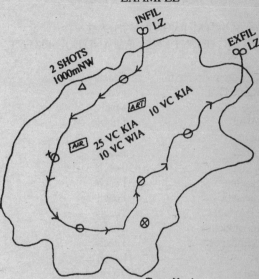

Team Nr. 1

	Team Leader	ROGERS	SFC
LEGEND	Asst Tm Ldr	JONES	SSG
	Tm Members	TELFAIR	PFC
Infiltration/Exfiltration LZ's ⌀		NICOLS	PFC
Route of march →→→→→		RETTER	PFC
		HAMILTON	PFC

Overnight halts ●–●–●–●

Arty called 10 VC KIA 〔ART〕

Air Strike called 25 VC KIA 10 VC WIA 〔AIR〕

2 shots heard 1000 M NW of team △

2 VC with weapons moving south on trail Ⓧ

2 VC KIA in ambush ①

Appendix 7

MACV RECONDO SCHOOL
5TH SPECIAL FORCES GROUP (AIRBORNE), 1ST SPECIAL FORCES
APO SAN FRANCISCO 96240

SPECIAL PATROL EQUIPMENT
ANNEX A—STUDENT UNIFORM AND EQUIPMENT

Camouflage fatigue uniform	1 each
Floppy brimmed hat	1 each
Jungle boots	1 pair
Insect repellent	1 bottle
Panel, signaling	1 each
Pen flare gun	1 each
Flares, pen gun	10 each
Mirror, signaling	1 each
Compass, lensatic	1 each
Triangular bandages	2 each
Ammunition pouches	2 each
Compress bandages	3 each
Magazines	11 each
Ammunition	200 rounds
Grenade, smoke	2 each (1 red, 1 yellow)
Grenade, fragmentation	3 each
Canteen, plastic	4 each
Cover, canteen	2 each
Water purification tablets	4 bottles
Pistol belt	1 each
Harness, pistol belt	1 each
Snap link	2 each
Bayonet with scabbard	1 each
Pouch, first aid	1 each
Rucksack, indigenous	1 each
Nylon rope, 12 feet	1 each

Gloves, rappelling	1 pair
Poncho, lightweight	1 each
Individual weapon	1 each

Appendix 8

MACV RECONDO SCHOOL
5TH SPECIAL FORCES GROUP (AIRBORNE),
1ST SPECIAL FORCES
APO SAN FRANCISCO 96240

SPECIAL MEDICAL DRUGS
HANDOUT 401-1 DESCRIPTIONS AND DOSAGES

1. Darvon	a. Appearance	Pink and gray capsule
	b. Action	Analgesic (relieves pain)
	c. Dosage	Two capsules, four times daily
2. Codeine	a. Appearance	Small white tablet
	b. Action	Analgesic (relieves pain)
		Antitussive (relieves cough)
	c. Dosage	Analgesic—one tablet, four times daily
		Antitussive—$1/2$ tablet, three times daily
3. Cold Tablet	a. Appearance	Large white tablet
	b. Action	Relieves symptoms of cold
	c. Dosage	One tablet, four times daily
4. Dextro-amphetamine	a. Appearance	Medium-sized white tablet
	b. Action	Central nervous system stimulant
		Appetite depressant
	c. Dosage	Maximum of eight tablets in 24-hour period
5. Chloroquine Primacuine	a. Appearance	Large orange tablet
	b. Action	Malaria suppressant
	c. Dosage	One tablet weekly
6. Polymagma	a. Appearance	Large pink tablet
	b. Action	Antidiarrheal
	c. Dosage	Two tablets after each watery bowel movement

7. Tetracycline	a. Appearance	Yellow tablet
	b. Action	Antibiotic
	c. Dosage	One tablet, four times daily
8. Morphine	a. Appearance	Syrette
	b. Action	Analgesic (relieves pain)
	c. Dosage	No more than three syrettes in a 24-hour period and not less than two hours apart.
	d. Contra-indications	1) Head and chest wounds
		2) Patient with depressed respiration below 12 breaths per minute
		3) As a sedative for anxiety, fear, hysteria

Appendix 9

ARM AND HAND SIGNALS
แบบขันและสัญญิป ประกาศ
HIÊU-BÁO BĂNG TAY

STOP
หยุก
DŪNG LAI

GO
ไป
ĐI

REST (BREAK)
พัก (หัก)
NGHI[2]

SMOKE
สูบยา
HÚT THUỐC

COVER ME
(WITH FIRE)
ยิงสกัดให้ ฉัน
YỂM TRỢ CHO TÔI
(BẰNG HỎA LỰC)

RADIO FORWARD
สงวิทยุมา
LIÊN LẠC MÁY PHÍA
TRƯỚC

LEADER FORWARD
หัวหน้ามา
TRƯỞNG TOÁN ĐẰNG TRƯỚC

KILL
(ADD SILENT SIGN
FOR SILENT KILL)
ฆ่าเลย
(ให้สัญญาณเงียบ
เพิ่มเข้าว่า ฆ่าเงียบ)
GIẾT
THÊM DẤU HIỆU IM LẶNG
ĐỂ giết một cách im Lặng

ARE YOU READY?
I AM READY
แบกพร้อมหรือยัง
ฉัน ทองพ้มแล้ว
ANH SẴN SÀNG CHƯA ?
TÔI SẴN SÀNG

ASSEMBLE
ประชุม
TẬP HỌP

RECON
ลาดตระเวน
THÁM SÁT

AMBUSH (POINT)
ที่ช่ม (ธีที่สำทาง)
PHỤC KÍCH (ĐỊA ĐIỂM)

HIDE
(INDICATE DIRECTION)
ซ่อนอยู่ (ชี้ทิศทาง)
TRỐN
(CHỈ² PHƯƠNG HƯỚNG)

DOWN AND FREEZE
หลบนิ่ง
NẰM XUỐNG VÀ GOM LẠI

MAKE CAMP
สร้างค่าย
DỰNG LỀU

LISTEN
ฟัง
NGHE

SILENCE
เงียบ
IM LẶNG

EAT
กิน
ĂN

ENEMY
ศัตรู
ĐỊCH

ALL CLEAR
ปลอดครัย
AN TOĀN

HOUSE
บ้าน
NHA

VILLAGE
หมู่บ้าน
LÀNG

Appendix 10

MACV RECONDO SCHOOL
5TH SPECIAL FORCES GROUP (AIRBORNE),
1ST SPECIAL FORCES
APO SAN FRANCISCO 96240

COMMUNICATIONS PROCEDURES
HANDOUT 505-2 PROWORDS AND
THEIR MEANINGS

PROWORD	MEANINGS
THIS IS	This transmission is from this station whose designation immediately follows.
OVER	This is the end of my transmission to you and a response is necessary. Go ahead and transmit.
OUT	This is the end of my transmission to you and no answer is required or expected.
GROUPS	This message contains the number of groups indicated by the number following.
TIME	That which immediately follows is the time or date time group of this message.
BREAK	I hereby indicate the separation of the text from other portions of the message. To be used when there is no clear distinction between the text and other portions of the message.
SAY AGAIN	Say again all of your last transmission.
I SAY AGAIN	I am repeating transmission or portion indicated.
ALL AFTER	The portion of the message of which I have reference is all that which precedes . . .
ALL BEFORE	The portion of the message to which I have reference is all that which precedes . . .

WORD AFTER	The word of the message which I have reference is that which follows . . .
WORD BEFORE	The word of the message which I have reference is that which precedes . . .
I SPELL	I shall spell the next word phonetically.
WAIT	I must pause for a few seconds.
WAIT OUT	I pause longer than a few seconds.
WILCO	I have received your message, understand it, and will comply.
ROGER	I have received your last message satisfactorily.
CORRECTION	An error has been made in this transmission (or message indicated) the correct version is . . .
WRONG	Your last transmission was incorrect. The correct version is . . .
THAT IS CORRECT	You are correct, or what you have transmitted is correct.
GROUP NO COUNT	The groups in this message have not been counted.
I READ BACK	The following is my response to your instructions to read back.
MESSAGE FOLLOWS	A message which requires recording is about to follow. Transmitted immediately after the call.
NUMBER	Station serial number.
READ BACK	Repeat this entire transmission back to me exactly as received.
RELAY (TO)	Transmit this message to all addresses or to the address designated immediately following.
SPEAK SLOWER	Your transmission is at too fast a speed. Reduce speed of transmission.
UNKNOWN STATION	The identity of the station with whom I am attempting to establish contact is unknown.

Appendix 11

MACV RECONDO SCHOOL
5TH SPECIAL FORCES GROUP (AIRBORNE),
1ST SPECIAL FORCES
APO SAN FRANCISCO 96240

SOI AND MESSAGE WRITING
HANDOUT 504-1 SOI AND MESSAGE WRITING

A RECONDO SOI SHOULD BE:
1. SIMPLE
2. COMPACT
3. CONCISE
4. COMPLETE
5. FLEXIBLE
6. EASILY MEMORIZED
7. WATER PROOF
8. EASILY CARRIED
AND ABOVE ALL
9. SECURE!!!!

A RECONDO SOI MUST CONTAIN THE FOLLOWING:
1. CALL SIGNS
2. FREQUENCIES
3. OPERATIONAL CODE*
4. BREVITY CODE**

*NORMAL TRAFFIC, SITREPS, ETC.
**EMERGENCY TRAFFIC
THE OPERATIONAL CODE AND THE BREVITY CODE
ARE *NEVER* USED TOGETHER.

A RECONDO SOI SHOULD ALSO CONTAIN:
1. MESSAGE FORMATS
2. CODED MESSAGE INDICATORS
3. GROUND TO AIR PANEL MARKINGS

Appendix 12

MACV RECONDO SCHOOL
5TH SPECIAL FORCES GROUP (AIRBORNE),
1ST SPECIAL FORCES
APO SAN FRANCISCO 96240

FIELD-EXPEDIENT ANTENNAE
HANDOUT 502-1 JUNGLE ANTENNA

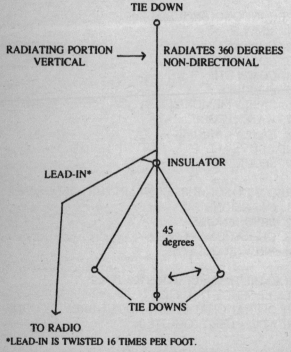

TIE DOWN

RADIATING PORTION
VERTICAL →   RADIATES 360 DEGREES
                  NON-DIRECTIONAL

LEAD-IN*   INSULATOR

45 degrees

TIE DOWNS

TO RADIO

*LEAD-IN IS TWISTED 16 TIMES PER FOOT.

FORMULA FOR RADIANT AND GROUND PLANES:
234 divided by the frequency in megacycles or 234/FMC

THE RADIANT SHOULD BE AT LEAST 15 FEET ABOVE THE GROUND, HOWEVER THE HIGHER THE BETTER.

MACV RECONDO SCHOOL
5TH SPECIAL FORCES GROUP (AIRBORNE),
1ST SPECIAL FORCES
APO SAN FRANCISCO 96240

FIELD-EXPEDIENT ANTENNAS
HANDOUT 502-2 HORIZONTAL DOUBLET
ANTENNA

RADIATES 90 DEGREES
BROADSIDE

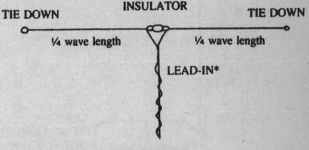

INSULATOR

TIE DOWN   TIE DOWN

¼ wave length   ¼ wave length

LEAD-IN*

TO RADIO

*LEAD-IN TWISTED 16 TIMES PER FOOT.

THE FORMULA FOR THE LENGTH OF THE RADIANT AND THE
GROUND IS 234/FMC.

THE ANTENNA SHOULD BE AT LEAST 15 FEET ABOVE THE
GROUND.

TO FIND THE LENGTH OF THE RADIANT OR GROUND OF AN-
TENNA FREQUENCY OF 46.80 MEGACYLCES . . .

$$234/46.80 = 5'$$

$$
\begin{array}{r}
5.0 \text{ feet} \\
46.80)\overline{234.00} \\
234.00 \\
\hline
0
\end{array}
$$

MACV RECONDO SCHOOL
5TH SPECIAL FORCES GROUP (AIRBORNE),
1ST SPECIAL FORCES
APO SAN FRANCISCO 96240

FIELD-EXPEDIENT ANTENNAS
HANDOUT 502-3 VERTICAL DOUBLET ANTENNA

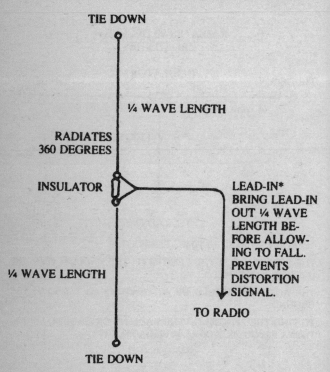

TIE DOWN

¼ WAVE LENGTH

**RADIATES
360 DEGREES**

INSULATOR

LEAD-IN*
**BRING LEAD-IN
OUT ¼ WAVE
LENGTH BE-
FORE ALLOW-
ING TO FALL.
PREVENTS
DISTORTION
SIGNAL.**

¼ WAVE LENGTH

TO RADIO

TIE DOWN

*LEAD-IN TWISTED 16 TIMES PER FOOT.

FORMULA SAME AS HORIZONTAL DOUBLET.

ADD SIX INCHES TO RADIANT AND GROUND PORTION, FOR TIE
DOWN.

Appendix 13

MACV RECONDO SCHOOL
5TH SPECIAL FORCES GROUP (AIRBORNE),
1ST SPECIAL FORCES
APO SAN FRANCISCO 96240

FO PROCEDURES AND ARTILLERY ADJUSTMENT
HANDOUT 803-4 BINOCULAR RETICLE

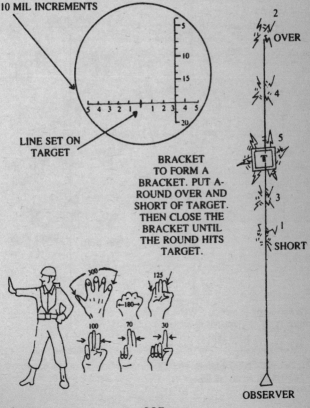

10 MIL INCREMENTS

LINE SET ON TARGET

BRACKET TO FORM A BRACKET. PUT A-ROUND OVER AND SHORT OF TARGET. THEN CLOSE THE BRACKET UNTIL THE ROUND HITS TARGET.

OVER

SHORT

OBSERVER

Appendix 14

MACV RECONDO SCHOOL
5TH SPECIAL FORCES GROUP (AIRBORNE),
1ST SPECIAL FORCES
APO SAN FRANCISCO 96240

FO PROCEDURES AND ARTILLERY ADJUSTMENT
HANDOUT 803-5 MIL RELATION

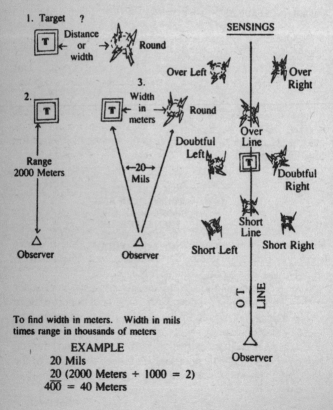

To find width in meters.   Width in mils
times range in thousands of meters

EXAMPLE
20 Mils
20 (2000 Meters ÷ 1000 = 2)
$\overline{400}$ = 40 Meters

Appendix 15

DEPARTMENT OF THE ARMY
CO L (RANGER) 75TH INF
101ST AIRBORNE DIVISION (AMBL)
APO SAN FRANCISCO 96383

Concept of Employment

Ranger teams are clandestinely inserted into areas of interest to discover or confirm evidence of enemy activity obtained from other sources (sniffer, infrared, and agent reports). The areas of interest may be anywhere in the division area of operations, but are generally confined to the division recon zone. Each team operates within its own recon zone, the size of which is determined by strength of the team. The team's recon zones are located in such a way as to saturate an area of interest for maximum intelligence value.

Missions Assigned

The basic mission of the Ranger company is ground reconnaissance. Specific missions, to include investigation of sniffer readings, infrared readings, agent reports, and sensor activations are centered around the basic mission.

The secondary mission of the Ranger company is prisoner snatch. This mission is assigned as a mission of opportunity, in effect, when it will not interfere with the primary mission.

The Ranger company has the capability of performing additional missions to include downed aircraft security and ambush, but is rarely used for these since they reduce the ability of the company to meet its ground reconnaissance responsibilities.

Techniques of Operation

Preparation

The company is notified of an area of interest by division G-2 [intelligence] through the S-3 [operations] section of the 2/17th Cavalry, and a company officer is dispatched to make an LZ reconnaissance of the area. This officer selects the insertion LZs and delineates the recon zones (generally a 2,000 meter square) based on his assessment of terrain and of the intelligence available. The officer conducts an overflight of the area with the patrol leaders and their assistants and with the insertion pilots, giving each the opportunity to see the recon zone and its LZs.

While this is taking place, the intelligence sergeant goes to division order of battle and obtains all available intelligence on the area, and the operations sergeant prepares the operations order, the [map] overlays, and the artillery preplotted fire concentrations. These are delivered to the 2/17th Cavalry S-2, who in turn distributes them to all of the supporting units and to division G-2 (the supporting units includes supporting artillery, the supporting cavalry troop for aircraft and immediate-reaction platoon, the supporting brigade for ready-reaction company, and any others). At this time, radio-relay teams are sent to advance fire support bases to provide communication as necessary with Ranger operations.

When the overflight is completed, the teams to be inserted draw their equipment, rations, and ammunition, pack their gear, receive the operations order, and practice immediate-reaction drills and any other techniques necessary to the accomplishment of the mission. The team leader gives a briefback before his final inspection.

Insertion

Ninety-nine percent of the insertions are made with rotary wing aircraft. The other methods are insertion by swift boat, walk-ins, and stay-behind missions. Each requires an overflight. Walk-in insertions are generally staged from a fire support base. Aircraft insertions are made using a slick for each team, a gunship, and a command-and-control ship. Feints, low leveling, false insertions, etc., are used to conceal the actual insertion from the enemy.

Ground Operations

Communications

Immediately upon insertion, the team moves to a secure position and attempts to establish communications with the radio-relay element and with the teams around it. The teams carry PRC-77s, PRC-74s (A1), and URC-10s. Every attempt is made to obtain FM communications, because A1* requires antennae which cannot be used in emergencies. The URC-10 provides emergency communications when both FM and AM fail. It is critical that good communications be established, first, in order to permit exploitation of fresh intelligence and, second, to protect the members of the team.

Security

The success of the mission depends entirely on the secrecy with which it is carried out. The team must move, eat, and sleep in such a manner as to insure they are not discovered. If the team is discovered, the mission is compromised, and the team stands a good chance of being attacked in force. Movement must be made with stealth and, as a result, slowly. Further, since the best way of finding the enemy is when he is moving and the team is not, considerable time is spent monitoring trails, streams, and other likely avenues of movement. All movement by the team is sterilized to prevent detection. During movement, each member of the team has a certain area for which he is responsible. These areas interlock and provide the team with 360-degree security.

Rations are restricted to those that can be eaten quietly and with a minimum of refuse. Teams never eat in an area where they remain any length of time, and all refuse is buried and camouflaged.

Teams sleep with only a poncho and poncho liner because of noise, size, and weight. At night, the teams do not dig in, but

*A1 refers to AM.

rather attempt to move into a concealed area. Twenty-four hour security is maintained, and additional security is provided by the placement of claymore mines around the position.

Enemy Contact

Unless the team is observed during insertion or something takes place to compromise their location (extraction of an injured man, attempt to resupply, etc.) the team usually discovers the enemy before the team is discovered. In such cases, the actions of the team depend on the size and location of the enemy force. If it is larger and far enough away, the team, after reporting it, attempts to destroy it with artillery or air strikes. If it is larger and too close, the team reports it, and avoids it until force can be brought to bear. If the force is of the same size or smaller and it is close, the team will attempt a prisoner snatch, if the mission calls for it.

Experience has shown that many LZs and trails have NVA/VC watchers, usually one man, but sometimes two. These individuals are usually responsible when a team is discovered. They employ two methods. The first is to move to the team and attempt to halt or slow down the team by wounding or killing one or more of its members. This accomplished, the watcher can go to his base and return with a larger force. The second method employed is for the watcher to go immediately to the base and return with reinforcements. In the first case, if the team has been alerted to the enemy presence, they have enough forewarning to call for gunship support, and can generally hold until the immediate-reaction force arrives. In the second case, the team may become surrounded before contact is initiated and must use smoke and gas to escape. More likely, however, the enemy's movement will be detected, and the gunships and reaction force can be called.

The final means of contact is the meeting engagement. Here, the Ranger team and enemy force meet by accident, and after an initial sporadic exchange of fire, both forces usually back off to maneuver and discover the other's true size. Again, this maneuvering provides the team with time to contact their own reinforcements.

In all cases, the arrival of a reaction force usually signals the withdrawal of the enemy force, coupled with his attempt to cover his tracks. Our enemy delights in battles where the odds are in his favor but shrinks away from those where they are not. It is for this reason that the enemy generally makes his attacks in force at night.

Contact of all kinds requires communications, not only between the team in trouble and Ranger operations, but between all teams operating. As soon as one team makes contact, all others must stop their movement and set up a defensive position. Problems involving two or more teams in contact increase exponentially.

Spot Reports

All sightings of any kind, from actual enemy to evidence of his presence, are reported to Ranger operations and to 2/17th Cavalry. A log of the sightings is kept with the team's mission folder.

Emergency Aircraft

During the time that teams are in the field, 2/17th Cavalry provides to the Ranger company a C & C aircraft on fifteen-minute standby. This gives the Ranger company the capability of providing air-relay and position fixes to the teams, if necessary.

Extractions

In addition to the occasions for use of the capabilities of Dustoff aircraft, there are two kinds of extractions and three ways of accomplishing them. The team or any of its members can be extracted by McGuire rig, from an LZ by ladders, or with a touchdown LZ. The teams are extracted by one of these means either on the day they are scheduled to return, or when contact with the enemy has been made and reinforcements cannot be inserted. The most common reason for emergency extraction is the need to remove several members of the team because they have been wounded, and to remove the remaining members because they cannot sustain themselves alone.

Debriefing

Once the team has been extracted, for whatever reasons, they return to Ranger operations for debriefing by S-2, 2/17th Cavalry. The debriefing report appears in the division INSUM [intelligence summary] and a record of the operation is kept at Ranger operations.

Team Organization

The Ranger team generally consists of six members, although it can operate with as many as eight or as few as four. A heavy team consists of two or more teams and may vary from ten to twenty-four members. All Ranger teams are built around the base six. They are:

- Team Leader
- Assistant Team Leader
- Senior Scout Observer
- Scout Observer
- Senior RTO (command frequency)
- Junior RTO (artillery frequency)

The team leader varies his team as required for the mission with the most frequent modification being that he carries the command frequency radio himself. When a heavy team is employed, it is created by combining two or more regular teams and giving overall command to one team leader. In this way, the team may split up and explore a greater area. One of the primary reasons for employing a heavy team is to provide more staying power in an area where adverse weather creates limited access. Additional reasons include providing a security element for a killer team, prisoner snatch, or cave search.

Kit Carson scouts are a recent addition to the Ranger company, and there has been no evaluation of their performance at this time.

The following list of equipment is the established minimum equipment that each patrol will carry to the field. Any amount of equipment over these standards may be carried at the discretion of the patrol leader. Additionally, special equipment such as M-79s, sensor devices, M-60s, etc., are left to the discretion of the team leader, based on his assigned mission and terrain.

20 magazines per member
 4 M-26 fragmentation grenades per member
 3 smoke grenades per member
 1 white phosphorous grenade per member
 3 CS grenades per team
 1 claymore mine per member
 1 gas mask per member
 3 strobe lights per team
 3 mirrors per team
 3 pen guns per team
 3 flash panels per team
 3 lensatic compasses per team
 1 penlite flashlight per team
 1 SOI per team
 1 poncho per member
 1 can foot powder per member
 1 extra pair of socks per member
 1 first-aid kit per team
 1 sling rope and snap link per member
 2 radios per team
 1 extra battery per radio
 1 extra handset per two radios per team
 1 field-expedient antenna per team
 1 field dressing per member
 5 quarts of water per member
 3 camouflage sticks per team

A Successful Operation

A Ranger heavy team was inserted on 1 November 1969 into the 101st recon zone, forty kilometers south of Hue. The team was scheduled for extraction on 5 November. For the first two days, the team explored its recon zone, reporting evidence of trails, unused bunkers, etc. On the third day, one man on the team was extracted by McGuire rig because of malaria. Later that same day, the team discovered three VC/NVA, apparently in a carrying party, and in their attempt to get a prisoner, they killed one and forced the others to drop their loads and flee. A reaction force was inserted, and a search of the area revealed one body, three rucksacks, and a blood trail. The rucksacks contained fifty-two 60mm mortar rounds, their firing devices, and point-detonating fuses. The reaction force removed the captured equipment, and the Ranger team remained as a stay-behind in an attempt to monitor further traffic in the area.

An Unsuccessful Operation

A Ranger Team consisting of five persons was inserted into an area in the 101st recon zone thirty-five kilometers southeast of Hue. The team was scheduled for a four-day mission. The insertion was early in the day, and the team moved without incident. That night, rain began to fall, and it continued into the early morning. Under the cover of the rain, an apparent trail watcher was able to move close enough to the team to fire an AK burst into their perimeter. Two of the team members were wounded and were later extracted by Dustoff. One other wounded man, the team leader, and the other two members of the team were McGuired out of the area. The team was unable to obtain communications with any other element for almost one hour after the contact because of poor commo conditions and distances involved.

Problems Encountered in Ranger Operations

Artillery

One of the greatest assets of the Ranger team is its ability to direct accurate artillery on targets of opportunity. In addition, artillery is often the only support that can reach the team in adverse weather. Operating in the 101st recon zone, however, means that the only artillery available is 175mm. With this size weapon, "danger close" is eight hundred meters. Since a team rarely observes VC/NVA at a distance greater than two hundred meters, the artillery is virtually useless.

Weather

During the periods of bad weather, teams cannot receive support from aircraft, and often artillery will not fire. This means that teams cannot move during this weather because they cannot afford to make contact. Bad weather also prevents insertion and extraction of teams. This means that teams must often be extended and that, coupled with another problem, causes our unit's flexibility to be severely reduced. Extended teams cannot deploy on schedule.

Ground Maneuver

a. Formations

Teams will normally move in a file formation due to the thick terrain in which operations can best be conducted. In more open areas, the file can be modified into a cigar-shaped column formation. Distance between each team member will ordinarily be five to ten meters apart, but never farther apart so as not to be within visual observation of the man immediately to the front and rear.

b. Order of and individual responsibilities during movement

(1) Senior scout observer: Will act as point man and is responsible for front security, early warning of enemy activity, and maintaining a general compass direction of the route of march. In the event the team leader and assistant team leader become casualties, assume command of the team.

(2) Team leader: Responsible for all actions of the team. Will be second in order of march and will direct the point man by arm and hand signals to maintain the specific route of march. With help of the assistant team leader, will assign team equipment, uniform, and weapons.

(3) Senior RTO: Will be third in order of march and is responsible for maintaining communications with company TOC or relay station. Also will observe designated flank for security and will maintain a pace count to assist the team leader in land navigation.

(4) Assistant team leader: Will be fourth in order of march and will monitor compass heading and pace count to maintain a constant awareness of the team's exact map location. In the event the team leader becomes a casualty, assumes leadership of the team. Will carry the team and bag and is the team medic.

(5) Junior RTO: Will be fifth in order of march and is responsible for security of designated flank. Responsible for communications as designated by team leader.

(6) Junior scout observer: Will be sixth in the order of march and is responsible for rear security and to sanitize the team's route of march by ensuring nothing is left behind to alert the enemy to the team's passage. This will include straightening branches, covering scuff marks, etc. (NOTE: On extended missions, the team leader may adjust the order of march and individual responsibilities to maintain alertness. In the event that the team is short of personnel, the team leader and/or assistant team leader may carry his own radio and assume the additional duty of RTO. The team leader is not confined by this portion of the SOP if the situation dictates otherwise.)

c. Actions at halts

(1) For short halts, the team will "herring bone," with the point man facing forward, the rear security man covering the rear, and the other team members facing in alternate directions down the file.

(2) For longer halts, including right positions, the team will

"wagon wheel," with their feet to the center and weapons facing outward. If terrain or situation so dictate, the team may set up in a linear position within arm's reach of each other. In any position occupied for more than a few minutes, claymores will be placed to provide 360-degree protection, with concentration on likely avenues of enemy approach.

d. Actions at danger areas

(1) Danger areas are defined as those areas where the terrain offers increased chances for detection of the team by the enemy. They are usually in the form of open areas, roads or trails, or streams.

(2) The best way to handle a danger area is to avoid it. The team should go around the area or wait for the hours of darkness before crossing. If the danger area must be crossed during daylight, the point man will cross and recon the far side before directing the remainder of the team to cross. Rally points will be designated by the team leader at both the near and far sides before the crossing in case the team is engaged by the enemy and becomes temporarily separated.

Immediate-Action Drills (IAD)

Immediate-action drills are defined as drills designed to provide swift and positive reactions to visual or physical contact with the enemy. They are single courses of action that require a minimum of signal or command to initiate and may be initiated by any member of the team. IAD may be defensive or offensive in nature. They must be simple and capable of quick execution. Common IAD include:

a. Chance contact

First man to spot the enemy freezes and signals the rest of patrol to do the same. The team remains motionless until the enemy passes. If spotted by the enemy, the team immediately opens fire.

b. Hasty ambush

A team member spots the enemy without being detected. He

signals the rest of the team of the spotting and the direction of the enemy. The team leader signals orientation of the team to engage while the enemy is allowed to proceed as far as possible into the kill zone. Any ambush formation may be used; however, linear will most often be employed due to simplicity, time available, and ease of control. Team leader initiates the ambush with well-aimed shots.

c. Immediate assault

The team and the enemy sight each other simultaneously. Nearest team member fires as rest of team swiftly moves on line and assaults.

d. Counterambush

(1) If part of the team is caught in the killing zone, they return fire and attempt to withdraw. The remainder of the team supports by fire or maneuvers to assault the flank of the enemy ambush.

(2) If the entire team is caught in the kill zone, return fire and attempt to withdraw. If in extremely close quarters, the only option may be to attempt to assault through the ambush. (NOTE: Smoke or CS grenades will assist in covering the team's withdrawal.)

e. Withdrawal by fire

In most chance contacts, the best course is to withdraw as rapidly as possible until the strength of the enemy can be determined. It is not the recon team's mission to stand and fight. Withdrawal by fire may best be accomplished by a leapfrog method of bounds while one part of the team covers the other.

f. Reaction to enemy mortar fire

If the team is engaged by mortar fire, it can be assumed that the fire is being adjusted by direct observation. The team should hit the ground on hearing incoming rounds and, after impact, move at a right angle to the direction of march as rapidly as possible. These same actions will be taken if hit by accidental friendly artillery or mortars with the addition of the RTOs immediately calling for an emergency "check fire" on all radio nets.

Extraction

a. The LRRP team may be extracted by helicopter or by walking out of the AO upon completion of the planned duration of the patrol.

b. Normal helicopter extraction will be conducted by either touchdown, ladder, or McGuire rig. Prior to the extraction, the company operations officer will notify the team of the time for the extraction and will request an LZ report from the team leader. The report will include:

    (1) Type (touchdown, ladder or McGuire rig)

    (2) Location (map grid coordinates)

    (3) Size (dimensions of the LZ in meters)

    (4) Vegetation (height, type, density, etc.)

    (5) Slope (degree and direction)

c. After submitting the LZ report, the team will conduct a thorough recon of the LZ to ensure it is secure and report their findings. As the command-and-control and lift ships near the LZ, the team will display the prescribed marking panel, signal mirror flash, smoke, or strobe light. When the lift chopper is on final approach, the team leader will consolidate the team from their security positions and prepare to be extracted.

d. Actions taken by the team during extraction include:

    (1) Touchdown: As the helicopter sits down on the LZ, the team boards as rapidly as possible. As soon as all are on board, the crew chief will notify the aircraft commander to lift off.

    (2) Ladder: As the helicopter hovers above the LZ, the bellyman will drop the ladders to the team. The team will approach the ladder in threes, attach their packs to the bottom of the ladder with snap links, and ascend the ladder. After all are aboard, the aircraft will take off to a higher altitude where the ladders and packs will be pulled on board.

    (3) McGuire rig: As the helicopter hovers above the LZ, the bellyman will drop the McGuire rigs. Normally, a helicopter will lift out only three men on the McGuire rigs, requiring two aircraft per team extraction. Once the three

men are in the rigs, the team leader will signal the belly-man and the helicopter will make a vertical ascent until all personnel are clear of the trees. The second aircraft will then repeat the process. Once the aircraft have flown to a friendly firebase, they will make a slow vertical descent until the team reaches the ground. The aircraft will then land so the team can load inside and return to the company base.

(4) Walk out: In a walk-out extraction the team will follow a planned route of march to a linkup with friendly units. On reaching the designated area, the team will notify the company TOC for further transportation.

(5) Vehicle or boat: The team will move to and secure the pickup position at the edge of the road or stream. The vehicle or boat will proceed to and beyond the pickup point. As the transportation passes the team, they will make the appropriate signal. Upon verification of the team's position by the operations officer, the vehicle or boat will turn around and return to the pickup point where they will briefly stop while the team loads.

Emergency Extraction

Emergency extractions are those that are conducted when in or anticipating enemy contact. They will be conducted in the same manner of normal extractions except for emergency night pickups by McGuire rig and emergency walk outs. In all instances, the team will keep the operations officer informed of the developing enemy situation. Procedures for emergency night McGuire rig and walk-out extractions are as follows:

a. Night McGuire

The team will use one strobe light to mark the LZ. A second strobe will be turned on when the first load of three men is ready to be lifted from the LZ. A third strobe is lit when the second group is prepared to be lifted out. Each group of three will keep a strobe lit while in flight to assist the aircraft pilot in lowering the team to the ground once they arrive at a secure area.

b. Emergency walk out

The team follows a predesignated escape and evasion (E & E) route when in contact with a superior enemy force. The team leader informs the operations officer of the enemy situation and that they are moving on their E & E route. The team may also decide to perform an emergency walk out in the event communications are lost and all efforts to contact the TOC, radio relay, or other friendly elements has failed.

Reporting

LRRP teams will report to the company TOC, which will relay appropriate messages to higher headquarters. Reports include:

a. Insertion report

On reaching the insertion point the team will report:

(1) Location of the insertion

(2) Time of insertion

(3) Enemy situation (hot or cold)

b. Situation report

Current situation reports will be rendered at 0600, 0900, 1200, 1500, and 1800 hours and hourly on the half hour during hours of darkness. This schedule may vary in the event the team is beyond normal radio communications and must relay through aircraft. At no time will the team be without radio-relay support for more than four hours. Situation reports (sitreps) will include:

(1) Team location

(2) Enemy situation (NOTE: Reports at night or when designated by the team leader will be initiated by the TOC or radio relay rather than by the team. To maintain as much silence as possible the TOC will call requesting a sitrep. The RTO can answer by a predetermined set of keying the radio handset to break squelch. Other questions can be answered in similar manner with one squelch meaning yes, two for no, and three for ask again.)

c. Spot report

Spot reports will be made immediately when a significant

sighting or enemy contact is made. The spot report will follow the acronym SALUTE:

(1) Size of enemy force
(2) Activity
(3) Location
(4) Unit or uniform description
(5) Time
(6) Equipment observed

(NOTE: In the event contact is made, remarks should be added as to results in body count and weapons and equipment captured.)

d. Other reports will be made in accordance with other paragraphs of this SOP (LZ, extraction, etc.) or as designated by the company commander or operations section.

Debriefing

a. Patrols will be debriefed immediately on return to the company base. Debriefings will be conducted by the company intelligence NCO or by the company commander. Intelligence officers of higher commands may attend and participate in the debriefing if approved by the company commander. Debriefings will take place in the company debriefing tent or in another location that is secure and free of interruption or distractions. A formal, written report of the debriefing will be made and signed by the team leader and the debriefing official. Copies of the report and appropriate maps and map overlays, which will be classified at least at the confidential level, will be filed in the company intel section with copies forwarded to division and to units operation in or near the AO.

b. Debriefing will include:

(1) Name, rank, and position of each team member
(2) Mission
(3) Time, location, and method of insertion and extraction
(4) Routes of movement by the team
(5) Terrain (vegetation, height of canopy, trails, water sources, LZs)

(6) Enemy (strength, location, activity, equipment, weapons, morale, estimate activity)

(7) Results of enemy contact (body count, captured weapon description and serial number, description of documents and equipment)

(8) Map corrections

(9) Communications

(10) Condition of patrol (including time needed before next mission)

(11) Conclusions and recommendation

Fire Support

Coordination and planning with fire support elements is essential to the success of LRRP operations. Fire support includes:

a. Artillery

Artillery fire support will be coordinated with the division and the artillery battery in range of the AO through the company operations section. A fire support plan will be prepared with preplanned targets and numbers so that the data can be preplotted by the artillery fire direction center. On the mission, the team leader will communicate directly with the supporting battery on the artillery radio net. Artillery fires may be used to:

(1) Destroy or neutralize enemy personnel or equipment

(2) Deceive the enemy as to the patrol's location or intention

(3) Deny the enemy freedom of movement

(4) Defend the patrol while in contact or withdrawal

(5) Direct the patrol during movement by firing navigation rounds at preplotted locations

(6) Delay enemy reinforcements and pursuit

b. Naval gunfire

When in range, naval gunfire can be used similarly to artillery. Naval gunfire will be coordinated through the naval liaison officer at division.

c. Air support

(1) Army: AH-1 Cobra gunships will be employed in support of all team insertions and extractions. During

missions, gunships will be on strip alert or in the air near the AO and will be able to support in no more than ten minutes from the time requested by the team through company operations.

(2) Air force: The patrol teams will be supported by the air force forward air controller (FAC) of the brigade headquarters nearest the AO. Company operations section will also inform the division air force liaison of planned missions. Tactical air support will generally be available within fifteen minutes of request.

(NOTE: All AOs, while patrols are in the zones, will be no-fire/no-fly zones to all other elements. No fires of any type will be put into the AO without the coordination and approval of the team leader. The same rules apply to a one thousand meter buffer area around the AO.)

Coordination

An LRRP liaison from the operation section will conduct the coordination with all supporting units. Coordination will include:

a. Artillery

Coordination will be made with all batteries within range of the recon zones.

b. Air force

Coordination will be made with the division air force liaison officer when the teams are deployed outside the brigade operational areas. When patrols are within a brigade's sector, coordination will be made with the brigade air force liaison officer.

c. Ready reaction force (RRF)

An RRF of either an infantry platoon or company will normally be on ten-minute alert to reinforce teams in contact that cannot withdraw under their own firepower or to exploit a finding by the recon team or to assist in an emergency extraction. Coordination will be made directly with the commander of the RRF and with the RRF unit's higher headquarters.

(NOTE: Operations orders, including map overlays, will be distributed to the air force liaison, supporting artillery, the division G-2, the division G-3, the RRF, and to the brigade(s) next to or near the recon zones. Radio call signs and frequencies and the exact location and dimensions of the recon zones will also be provided.)

To TAC SOP: Rigging of Helicopters

General

This annex describes the techniques and procedures employed in rigging the UH-1 helicopter for the following:

1. Ladder
   a. Materials required
      (1) 1 cargo ladder, 30 feet long
      (2) 6 snap links
      (3) 2 sling ropes
   b. Procedures
      Depending on the vegetation of the landing zone, as reported in the LZ report, the operations officer will instruct the bellyman on the length of ladder that must be available for the insertion/extraction. The standard method will be to have equal lengths of the ladder extending out both sides of the aircraft. The middle portion of the ladder will be connected to the floor rings of the aircraft's cargo area with the six snap links. The free portion of the ladder will be coiled to the sides of the aircraft and secured with a sling rope tied with a slip knot for quick release. If high vegetation requires, a maximum length of twenty-eight feet may be achieved by extending all the ladder out of one side of the aircraft. At least two ladder rungs must be inside the aircraft so they can be connected with all six snap links.

2. Rappelling
   a. Materials required
      (1) 2 nylon ropes per station, each 120 feet by $7/16$ inch
      (2) 1 donut ring (composed of 10 feet of $1/2$-inch cable

with the ends overlapping and connected by 4 U-bolt clamps)

(3) 1 floating safety ring composed of two snap links taped together with gates opening in opposite directions connected to a 12-inch-long, 3/8-inch-diameter steel cable.

(4) 1 log or board 2 feet in length and 4 inches in diameter per station

(5) Each rappeller will have a sling rope, for tying a Swiss seat with a snap link, and leather gloves

b. Procedures

(1) The donut ring will be connected in a circular pattern to the floor of the aircraft and connected by six snap links. The floating safety ring will be connected to a different ring in the floor at the center of the ring with the twelve-inch cable running from the floating safety to the donut ring and connected with a snap link.

(2) A middle-of-the-rope bowline with a bight will be tied eighteen inches from the end of the rope. At the end of the rope, an end-of-the-rope bowline will be tied. A snap link will then connect the end-of-the-rope bowline to the donut ring with another snap link connecting the middle-of-the-rope bowline to the floating safety ring.

(3) The rappel rope is then rolled onto the board or log.

(4) Individuals will snap link their Swiss seat to the rappel rope, and the aircraft is prepared for departure.

3. McGuire rig

a. The interior aircraft donut ring and floating safety ring are prepared in the same manner as for rappelling.

b. At the ground end of the rope, a bowline with a bight is tied eight feet from the end of the rope. At the end of the rope is tied an end-of-the-rope bowline, which connects to a rope harness or one made from a parachute harness. A safety line will connect the harness to the upper bowline with a snap link.

To TAC SOP: Handling of Enemy POWs and KIAs

1. POWs

   Enemy POWs will be handled according to the five Ss, which are:
   a. Search
   b. Silence
   c. Safeguard
   d. Segregate
   e. Speed

2. When a prisoner is taken, an immediate request for evacuation will be made. If the POW is wounded, he will be treated and all efforts will be made to keep him alive. If more than one POW is taken, they should be separated and not allowed to communicate. They should be blindfolded and secured against escape. A POW may be a tremendous source of intelligence—a POW is far more valuable than a body count—they will be brought in alive if at all possible.

3. Enemy KIA

   Dead enemy will be stripped of all weapons and equipment, including their uniforms and footgear, which will be extracted with the team. Bodies should not be mutilated.

Appendix 16

NVA TRAIL MARKING AND FIELD-EXPEDIENT MESS FACILITIES

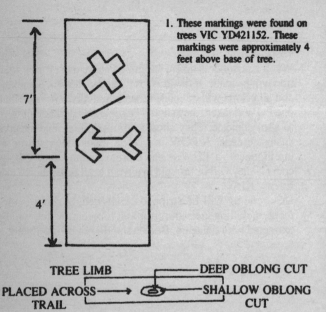

1. These markings were found on trees VIC YD421152. These markings were approximately 4 feet above base of tree.

TREE LIMB — DEEP OBLONG CUT
PLACED ACROSS → — SHALLOW OBLONG
TRAIL — CUT

2. This marking was found on a limb placed across trail VIC YD419159. Complete oblong sign was about the size of a tennis ball with center about the size of a half dollar.

3. Two stumps were found VIC YD27157 possibly used as table: There were two of these smaller stumps, one pulled out of ground approx 2 feet parallel from taller ones—possibly a bench.

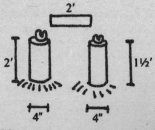

Appendix 17

NINE RULES
FOR PERSONNEL OF U.S. MILITARY
ASSISTANCE COMMAND, VIETNAM

The Vietnamese have paid a heavy price in suffering for their long fight against the communists. We military men are in Vietnam now because their government has asked us to help its soldiers and people in winning their struggle. The Viet Cong will attempt to turn the Vietnamese people against you. You can defeat them at every turn by the strength, understanding, and generosity you display with the people. Here are nine simple rules:

DISTRIBUTION—1 to each member of the United States
Armed Forces in Vietnam
USARV GTA NO. 21-2 (SEPTEMBER 1967)

1. Remember we are guests here: We make no demands and seek no special treatment.
2. Join with the people! Understand their life, use phrases from their language, and honor their customs and laws.
3. Treat women with politeness and respect.
4. Make personal friends among the soldiers and common people.
5. Always give the Vietnamese the right of way.
6. Be alert to security and ready to react with your military skill.
7. Don't attract attention by loud, rude, or unusual behavior.
8. Avoid separating yourself from the people by a display of wealth or privilege.
9. Above all else you are members of the U.S. Military Forces on a difficult mission, responsible for all your official and personal actions. Reflect honor upon yourself and the United States of America.

Glossary

Acid pad   Helicopter landing pad.

aerial recon   Reconning a specific area by helicopter prior to the insertion of a recon patrol.

AFB   Air force base.

air burst   Explosive device that detonates above ground.

air strike   Surface attack by fixed-wing fighter-bomber aircraft.

AIT   In the U.S. Army, Advanced Individual Training that follows Basic Combat Training.

AK   A Soviet bloc assault rifle, 7.62 mm., also known as the Kalashnikov AK-47.

AO   Area of Operations, specified location established for planned military operations.

ao dai   Traditional Vietnamese female dress, split up the sides and worn over pants.

ARA   Aerial Rocket Artillery.

Arc Light   A B-52 air strike.

Artillery or **Arty fan**   An area of operations which can be covered by existing artillery support.

ARTO   Assistant radio/telephone operator.

ARVN   Army of the Republic of (South) Vietnam.

Arty   Artillery.

ATL   Assistant team leader.

A Team   Special Forces operational detachment that normally consists of a single 12-man team composed of eleven enlisted men and one officer.

A Troop or **Alpha Troop**   Letter designation for one of the aerorifle companies of an air cavalry squadron.

baseball   Baseball-shaped hand grenade with a 5-meter kill range.

BCT   In the U.S. Army, every trainee must complete Basic Combat Training upon entering service.

BDA   Bomb Damage Assessment.

beat feet   Running from danger.

beaucoup (**boo koo** in GI slang)   French for many.

beehive   Artillery round filled with hundreds of small metal darts designed to be used against massed infantry.

berm   Built-up earthen wall used for defensive purposes.

Big Pond   Pacific Ocean.

Bird Dog   A small fixed-wing observation plane.

black box   Sensor device that detects body heat or movement. They were buried along routes used by the enemy to record their activity in the area.

black PJs   A type of local garb of Vietnamese farmers, also worn extensively by Viet Cong guerrillas.

blasting cap   A small device inserted into an explosive substance that can be triggered to cause the detonation of the main charge.

blood trail   Spoor sign left by the passage or removal of enemy wounded or dead.

Blues   Another name for the aerorifle platoons or troops of an air cavalry squadron.

body bag   A thick black plastic bag used to transport American and allied dead to Graves Registration points.

break contact   Disengaging from battle with an enemy unit.

bring smoke   Placing intensive fire upon the enemy. Killing the enemy with a vengeance.

B Troop or **Bravo Troop**   Letter designation for one of the aerorifle companies of an air cavalry squadron.

bush   The jungle.

buy the farm   To die.

C-4   A very stable, pliable plastique explosive.

C & C   Command and Control.

CA   Combat assault.

cammies   Jungle-patterned clothing worn by U.S. troops in the field.

cammo stick   Two-colored camouflage applicator.

CAR-15   Carbine version of the M-16 rifle.

Capt.   Abbreviation for the rank of captain.

Cav   Cavalry.

CCN   Command and Control (North), MACV-SOG.

Charlie, Charles, Chuck   GI slang for VC/NVA.

cherry   New arrival in country.

ChiCom   Chinese Communist.

Chieu Hoi   Government program that encouraged enemy soldiers to come over to the South Vietnam side.

Chinook   CH-47 helicopter used for transporting equipment and troops.

chopper   GI slang for helicopter.

chopper pad   Helicopter landing pad.

CIDG   Civilian Irregular Defense Group. South Vietnamese or Montagnard civilians trained and armed to defend themselves against enemy attack.

clacker   Firing device used to manually detonate a claymore mine.

CO   Commanding officer.

Cobra   AH-1G attack helicopter.

cockadau   GI slang for the Vietnamese word meaning kill.

Col.   Abbreviation for the rank of colonel.

cold   An area of operations or a recon zone is "cold" if it is unoccupied by the enemy.

commo   Communication by radio or field telephone.

commo check   A radiotelephone operator requesting confirmation of his transmission.

compromise   Discovered by the enemy.

contact   Engaged by the enemy.

CP   Command post.

Cs   Combat field rations for American troops.

CS   Riot gas.

*   *   *

daisy chain Wiring a number of claymore mines together with det cord to achieve a simultaneous detonation.

debrief The gleaning of information and intelligence after a military operation.

DEROS The date of return from an overseas tour of duty.

det cord Timed-burn fuse used to detonate an explosive charge.

didi Vietnamese for to run or move quickly.

diddy boppin' Moving foolishly, without caution.

DMZ Demilitarized Zone.

Doc A medic or doctor.

double canopy Jungle or forest with two layers of overhead vegetation.

Doughnut Dollies Red Cross hostesses.

drag The last man on a long-range reconnaissance patrol.

D Troop or Delta Troop Lettered designation for one of the aerorifle companies of an air cavalry squadron.

dung lai Vietnamese for don't move.

Dustoff Medical evacuation by helicopter.

DZ Drop zone for airborne parachute operation.

E-1 or E-2 Military pay grades of private.

E-3 Military pay grade of private first class.

E-4 Military pay grade of specialist fourth class or corporal.

E-5 Military pay grade of specialist fifth class or sergeant.

E-6 Military pay grade of specialist sixth class or staff sergeant.

E-7 Military pay grade of sergeant first class or platoon sergeant.

E-8 Military pay grade of master sergeant or first sergeant.

E-9 Military pay grade of sergeant major.

E & E Escape and evasion, on the run to evade pursuit and capture.

ER Enlisted Reserve.

ETS Estimated Termination of Service.

exfil Extraction from a mission or operation.

extension leave A 30-day furlough given at the end of a full tour of duty after which the recipient must return for an extended tour of duty.

FAC Forward Air Controller. Air force spotter plane that coordinated airstrikes and artillery for ground units.

fast mover Jet fighter-bomber.

firebase or fire support base Forward artillery position usually located on a prominent terrain feature used to support ground units during operations.

finger A secondary ridge running out from a primary ridgeline, hill, or mountain.

firefight A battle with an enemy force.

Firefly An LOH observation helicopter fitted with a high intensity searchlight.

fire mission A request for artillery support.

fix The specific coordinates pertaining to a unit's position or to a target.

flare ship Aircraft used to drop illumination flares in support of ground troops in contact at night.

flash panel A fluorescent orange or yellow cloth used to mark a unit's position for supporting or inbound aircraft.

field Anywhere outside friendly control.

FNG Fucking New Guy. Slang term for a recent arrival in Vietnam.

FO Forward Observer. A specially trained soldier, usually an officer, attached to an infantry unit for the purpose of coordinating close artillery support.

fougasse (in GI slang **foo gas** or **phou gas**)   A jellied gasoline explosive that is buried in a 55-gallon drum along defensive perimeters and, when command detonated, sends out a wall of highly flammable fuel similar to napalm.

freak or **freq**   Slang term meaning a radio frequency.

G-2   Division or larger intelligence section.

G-3   Division or larger operations section.

ghost or **ghost time**   Taking time off, free time, goofing off.

gook   Derogatory slang for VC/NVA.

grazing fire   Keeping the trajectory of bullets between normal knee to waist height.

grease   Slang term meaning to kill.

Green Beret   A member of the U.S. Army Special Forces.

ground pounder   Infantryman.

grunt   Infantryman.

gunship   An armed attack helicopter.

H & I   Harrassment and Interdiction. Artillery fire upon certain areas of suspected enemy travel or rally points, designed to prevent uncontested use.

HE   High explosive.

heavy team   In a long-range patrol unit, two five- or six-man teams operating together.

helipad   A hardened helicopter landing pad.

Ho Chi Minh trail   An extensive road and trail network running from North Vietnam, down through Laos and Cambodia into South Vietnam, which enabled the North Vietnamese to supply equipment and personnel to their units in South Vietnam.

hootch   Slang for barracks or living quarters.

horn   Radio or telephone handset.

hot   A landing zone or drop zone under enemy fire.

HQ   Headquarters.

Huey   The Bell UH helicopter series.

hug   To close with the enemy in order to prevent his use of supporting fire.

hump   Patrolling or moving during a combat operation.

I Corps   The northernmost of the four separate military zones in South Vietnam. The other divisions were II, III, and IV Corps.

immersion foot   A skin condition of the feet caused by prolonged exposure to moisture that results in cracking, bleeding, and sloughing of skin.

incoming   Receiving enemy indirect fire.

Indian country   Territory under enemy control.

indigenous   Native peoples.

infil   Insertion of a recon team or military unit into a recon zone or area of operation.

intel   Information on the enemy gathered by human, electronic, or other means.

jungle penetrator   A metal cylinder lowered by cable from a helicopter used to extract personnel from inaccessible terrain.

KCS   Kit Carson scout. Repatriated enemy soldiers working with U.S. combat units.

Khmer   Cambodian.

Khmer Rouge   Cambodian communist.

Khmer Serei   Free Cambodian.

KIA   Killed in Action.

Killer team A small LRRP/Ranger team with the mission of seeking out and destroying the enemy.

LAW Light Antitank Weapon.

lay dog Slang meaning to go to cover and remain motionless while listening for the enemy. This is SOP for a recon team immediately after being inserted or infiltrated.

LBJ Long Binh jail. The in-country military stockade for U.S. Army personnel convicted of violations of the U.S. Code of Military Justice.

Lifer Slang for career soldier.

LMG Light machine gun.

LOH or **Loach** OH-6A light observation helicopter.

LP Listening post. An outpost established beyond the perimeter wire, manned by one or more personnel with the mission of detecting approaching enemy forces before they can launch an assault.

LRP Long Range Patrol.

LRRP Long Range Reconnaissance Patrol.

LSA Government issue lubricating oil for individual weapons.

Lt. Lieutenant.

Lt. Col. Lieutenant Colonel.

LZ Landing zone. A cleared area large enough to accommodate the landing of one or more helicopters.

M-14 The standard issue 7.62mm semiautomatic/automatic rifle used by U.S. military personnel prior to the M-16.

M-16 The standard issue 5.56mm semiautomatic/automatic rifle that became the mainstay of U.S. ground forces in 1967.

M-60 A light 7.62mm machine gun that has been the primary infantry automatic weapon of U.S. forces since the Korean War.

M-79 An individually operated, single-shot 40mm grenade launcher.

MAAG Military Assistance Advisory Group. The senior U.S. military headquarters during the early American involvement in Vietnam.

MACV Military Assistance Command Vietnam. The senior U.S. military headquarters after full American involvement in the war.

MACV Recondo School A three-week school conducted at Nha Trang, South Vietnam, by cadre from the 5th Special Forces Group to train U.S. and allied reconnaissance personnel in the art of conducting long-range patrols.

MACV-SOG Studies and Observations Group under command of MACV that ran long-range reconnaissance and other classified missions over the borders of South Vietnam into NVA sanctuaries in Laos and Cambodia.

mag Short for magazine.

McGuire rig A single rope with loops at the end that could be dropped from a helicopter to extract friendly personnel from inaccessible terrain.

Main Force Full-time Viet Cong military units, as opposed to local, part-time guerrilla units.

Maj. Major.

Marine Force Recon U.S. Marine Corps divisional long-range reconnaissance units similar in formation and function to U.S. Army LRP/Ranger companies.

MARS Military/civilian radio/telephone system that enabled U.S. personnel in Vietnam to place calls to friends and family back in the United States.

Medevac or **Dustoff** Medical evacuation by helicopter.

MG Machine gun.

MIA   Missing in Action.

Mike Force   Special Forces mobile strike force used to reinforce or support other Special Forces units or camps under attack.

Montagnard   The tribal hill people of Vietnam.

MOS   Military Occupation Skill.

MP   Military police.

MPC   Military Payment Certificates. Paper money issued to U.S. military personnel serving overseas in lieu of local or U.S. currency.

NCO   Noncommissioned officer.

NDP   Night defensive position.

net   Radio network.

NG   National Guard.

no sweat   With little effort or with no trouble.

Number One   The best or highest possible.

Number Ten   The worst or lowest possible.

nuoc mam   Strong, evil-smelling fish sauce used to add flavor to the standard Vietnamese food staple—rice.

Nungs   Vietnamese troops of Chinese extraction hired by U.S. Special Forces to serve as personal body guards and to man special strike units and recon teams. Arguably the finest indigenous forces in Vietnam.

NVA   North Vietnamese Army.

ONH   Overnight halt.

OP   Observation post. An outpost established on a prominent terrain feature for the purpose of visually observing enemy activity.

op   Operation.

op order   Operations order. A plan for a mission or operation to be conducted against enemy forces, covering all facets of such mission or operation.

overflight   An aerial reconnaissance of an intended recon zone or area of operation prior to the mission or operation, for the purpose of selecting access and egress points, routes of travel, likely enemy concentrations, water, and prominent terrain features.

P-38   Standard manual can opener that comes with government issued C rations.

pen flare   A small spring-loaded, cartridge-fed signal flare device that fired a variety of small colored flares used to signal one's position.

peter pilot   Military slang for the assistant or copilot on a helicopter.

PFC   Private first class.

Pink Team   An aviation combat patrol package comprised of an LOH scout helicopter and a Charlie model Huey gunship or an AH-1G Cobra. The LOH would fly low to draw enemy fire and mark its location for an immediate strike from the gunship circling high overhead.

pith helmet   A light tropical helmet worn by some NVA units.

point   The point man or lead soldier in a patrol.

POW   Prisoner of War.

PRC-10 or **Prick Ten**   Standard issue platoon/company radio used early in the Vietnam War.

PRC-25 or **Prick Twenty-five**   Standard issue platoon/company radio that replaced the PRC-10.

PRC-74   Heavier, longer range radio capable of voice or code communication.

Ps or **piasters** South Vietnamese monetary system. During the height of the Vietnam War, 100P was equal to about $0.85US.

PSP Perforated steel planking used to build airstrips, landing pads, bridge surfaces, and a number of other functions.

P-training Preparatory training. A one-week course required for each new U.S. Army soldier arriving in South Vietnam, designed to acclimatize new arrivals to weather conditions and give them a basic introduction to the enemy and his tactics.

Puff the Magic Dragon AC-47 or AC-119 aircraft armed with computer-controlled miniguns that rendered massive support to fixed friendly camps and infantry units under enemy attack.

pulled Extracted or exfiltrated.

punji stakes Sharpened bamboo stakes, imbedded in the ground at an angle designed to penetrate into the foot or leg of anyone walking into one. Often poisoned with human excrement to cause infection.

Purple Heart A U.S. medal awarded for receiving a wound in combat.

PX Post Exchange.

R & R Rest and Recreation. A short furlough given to U.S. forces while serving in a combat zone.

radio relay A communications team located in a position to relay radio traffic between two points.

Rangers Designation for U.S. long-range reconnaissance patrollers after January 31, 1969.

rappel Descent from a stationary platform or a hovering helicopter by sliding down a harness-secured rope.

reaction force Special units designated to relieve a small unit in heavy contact.

rear security The last man on a long-range reconnaissance patrol.

redleg Military slang for artillery.

REMF Rear echelon motherfucker. Military slang for rear echelon personnel.

rock 'n' roll Slang for firing one's weapon on full automatic.

Roundeye Slang for a non-Asian female.

RPD/RPK Soviet bloc light machine gun.

RPG Soviet bloc, front-loaded antitank rocket launcher used effectively against U.S. bunkers, armor, and infantry during the Vietnam War.

RT Recon Team.

RTO Radio/telephone operator.

ruck Rucksack or backpack.

Ruff-Puff or **RF** South Vietnamese regional and popular forces recruited to provide security in hamlets, villages, and within districts throughout South Vietnam. A militia-type force that was usually ineffective.

saddle up Preparing to move out on patrol.

same-same The same as.

sapper VC/NVA soldiers trained to penetrate enemy defense perimeters and to destroy fighting positions, fuel and ammo dumps, and command and communication centers with demolition charges, usually prior to a ground assault by infantry.

satchel charge Explosive charge usually carried in a canvas bag across the chest and activated by a pull cord. The weapon of the sapper.

Screaming Chickens or **Puking Buzzards** Slang for members of the 101st Airborne Division.

SEALs   Small U.S. Navy special operations units trained in reconnaissance, ambush, prisoner snatch, and counterguerrilla techniques.

search and destroy   Offensive military operation designed to seek out and eradicate the enemy.

SERTS   Screaming Eagle Replacement Training School. Rear area indoctrination course that introduced newly arrived 101st Airborne Division replacements to the rigors of combat in Vietnam.

SF   U.S. Special Forces or Green Berets.

SFC   Sergeant First Class (E-7).

Sgt.   Sergeant.

shake 'n' bake   A graduate of a Stateside noncommissioned or commissioned officer's course.

short-timer   Anyone with less than 30 days left in his combat tour.

short rounds   Artillery rounds that impact short of their target.

single canopy   Jungle or forest with a single layer of trees.

sitrep   Situation Report. A radio or telephone transmission, usually to a unit's tactical operations center, to provide information on that unit's current status.

Six   Designated call sign for a commander, such as Alpha-Six.

SKS   Communist Bloc semiautomatic rifle.

sky   To run or flee because of enemy contact.

Sky Pilot   Chaplain.

slack   Slang for the second man in a patrol formation. The point man's backup.

slick   Slang for a lightly armed Huey helicopter primarily used to transport troops.

smoke   A canister-shaped grenade that dispenses smoke used to conceal a unit from the enemy or to mark a unit's location for aircraft. The smoke comes in a variety of colors.

Snake   Cobra helicopter gunship.

snatch   To capture a prisoner.

Sneaky Pete   A member of an elite military unit who operates behind enemy lines.

snoop and poop   A slang term meaning to gather intelligence in enemy territory and get out again without being detected.

socked in   Unable to be resupplied or extracted due to inclement weather.

SOI   Signal Operations Instructions. The classified code book that contains radio frequencies and call signs.

Sp4, or Spec Four   Specialist fourth class (E-4).

Spectre   An AC-130 aircraft gunship armed with miniguns, Vulcans, and sometimes a 105mm howitzer with the mission of providing close ground support for friendly ground troops.

spider hole   A camouflaged one-man fighting position, frequently used by the VC/NVA.

Spooky   AC-47 or AC-119 aircraft armed with Gatling guns and capable of flying support over friendly positions for extended periods. Besides serving as an aerial weapons platform, Spooky was capable of dropping illumination flares.

spotter round   An artillery smoke or white phosphorous round that was fired to mark a position.

S.Sgt.   Staff Sergeant (E-6).

staging area   An area in the rear where final last-minute preparations for an impending operation or mission are conducted.

stand-down   A period of rest after completion of a mission or operation in the field.

star cluster   An aerial signal device that produces three individual flares. Comes in red, green, or white.

starlight scope   A night vision device that utilizes any outside light source for illumination.

Stars and Stripes   U.S. military newspaper.

Glossary

stay behind   A technique involving a small unit dropping out of its larger parent unit or remaining behind when the larger unit moves out on an operation. A method of inserting a recon team.

strobe light   A small device employing a highly visible, bright flashing light used to identify one's position at night. Normally used only in emergency situations.

TA   Target Area. Another designation for AO or area of operations.

TAC Air   Tactical air support.

tail gunner   Rear security or the last man in a patrol.

TAOR   Tactical Area of Responsibility. Another designation for a unit's area of operations.

TDY   Temporary duty.

tee tee or *ti ti*   Very small.

ten forty-nine or **1049**   Military Form 1049 used to request a transfer to another unit.

thumper or **thump gun**   Slang terms for the M-79 grenade launcher.

Tiger Force   The battalion reconnaissance platoon of the 2/327, 101st Airborne Division.

tigers or **tiger fatigues**   Camouflage pattern of black and green stripes usually worn by reconnaissance teams or elite units.

time pencil   A delayed-fuse detonating device attached to an explosive charge or a claymore antipersonnel mine.

TL   Team leader.

TM   Team.

TOC   Tactical Operations Center or command center of a military unit.

toe popper   Small pressure detonated antipersonnel mine intended to maim, not kill.

Top   Slang term for a first sergeant meaning top NCO.

tracker   Soldiers specializing in trailing or tracking the enemy.

Tri-Border   The area in Indochina where Laos, Cambodia, and South Vietnam come together.

triple canopy   Jungle or forest that has three distinct layers of trees.

troop   Slang term for a soldier, or a unit in a cavalry squadron equal to an infantry company in size.

tunnel rat   A small-statured U.S. soldier who is sent into underground enemy tunnel complexes armed only with a flashlight, knife, and pistol.

URC-10   A pocket-sized, short-range emergency radio capable of transmitting only.

VC   Viet Cong. South Vietnamese communist guerrillas.

Viet Minh   Short for Viet Nam Doc Lap Dong Minh, or League for the Independence of Viet Nam. Organized by communist sympathizers who fought against the Japanese and later the French.

VNSF   South Vietnamese Special Forces.

warning order   The notification, prior to an op order, given to a recon team to begin preparation for a mission.

waste   To kill the enemy by any means available.

White Mice   Derogatory slang term for Saigon police.

WIA   Wounded in Action.

World   Slang term for the United States of America or home.

WP or **willy peter**   White phosphorous grenade.

XF   Exfiltration. Extraction from the field, usually by helicopter.

xin loi/sin loi   Vietnamese for sorry or too bad.

XO   Executive officer.

Xray team   A communication team established at a site between a remote recon patrol and its TOC. Its function is to assist in relaying messages between the two stations.

Yards   Short for Montagnards.

zapped   Killed or wounded.

RECONDO
LRRPs in the 101st Airborne

by Larry Chambers

The 5th Special Forces Recondo School at Nha Trang, Vietnam, was taught by the army's skilled Special Forces veterans to pass on to outstanding recon operators, from all U.S. military services and their allies, the skills that would enable them to infiltrate VC and NVA sanctuaries and return with reliable intelligence on the enemy.

This unforgettable account follows author Larry Chambers every step of the way—from joining the volunteer-only training program in Nha Trang to the hair-raising graduation mission that turned out to be very real to finally leading his own team on white-knuckle missions in the jungles of Vietnam to scout out, locate, and out-guerrilla the NVA.

Published by Ivy Books.
Available in bookstore everywhere.

*They did it—
and saw it—
all. . . .*

THE EYES OF THE EAGLE
F Company LRPs in Vietnam, 1968
by Gary A. Linderer

Gary Linderer volunteered for the army, then volunteered for Airborne training. When he reached Vietnam in 1968, he was assigned to the famous Screaming Eagles, the 101st Airborne Division. Once there, he volunteered for training and duty with F Company, 58th Infantry, the Long Range Patrol company that was known as "The Eyes of the Eagle."

F Company pulled reconnaissance missions and ambushes, and Linderer recounts night insertions into enemy territory, patrols against NVA antiaircraft emplacements and rocket-launching facilities, the fragging of an unpopular company commander, and one of the bravest demonstrations of courage under fire that has ever been described. *The Eyes of the Eagle* is a riveting look at the recon soldier's war. There are none better.

THE EYES OF THE EAGLE
F Company LRPs in Vietnam, 1968
by Gary A. Linderer

Published by Ivy Books.

The suffering and the courage . . .

EYES BEHIND THE LINES
L Company Rangers in Vietnam, 1969
by Gary A. Linderer

In mid-December 1968, after recovering from wounds sustained in a mission that saw four members of a twelve-man "heavy" team killed and five more sent back to the States, Gary Linderer returned to Phu Bai to complete his tour of duty as an LRP.

The job of the all-volunteer Rangers was to find the enemy, and observe him or kill him—all the while behind enemy lines, where discovery could mean a quick but violent death. Whether inserting into hot LZs, ambushing NVA soldiers, or rescuing downed aircrews, the Rangers demanded—and got—extraordinary performances from their dedicated and highly professional troops.

EYES BEHIND THE LINES
L Company Rangers in Vietnam, 1969
by Gary A. Linderer

Published by Ivy Books.
Available in your local bookstore.

FORTUNE FAVORS THE BOLD
A British LRRP with the 101st

by James W. Walker

Born in England to a British father and a Canadian mother, James Walker was raised at the British Sailors Orphan Home following the divorce of his parents. After he joined the British army as a teen, his mother, who was by then living in the States, bought his way out of the military and brought him to America— where he volunteered for the army, then went Airborne. In 1965, as an Airborne trooper in the 82d Airborne Division, he took part in the invasion of Santo Domingo.

But in 1967, in Vietnam, James Walker became "Limey," the only British citizen in the 101st LRRPs. He and the other LRRPS were given every sort of assignment: long-range recons, surprise raids on villages, trail watching, even herding stray cattle with helicopters. Back in camp, however, they did nothing to diminish their reputations as hell-raisers—especially Walker, whose outlandish behavior eventually made him possibly the only healthy enlisted man ever denied the "privilege" of an extension of his tour in Nam.

Published by Ivy Books.
Available in bookstores everywhere.